SUMMER'S LEASE

THE AUTHOR *aet.* 26, BY JACQUES-EMILE BLANCHE

SUMMER'S LEASE

AUTOBIOGRAPHY

1901-1938

JOHN ROTHENSTEIN

HAMISH HAMILTON
LONDON

PRINTED IN GREAT BRITAIN BY
WESTERN PRINTING SERVICES LTD, BRISTOL

Rough winds do shake the darling buds of May,
And Summer's lease hath all too short a date.

ACKNOWLEDGMENTS

The author wishes to record his indebtedness to those who have granted him permission to make use of copyright material: Mrs. Reichmann and the trustees of the late Sir Max Beerbohm; Mrs. Dorothy Cheston Bennett (©, 1965); Messrs. Jonathan Cape; Messrs. Cassell & Co.; the executors of the late Joseph Conrad; Mr. Edward Gordon Craig; Messrs. Peter Davies; Messrs. J. M. Dent; les Editions Gallimard; Mr. William Gerhardi; Madame Catherine Gide; the executors of the late Eric Gill; Admiral Sir Angus Cunninghame Graham; Mrs. Joanna Hague; Messrs. William Heinemann; Mrs. Augustus John; Professor A. W. Lawrence; Mrs. G. W. Dickson, Miss Eleanor Manning and Mr. O. W. Manning; Monsieur Mévil-Blanche; Mr. John Nash and the executors of the late Paul Nash; Mr. Peter Quennell; Mr. David Rutherston; Mr. Siegfried Sassoon; Sir Osbert Sitwell; the executors of the late Stanley Spencer; Mr. Dudley Tooth; and the Directors of the National Portrait Gallery and the City Art Gallery, Manchester; to Father Vincent Turner, S.J. for his invaluable assistance in the correction of the proofs and to Miss Corinne Bellow for her deciphering and typing of this book.

CONTENTS

ILLUSTRATIONS

CHAPTER ONE

A HAMPSTEAD CHILDHOOD

THERE are people who continue to look nostalgically at their childhood, but I am not one of them. Now that I have occasion to give a hard purposive backward look I see little of my earliest years. A very few memories, but these perfectly clear like fragments of coloured glass, are all that remain. A corner of a small upper room (the room where I was born). Sitting, naked in an armchair, posing, involuntarily, for my first photograph: I still see quite plainly the green-check pattern of the chintz and feel its coldness. Not long ago I came upon the photograph itself, which suggests that I was some six months old. Then a strange landscape with tall pointed trees of a blackish green. This particular memory I long considered a fancy or a dream. A quarter of a century later I stayed at his house in Silesia with Gerhart Hauptmann, and walking with him in his garden we came upon a place where, I told him, I had an eerie sense of having been before, and that everything was just as it had been, except for a clump of trees which I pointed out. 'But you *have* been here before,' Hauptmann said. 'Your parents brought you to visit us when you were one year old; your perambulator used to rest just here, and the trees you don't remember, quick-growing pines, weren't planted then.'

When I was about two years old my parents left the house where I was born on 11th July 1901, 1 Pembroke Cottages, in Edwardes Square, Kensington, and moved to 26 Church Row, Hampstead. Pembroke Cottages—there are only two of them—together formed a little cube of a house which, like the rest of Edwardes Square, was built by French prisoners taken during the Napoleonic Wars. The Hampstead house was a fine red-brick Queen Anne house, with white panelling; but its perfection came to irk my father, who found that it frustrated the expression of his own extremely decided and far from antiquarian taste. We lived for some ten years in Church Row, where my two sisters and my brother were born, but I remember

I

little about our life there. I do remember well a tall, spare man, in light-coloured, shabby tweeds, who spoke to us with a rather wintry kindliness, and who lived two doors away, at number 28. This man—who seemed to me to be extremely old—was Charles Aitken, whom, decades later, I was to succeed, only eight years after his retirement, as Director of the Tate Gallery.

I was baptised in the parish church at Hingham, in Norfolk, where my parents spent the summer of 1901. Augustus John liked to think that I was named after him. 'And you have called him John,' he wrote to my father, 'my vainest of hearts refuses to deny itself the gratification of the pride you have unwittingly but fatally laid in its way, like a snare, tho' my mind is well aware of your intention in thus reviving the memory of that distinguished figure John of Gaunt (or can it be Prester John?). I hope in expressing such a weakness I exonerate myself from a portion of it.' In fact this commonest of Christian names had been given over many generations to sons of the Knewstub family.

Eventually, to my father's impatience with the ready-made perfection of his Queen Anne house was added my mother's protestations that it was not large enough to accommodate a family of six, and we accordingly moved again. The new house, 11 Oakhill Park, was large, early Victorian, classical, and situated at the top of Frognal, high up on Hampstead Hill. I have not seen it for more than forty years, but with our establishment in this light and spacious house my memory of events becomes much clearer, and in particular of the house itself and our life there. There was a panoramic view over London and there was a long, narrow garden with a great elm tree at the far end of it.

Pembroke Cottages and Church Row still stand, but when I visited the Oakhill Park area a few years ago I found number 11 and its neighbours demolished, and the whole lie of the land so altered by the bulldozer that I could not even approximately locate their sites.

During these years I attended two preparatory schools. The first, University College School, where I remained only for a term or so, leaving on account of illness. Of 'U.C.S.' I remember nothing except its hideous buildings, and the funny-sounding name of one boy. The second, King Alfred's, then situated in Ellerdale Road, was as eccentric as the other was drably conventional. It was a small co-educational 'progressive' school run on benevolently paternal lines.

Discipline was lax and instruction amateurish, but although there was much roughness—of which I will presently give an example which had far-reaching results for me—King Alfred's was a place where fair and kindly relations subsisted, both between the boys and girls and between them and the staff. The example of the roughness to which I have just alluded I encountered at the end of my first day. As I was leaving to walk home, I was set upon by two older boys, not viciously but pretty roughly, and for a few moments I was hard pressed. Then I noticed another boy approaching, and I said to myself, 'I wonder what will become of me now, against three of them,' but the other boy pushed a fist hard into the face of one of my attackers, and a moment later he caused the second to gasp with pain. I took heart and began to enjoy myself, at their expense. Presently we were left alone together. The first thing I noticed about this boy was the way in which his wonderfully handsome face remained smilingly composed as he administered his savage, well-placed blows: I was aware of a magnanimous presence. He was very tall, with black hair and light blue eyes. 'Why don't you come home and have some tea with us?' he asked. I did, and so began one of the closest friendships of my life. After tea we went upstairs to a room given over to his own activities. Draped over the furniture, looking like a punctured balloon, was a vast object. 'That,' he said, 'is thirty-six yards of brown paper that I'm making into scenery for some theatricals.' Above the mantelpiece hung a large reproduction of Van Dyck's equestrian 'Portrait of Charles I'. Some casual allusion to it of mine led to a discussion of the Civil War, and to my surprise I learnt that my new friend's sympathies were unquestioningly with the King and against Cromwell. Another boy might have accepted such sympathies as natural even if he did not share them, but for someone such as myself, whose life was suffused with Liberalism, they seemed to me perverse, but when he went on to justify his loyalties (which extended to emotional Jacobitism) with perspicacious argument I was still more surprised. That afternoon was in one respect crucial for me. I am in a qualified sense a Liberal still, but what, from this insignificant beginning, I came ever more clearly to understand, was that almost every gain made by the forces of political progress is purchased by the sacrifice of something of value; that even Jacobitism was not, as I had vaguely supposed, a matter of fancy-dress heroics. It would be premature to say more of this matter here:

but that talk, and the friendship it began, started a train of thought
for me that has persisted. This boy was named Tom Rowat; he was a
Scot, his father, a Lowlander, was a director of a shipping line, and
his mother was of Highland descent. The one, shrewd and cautious,
was impatient of 'nonsense', which for him included many of the less
tangible values, as well as true nonsense; the other frankly delighted
in fantasy of every sort. From the time of my first visit the Rowat's
house was my second home. Tom inherited his mother's sense of
fantasy. I remember, years later, indeed in the last year of his life,
when he was serving in a smart cavalry regiment, his father offered
him, as a twenty-first birthday present, the choice between a horse
and a motor-car. Tom chose the car, shocking his father's sense of
where a cavalry officer's preference ought to lie. 'You see, father,'
Tom explained, 'one could get *fond* of a car.'

The Liberalism in me that was challenged by the political attitudes of my new friend owed something to personal predisposition,
but far more to environment, that is to say, to the particular sort
of Liberalism in which I grew up. It was undogmatic, very humane,
and placed the individual near the centre of things. My grandfather
was a liberal-minded man who was also a Liberal in the political
sense, in particular an ardent supporter of Free Trade. He was
invited to stand for the Bradford City Council in the interest of his
party with a view to his becoming Mayor, but he declined. As a boy
my father, too, was a Liberal in this sense. He has related how he
went to Manningham station to watch a train pass without stopping
because he believed that it carried Mr. Gladstone. As he grew up,
especially after his return from his studies in Paris, his Liberalism
was infused with the teachings of Tolstoy; it became broader, even
less susceptible of exact definition, yet more pervasive. It was shown
in his instant response to any high ideal, also, for instance, in his
sending me to a co-educational school in which there was little
attempt at formal education, in his friendships with Radicals such as
H. G. Wells—a near neighbour of whose two sons I was at one time
a constant companion—H. N. Brailsford and J. L. Hammond. I do
not suggest that this Liberalism was more than one, albeit important,
aspect of a many-sided man. But I know that whenever I went outside its ambience I became instantly aware of entering different
worlds of thought and feeling. In all this my mother had herself no
part—she was an inflammable compound of Toryism and anarchy—

yet her father, Walter John Knewstub, who ended his days with us in Church Row, had also been something of a Radical. When I knew him he was a sad old gentleman, but as a young man he had recoiled violently from the gloomy evangelicalism of his family, become a rationalist, and an impassioned advocate of the evolutionary theories of Darwin and a pupil and disciple of Ruskin.

I learnt nothing in the short time I spent at University College School, and little at King Alfred's, where I was happy and content to swim with the tide of its slightly cranky progressivism. What I remember most clearly were the meetings we had with the Head-master, with which our working days began. One morning he announced to us that George Meredith had died, and he explained in simple terms what Meredith had contributed to English literature. On another occasion he confessed that he was going bald, and asked us whether we preferred him bald or wigged and undertook to abide by our vote. We voted for the wig. For a term he read out *Sorab and Rustom*, and I was so moved by the story of the heroic friendship of these noble Persians that when later on I came to know a little about the history and literature of the Ancient World I found it difficult for a time to share the philhellenic bias of both and to see the Persians as the threat to the civilized values represented by the Greeks. If I remember little of the little I learnt at school I remember with clarity and gratitude my readings with my father after tea: the quiet drawing-room, the Queen Anne settees and chairs covered with dark green fabric, the brass table-lamp with the pleated dark green shade the only light. My father read to me, and made me read out, the historical plays of Shakespeare, from the English poets, *Ivanhoe* and *Treasure Island*, Froissart's *Chronicles* and lives of great Englishmen, in particular from Lockhart's *Life of Nelson*. The immediate effect of these readings, passionately as I enjoyed them, was to drive me to find secret solace in 'penny dreadfuls', which really could be bought for a penny in those days. But they implanted in me a love of English literature that grew stronger with every year of my life. They also revealed one of the most grievous of my intellectual shortcomings: an almost total inability to learn anything by heart. I can recall the sense of what I read, but envy those who carry in their heads such celestial baggage as Shakespeare's sonnets. These readings had a further effect—an effect which, had I passed my life as a butcher or a baker, outside the intellectual and artistic world, would hardly merit notice. They inspired in me an ardent love of my own country. In the societies in which I have passed the greater part of my life there are many who acquire an attitude of mind which leads them to regard themselves as citizens of the world and to consider too warm an attachment to a particular part of the earth's surface as parochial, as anachronistic and even dangerous, as liable to hinder the formation of those larger groupings of peoples which, they feel, represent the sole chance of avoiding war.

Not long ago, an anonymous (but easily identified) critic commented upon 'the singular partiality for British art of certain persons whose own antecedents are not entirely British'. The words were written in malice and they were intended to refer to me, but they were truer in their implications than the writer knew. There is an intimate connection between my love of British art (and of the civilization from which it springs) and my 'not entirely British antecedents'. My paternal grandfather came to England as a very young man from his Hanoverian village partly because he disliked the oppressive atmosphere which prevailed in Germany after the failure of the Revolution of 1848; but a stronger motive was a romantic love for England, for its liberties, its just laws, for the language of Shakespeare and Milton. This romantic love survived, indeed was enchanced by, an adult lifetime spent in the grey twilight and the grim environment of industrial Yorkshire. This romantic love was inherited by my father, and suddenly kindled in me by these readings of English poetry and English history between tea and dinner at Oakhill Park. And the probability that my ancestors on my mother's side had been long settled in England before the Norman ships appeared off Pevensey, indeed throughout most of its recorded history, gave to this romantic love an enchanted actuality.

Much as I delighted in these readings and fruitful though they were, England and English literature were matters only of peripheral concern: the theatre of my activities was neither home nor school. This, for me, as it was for many boys who lived in the neighbourhood, was Hampstead Heath. It was a good deal wilder than it is now, and less frequented. This stretch of country, with its dense, ragged clumps of thorn, bracken and gorse, its woodland of silver birch, its stately chestnut groves, and its ponds, was a vast playground in which rough but elaborate games were played by groups of boys drawn from our own and other Hampstead schools, in which working-class boys also intervened. The games were mostly war games played over a wide area which offered endless cover. Considering that the participants were armed with sticks and often engaged in close combat, it is surprising how little harm was done. There was an insuperable obstacle to co-operation between the working-class boys ('street boys' as they were called) and the private schoolboys. This was a curious class distinction: they were apt to throw stones, which we never did.

There were other war-games, far more elaborate, in which I was an absorbed participant. These were invented and played by H. G. Wells with his sons, G. P. (Gyp) and Frank, and myself. Wells was an enjoyable companion: he was immensely zestful and he took his (very occasional) defeats so badly, and there was so little trace of the condescending elder for whom the game was 'only a game', that he was one of ourselves, but one of ourselves who earned by his superior inventiveness and powers of organization the authoritative position he assumed. He gave himself wholly to the game, and I can still hear his always high voice ascend into a scream of protest at the slightest infringement of the complicated rules. Between the warfare on the Heath and on floor and table at the Wells' house I was able, I think, to visualize the fighting in the First War more vividly than many of my contemporaries. Wells was a welcoming and genial host, who talked to me of how the world was being transformed by science in a way that held me spellbound, but I sensed a slight reserve in his attitude towards me. It was not until later that I understood its cause: a contempt, wholly justified, for the poor quality of my education, which was in the sharpest possible contrast to that of his sons. I have already referred to the sketchiness of the instruction at King Alfred's, but I would not have it supposed that I was an apt pupil. Moreover, one of my few aptitudes made matters worse—then and afterwards—by disguising from my teachers the full extent of my deficiencies. I possessed some small power of seeing relationships between apparently disconnected facts, of apprehending situations as a whole. This must have given me the appearance of possessing more knowledge than I in fact possessed. The full extent of my ignorance was only perceived when it had brought me to the brink of disaster, and this too late for anything but patchwork repair.

CHAPTER TWO

SCHOOL AT BEDALES

I LOVED my parents passionately. When they went out at night I imagined as I lay in bed the dangers they would be exposed to, and I prayed fervently that they should be spared. From time to time I would creep down the stairs to find out whether they had returned, and I could not rest peacefully until I was reassured.

During our years in Hampstead my life was happy: there was my friendship with Tom Rowat and his family; there were also other warm but ephemeral friendships, and there was the Heath. Our home life was serene. My sisters Rachel Mary and Bertha Strettell (Betty) attended a small private school, and their life was at this time rather remote from mine, as was that of my brother, Michael, since he was six years my junior. But there was one unusual feature of our home life which at first I apprehended only very vaguely but which became gradually clearer.

Many husbands and wives, after some years of marriage, grow into a single entity: however individual their personalities they evolve a coherent personality of which they each represent different aspects. One, for instance, is the 'strict', the other the 'lenient'. The personalities of my own parents were in almost everything so much opposed that the composite personality never evolved. No two people could have been more unlike. I do not propose to attempt here anything in the nature of a full study of my father. He himself has written extensive memoirs;[1] these, however, are so much more informative about his contemporaries than about himself as to justify our friend, Robert Speaight, in writing his biography.[2] I have in any case myself written a longish essay on his life as an artist.[3] It is accordingly sufficient for my purpose to indicate those aspects of his earlier life and circumstances which stand out in particular contrast

[1] *Men and Memories*, Vol. I, 1931, Vol. II, 1934; *Since Fifty*, 1939.
[2] *William Rothenstein: the Portrait of an Artist in his Time*, 1963.
[3] *Modern English Painters*, Vol. I, 1952.

8

to those of my mother. He came of a family which, never indigent, had become reasonably prosperous. His father, Moritz Rothenstein, was idealistic, gentle, of an openness that expected openness in others, in which he was sometimes deceived. It is certain that without the shrewd judgment and the energy of Charles, his eldest son, the family textile firm would not have prospered as it did. My grandfather's appearance precisely expressed the qualities I have mentioned. One of his brothers served in the Hanoverian Army in the War of 1870; another settled in Paris. About the Rothenstein family very little is known. They were farmers long established in the village of Gröhnde, near Hamlin in the Kingdom of Hanover, and it was here that my grandfather was born on 1st December 1836. It seems that one of his ancestors acquired the village mill and thus became rather better off than his neighbours.

This ignorance is due partly to the fact that until my grandfather's generation they lived uneventful lives, but even more because my grandfather himself, almost the only source of information, regarded his coming to England as marking the beginning of an entirely new life. He retained an affection for Germany—indeed he died of the shock he sustained from the outbreak of war in 1914 between the country of his birth and the country of his ardent adoption. My grandmother was born Bertha Henrietta Dux, in the small town of Hildesheim, also in the Kingdom of Hanover, on 5th May 1844. Her temperament and family were both very different from those of her husband. He was reflective and preoccupied with the future; she was the more energetic and practical—she ran her home with superlative efficiency—and was traditional in her cast of thought. He inclined to Unitarianism in belief and attended the Chapel Lane Unitarian Chapel; she was a pious Jewess. She belonged, in fact, to a Jewish family which counted men of talent among its members: her cousin Baron Ludwig Doczy—Doczy is the Hungarian form of Dux—distinguished himself in the Hungarian diplomatic service and as a writer. Her immediate ancestors owned a small private bank in Hildesheim, living above it in one of the ancient houses with carved wooden façades which formed one of the town's most picturesque features.

Whatever the differences between my grandparents of temperament, of belief, of social origin, they formed, as my parents never did, a single entity. Their house in Bradford was, so to say, under a firm and undivided rule. We used to look forward to our Christmas visits to 6 Walmer Villas, an ample stone-built, Victorian middle-class house, rather dark, solidly furnished. I well remember the fine 'library editions' of Carlyle, Dickens, Mill, Ruskin, Macaulay and Goethe, and, among the pictures, a small steel engraving of Cardinal Newman. (How surprised my grandparents would have been at my reasons for recalling this little print.) But the room I remember best was the bathroom, a dark room panelled in mahogany, with a bath, encased in mahogany, which made a noise so terrifying when the plug was removed that we were afraid of taking our baths alone!

It would be difficult to imagine circumstances more differing than those attendant upon the upbringing of my mother. The very word upbringing is inappropriate, for in a sense she had none.

The Knewstub family was an old one, never of sufficient importance to be strictly traced. The most notable member of it was John Knewstub, born in 1544, puritan divine and friend of Queen Elizabeth, Vice-Master of St John's College, Cambridge, and Rector of Cuckfield, Suffolk, where he died in 1624. The family came originally from Kirby Stephen in Westmorland but they were to be found later on in the eastern counties, perhaps on account of John Knewstub's migration there.

My mother's father, Walter John Knewstub, was a painter. The son of a printer, he was born in Colchester on 11th March 1833 and educated at Mill Hill. As a boy he came to know Ruskin, who gave him instruction in drawing and set him to make pencil studies of baskets, insisting upon such minute detail that his eyesight was for a time impaired. Settling in London he entered the Royal Academy Schools, where he met Rossetti and became his only pupil, living for a time at 16 Cheyne Walk, the splendid house in Chelsea which Rossetti took after his wife's death in 1862, which Swinburne shared and where he wrote a number of his *Poems and Ballads*, and where Meredith also briefly lodged.

Walking together, Rossetti and Knewstub saw a young woman whose beauty moved them deeply; they followed her home and asked her father for his permission to call again and make portraits of her. Deeply suspicious of 'artists', he consented with reluctance. My grandfather fell in love with her and, anxious to remove her from a bohemian circle around Rossetti (she was quickly acclaimed as one of the Pre-Raphaelite 'stunners'), he married her before he could maintain her otherwise than precariously. The marriage seems to have been unhappy. The Knewstub parents disapproved of the marriage and disinherited their son. The reason, perhaps, for parental disapproval was Emily Renshaw's Catholicism, for the Knewstub family was dourly evangelical. If this was in fact the reason, it was well founded: the household was harried by theological argument between the ardent Catholic convert and the not less ardent rationalist, emancipated from the family evangelicism. Knewstub's means of earning a livelihood were further impaired by an estrangement with Rossetti, with whom he worked as an assistant in his studio. Rossetti used Emily Knewstub's head for his 'Venus Verticordia', a half-nude Venus (of which two versions exist), and Knewstub was deeply offended. When I myself became a Catholic early in my life it was from intellectual conviction; so far was my conversion from deriving from my mother that it was not even disclosed to her, although by baptism and earliest upbringing she also was a Catholic; yet there is a sort of material sense in which I inherit it from this ill-fated Pre-Raphaelite beauty. She herself was first drawn to the Catholic faith by Lady Mount Temple (whose husband was Knewstub's principal patron), whom Ruskin followed, as the golden-haired Miss Tollemache, from church to church in Rome. She died young, worn out by child-bearing and poverty and theological dispute. Knewstub had a genuine talent that is perceptible, in spite of the pervasive influence of Rossetti, in his 'Portrait of Mrs. W. J. Knewstub and her Daughter'; but it was small, and small talents are apt to suffer when too much is required of them. He had a talent for comic drawing that reflected his genial but penetrating wit, and he contributed illustrations to a number of periodicals. In his struggle to provide for his family he was compelled at times to produce work inferior to his best. Ford Madox Brown, however, had a particular admiration for his work, which he praised with characteristic warmth. Knewstub assisted him in carrying out the twelve wall paintings in the Great Hall in the Town Hall, Manchester, on which he was engaged from 1879 to 1891. In spite of the active friendships of members of the Pre-Raphaelite circle, things went badly with Knewstub and his children: there were times when they were short of food. (At a time of acute distress he was compelled to sell the numerous letters he had received from Rossetti and other members of the Pre-Raphaelite circle, which would appear to have been lost sight of.)

As soon therefore as my mother—the *daughter* who figures in the
picture by her father referred to just now—was old enough (and that
was not very old) she assumed the responsibility of providing for the
family. Having received but a sketchy education and no vocational
training she could think of only one way of meeting their urgent
need. She was far from being a great actress, but her extraordinary
beauty and her combination of dignity and high spirits enabled her
to obtain parts. When she and my father met—at a reception for
Maeterlinck—she was playing the part of Miss Ansell in *Walker*,
London, with Irene Vanbrugh and Toole.

Such were the backgrounds of my parents, and they served to
accentuate the innate differences between them. My father, though
a close friend of such bohemians as Lautrec, Wilde, Conder and
Augustus John, retained the middle-class virtues which he learnt at
home in Bradford: he was at heart methodical, temperate, punctual
and considerate. My mother, going straight from a home beset by
poverty, where her whole energies were given to the care of her
brothers and sisters, into the exhilarating and undisciplined life of
the theatre, was denied the opportunity of reflection, or of forming
settled habits of any kind. She remained all her life a being moved
solely by impulse, moreover by violent impulse, and above all
tigerishly devoted to her family and friends. Aware that my father
must necessarily disapprove of much that she did, or failed to do,
of much that she thought and said, she tended to conceal it from him.
Therefore, although my parents in their entirely different ways were
deeply attached they never, until the last years of my father's life,
came to terms with one another; and our home was never subject
to one head, but to two, each opposed in almost every thought and
impulse. The contrast between my parents—above all between my
father's gravity and my mother's frivolity and indiscretion—was a
source of amusement to their friends.

Each of them came to feel that there was, so to say, a super-
abundance in their household of the qualities that the other provided.
Were my father tempted to impulsiveness or extravagance, he would
reflect that these already had sufficient scope, while my mother, had
she been tempted by high purpose, would feel that this was a quality
which, while respecting, she dreaded as one which jeopardized the
security of the family. (My father used to borrow money to lend to
writers and painters in need at times when he himself had nothing in

the bank.) And so they each acquired a settled suspicion of the purposes of the other. They had a few characteristics in common: both were courageous; both were physically strong (they used to walk and bicycle distances, to our generation incredible, about England and France) and, although my father was liable to fits of melancholy, both were immensely good company, and both had highly developed taste which invariably enhanced their surroundings. Even here, however, differences were conspicuous: my father's austerity was expressed in a preference for straight-backed, uncushioned chairs and the like. When they married and settled in Edwardes Square, my mother told me there was no single chair brought from the Glebe Place studio (where he lived before their marriage) that was fit to sit on. The furniture, mostly provided then and afterwards by my mother, was always well padded, though without sacrifice of style.

My parents shared a love for many friends and for one aesthetic movement, Pre-Raphaelitism. The Pre-Raphaelites were the heroes of my mother's early life. She remembered D. G. Rossetti, and more clearly still the dimly-lit rooms of 16 Cheyne Walk and their dark and heavy hangings. With William Michael, his brother who outlived him by many years, Ford Madox Brown and likewise Swinburne (of whom her father made a portrait which hung at No 2 The Pines, Putney, where Swinburne spent his last years under the vigilant tutelage of Theodore Watts-Dunton), my mother continued on terms of friendship until the end of their lives. Watts-Dunton himself developed an embarrassing passion for her, which misled him into hiring cabs to follow her about, himself kneeling, in order to remain unobserved and unrebuked, on the floor, and peering intermittently over the lower edge of the window. My father's attitude towards the Pre-Raphaelites was entirely different. Before his return from Paris in 1894 he had never lived in London—except for a year as a student at the Slade—and he had become a member of the French School. It was not until my mother introduced him into the William Michael Rossetti household that he was brought in direct contact with some of the survivors of the Pre-Raphaelite circle and that he received with a shock of pleasure the belated impact of its passionate flowering of the imagination, hitherto known to him only through legend. There was accordingly, until the end of their lives, frequent talk between my parents of the doings and sayings of the Pre-Raphaelites.

At the time of which I am writing my parents' extreme dichotomy had little effect upon my mind, upon my conscious mind at least. In these days when writers of self-biography make, with the aid, perhaps, of some pointers from Freud, lurid revelations about their childhood selves, I have to confess, with the consciousness of being a dull dog, that up to the age of twelve or so I was a rowdy extrovert, ever drawn towards what attracted me as romantic. I had little inner life: I was preoccupied mostly with my parents, my friends and with the adventurous life shared with some dozens of other boys that was enacted upon Hampstead Heath. If I had done little good in the small world in which I moved, I had also, I think, done little ill; life was straightforward and I had little cause for behaving otherwise than well. In particular I was truthful, and that, with an affectionate heart, was perhaps my principal virtue. I can remember, as well as I can remember anything in my childhood, the happening that made me so. It was at Hawksworth, a village in the Yorkshire Dales, where we spent the summer of 1904. I was three years old, and it was a sunny morning. I still see plainly in my mind's eye the wreckage of the little yellow cart with red wheels that I had managed to destroy. I can still recall the beating my father gave me after I told him that the cart had simply fallen to pieces. The shock I received from this happening drew my attention to the importance that people attached to truth, and from that day I came to respect it also.

But the time when I was able to pursue this simple way of life was brought to a sudden end. It would have ended in any case, for I was arriving at an age when, without having any notion of what it might consist, I was vaguely aware of intimations of the need of a wider theatre of action. But when I was eleven years old my way of life was radically altered: I was sent away to school and my parents left London and made their home in Gloucestershire.

We spent the summer of 1912 in a thatched cottage in the village of Oakridge Lynch. Rabindranath Tagore, the Indian poet, with his son and daughter-in-law, came to stay and lodged in a cottage nearby. Tagore, wearing a shallow white turban and an outer garment resembling an off-white cassock, made, in an English village, a striking and exotic figure. One afternoon my father, my mother, Tagore and I, out walking together, came upon a big, ruinous farmhouse in the neighbouring hamlet of Far Oakridge. My mother, and shortly afterwards my father, were enraptured by the place and the splendid view across the valley it commanded. By winter, partially restored, it had become our home.

Inclined to look forward rather than back, I saw at a glance that there was a stretch of country beside which Hampstead Heath was only a playground. But who was there to share it with me? For the first time in my life I gave a nostalgic backward look. I found I could think most clearly when I walked not through wood or field, subject to the multitudinous distractions they offered both in the way of things to look at and minor physical obstacles, but along the straight roads that ran across the flat hilltop to Bisley or Oakridge Lynch. Along the dullest ways I walked, then and as long as we lived in Gloucestershire, when I wished to focus my thoughts, mostly occupied with London. In those days London was more quintessentially London than it is now: the buildings were more heavily coated with soot, and soot more densely permeated the atmosphere. There was a pervasive clatter of iron-rimmed wheels and of horses' hooves over stone-surfaced streets. Above this clatter the hoarse cries could be heard of cab drivers and street hawkers. There was street after street of Georgian houses, black-faced, neglected but intact, along which traffic seldom passed, and in these people's voices could be plainly heard, even from far away. Most people were dressed in black; there was, of course, a sharper distinction between rich and poor—the poor looked really poor, shabby and rough, but is it only in my memory that they were more genial, more high-spirited? And is it only in my memory that the railway stations were different, that they were great black iron skeletons in and out of which streamed locomotives freshly painted and with brasswork gleaming like burnished gold? What I do now remember clearly—but which, being an unprecocious boy, mattered nothing to me then—was the way women were muffled from head to foot: bulky black beings whose faces, however, were sometimes so lovely as to make me stare, stare with surprise that flowers so lovely could grow upon stems so drab and shapeless. I remember the way, before crossing a street with my mother or nurse, one had to pause for a perceptible time while skirts were gathered. Would I, I wondered, ever again enjoy the sense of danger, slight but exhilarating, of getting up into a hansom cab, a sense of danger gradually diminished but never entirely stilled; even when one was settled in the seat so far from the ground there remained a sense of precariousness. I used to be the prey of a disquieting fancy that the driver, perched up behind, were he heavy, would overbalance the cab and catapult the horse backwards between the shafts. But apprehension only heightened the pleasure of rattling through the fog, nothing visible but the gaslit streetlamps and the horse's jogging rump and swishing tail.

Walking quietly along the dull road from Oakridge to Bisley or Oakridge Lynch, I recalled, also in London, two Putawayo Indians —survivors of a massacre—whom Sir Roger Casement used to bring for my father to paint: they spoke no English, but I was sent for to try to divert them while they posed, wearing nothing but beads and feathers. I used to look intently into Sir Roger Casement's lean and furrowed face—as kind a face as I had ever seen. I would have looked more intently still if I had foreseen that within a few years he would be executed as a traitor. I recalled two in particular of the occasions when I had raced to forestall the maid in answering the front-door bell, for on each I found myself face to face with a singular being. The first was a tall stooping man with long swathes of lank, honey-coloured hair—the hair that might have belonged to a boy or girl—hanging over a face of a man who had the look of one already dead, so pallid the ravaged flesh, so sightless-seeming the light blue eyes. He told me who he was and asked for my father. This was my only conscious sight of the artist Charles Conder, whose *Life and Death*, decades later, I was to write. The second was with a being very much alive, a shortish handsome boy with apricot-coloured skin and a dense mop of dark brown hair so stiff that it stood on end. He looked nervous, sullen and somehow hectic. I took him for a barrow-boy but he told me he had been sent to see my father. This boy was Mark Gertler, who had indeed been sent to show him his precocious drawings. I do not know when the first encounter took place; doubtless just before Conder was placed under restraint. I must have been five or six. The second, research in connection with the chapter on Gertler in my *Modern English Painters* enabled me to date exactly: 7th October 1908.

I repined, of course, for Tom Rowat, the Wells brothers and half a dozen more, and a few of my parents' friends who had shown me special kindness. Of one of these I was only a few weeks ago reminded. Going through old books in an attic I was about to throw away a battered copy of *The British Boy's Annual*. From force of habit I glanced at the fly-leaf, and what I saw made it precious to me. 'To dear John Rothenstein,' ran the inscription, 'from his friends Jessie and Joseph Conrad.' The handwriting was Conrad's: I must have valued the gift then, for beneath it, in my own, is the date '1911–1912'. Other of my parents' friends who, like Conrad, entranced me by stories of dramatic happenings in remote parts of the world were Robert Cunninghame Graham and W. H. Hudson. All three talked to this unnoteworthy boy as though to an equal: more than that, as though he were an inspiring audience.

A letter written to me by Cunninghame Graham precisely expresses the benevolent interest of my parent's friends:

14 Washington House,
Basil Street, SW

July 1st 1911.

Dear Mr. Rothenstein,

I was greatly struck yesterday by your telling me that you were ten years of age to the day.

I had thought you were much older, for I remember your father long before he was your age. Believe me, Sir, it is by growing old young that we maintain our youth and illusions.

Therefore I have ventured to send you a knife. In it you will find all (or nearly all) the implements useful, nay necessary to a young man turning his back on youth, and looking forward to the indiscretions of riper years.

In point, there is (or should be) a button hook. This will serve to button ladies' boots. As to your own, you will no doubt borrow a hair pin from one of them, and do it more artistically.

Then there is a corkscrew, a most invaluable weapon in an age of temperance. Nothing sticks so hard as the cork in a bottle of Kop's ale. The only unlucky thing is that, when the fog of combat is past and the cork extracted, the ale is but little worth.

We next come to the punch, so useful to make holes in book covers, musical instruments, and anything that is handy. The blades of the knife are excellent for furniture repairing, and for writing the name on public monuments and thus securing at least municipal immortality. The tweezers, and the like, all good in their way, will, I have no doubt, receive novel applications, by one so ingeniously inclined as yourself.

Pray, Sir, accept once more my heartiest congratulations and
convey the same to your family,
Believe me,
Yours very faithfully,
R. B. Cunninghame Graham

I was not ten (to the day) until eleven days later than I was alleged
to have stated. Was I less truthful than I have claimed? Or was I
misheard? I recall one other gift, one that, on reflection, seems to
have a symbolic and a melancholy meaning. 'I'll make you a model
theatre,' Gordon Craig promised, 'a theatre with changes of scenery,
and actors . . .'—and he evoked a dazzling toy with his eloquent and
detailed description. 'I've brought you,' he said later, 'the steps leading up to the stage,' and he handed me a tiny set of stairs he had
carved, but like the great theatre of his own dreams my little theatre
was never to be.

These continuous recollections of London and my friends made
me sad. This migration meant, too, the end of the summer holidays,
on which our parents took the four of us to St. Seine l'Abbaye, in
Burgundy, and to Vaucottes-sur-Mer and to nearby Vattetot, in
Normandy. My memories of these places were of sunny hot days.
We came to know the farmers, labourers and fishermen better than
we knew those at home. In both regions we used to lend a little help
with the harvest, and off the Norman coast we were taken out fishing.
Until I saw the fishermen kill conger eels and octopuses I had never
seen anything, except insects, die. I remember my father—who
sometimes stayed up all night making notes for his 'nocturnes'—
waking me to hear nightingales sing, and I remember the long rows
of cornstooks burnished silver by the moon.

My sadness was better founded than I knew. In Gloucestershire
a year's languid honeymoon was soon over, and then, though I continued to admire—who could not?—the splendid landscape and
buildings, the Cotswolds never fully gained my love. There seemed
to me a pervasive bleakness about them that was expressed in the
prevailing climate: sky the colour of slate, pressing low upon the
land, which promised heavy rain that rarely fell; a high dry wind.

I could not, did not, wish to resist the infection of my father's
passionate love of the Cotswolds. He had never before owned a
house in the country, and the ruinous condition of his fine farmhouse

was a challenge which he ardently met. I have never known a man so charged with energy as he. Up by six, he often spent the first two hours of his day, axe or billhook in hand, clearing a copse which bordered his few acres of beech wood. Although without previous experience, he himself farmed some sixty acres of land, riding over it on a strong horse which served equally well as a hack, between the shafts of the carriage, or for pulling the plough. My father's energies were far from being confined to his own small estate: he quickly established friendly relations with the villagers both at Far Oakridge and at Oakridge Lynch, initiating many constructive activities and making the fullest use his modest means allowed of the local craftsmen for which the neighbourhood was noted. Although he played a leading part in the life of the two villages, he avoided accepting the part of squire, which would have been discordant with both his temperament and convictions as well as the independent and radical traditions of the district. To none of his local interests, however, did he give any part of his working day; it was an uncommon event if he did anything except paint while the light lasted. Ardently as he loved Oakridge, it satisfied my father's needs just a degree less fully than he supposed. His manifold activities often called him away, but when he remained there for more than a few weeks he was subject to fits of depression which only the arrival of a friend could lift. I would have responded more readily to the attractions of life at Far Oakridge and shared more fully than I did my father's attachment to it had I been happier at school.

I was sent in the autumn term, 1912, to Bedales, which was in some respects a peculiar school, although its peculiarities are not those generally attributed to it. I do not remember why I was sent there, but it may have been due in part to my intimate friendship with Tom Rowat, who had entered the year before. That this Jacobite, destined for the regular army, came to attend so unconventional and so 'progressive' a school illustrates the pervasive Liberalism of the environment in which so many of my generation grew up. Tom's mother, although in many ways a traditional Highlander, was a relative of H. N. Brailsford, and she had contacts as a girl with that enterprising and liberal-minded Glasgow society especially active at the beginning of the century, in which such men as the pioneer architect Charles Rennie Mackintosh were leading figures. Bedales was not therefore so improbable a place for her to send her son to.

Bedales is a co-educational school, the most successful of its kind in England. Co-education seemed to me to play a far less influential part in the formation of the school than is generally supposed. In my day it would have made little difference to Bedales had there been no girls there: some boys—the majority, I fancy—would have preferred it; others were indifferent. The girls were positively welcome, in fact, only to a smallish minority. That is not to say that the girls were regarded as inferiors: there existed between the boys and the girls, on the whole, feelings of mutual friendliness and respect, but had Steephurst, the Girls' House, been two hundred miles away instead of two hundred yards, it would have mattered little to the boys. Among the majority of the boys the prevailing spirit was not very different from that at the average public school, but among the seniors, the prefects especially, there existed a small but active group imbued with the ideals of the founder and with the spirit that had animated the school in its early and formative years. Bedales first opened in 1893 in an old house on Bedales Hill, near Lindfield in Sussex, as a school for boys. Five years later four girls joined the sixty boys already there. In 1900 the school—by then numbering sixty-eight boys, seven girls and a staff of nine—was moved to an estate of some hundred and twenty acres by the village of Steep near Petersfield in Hampshire. Therefore at the time of my own entry something of the fervour and of the prejudices, too, engendered during the early years, were still strong among these older boys. The 'Early Christians', so to say, among them could be distinguished by certain outward signs: they affected sandals, and coats that looked as though they had been made at home or else in some remote fishing village, and they showed a predilection for cold baths, a vegetable diet, for brown bread, and in season and out of it for fresh air, the colder the better. The outlook expressed by these outward signs was in politics Liberal or Socialist, but Socialist according to Morris rather than to Marx. This was due partly to the fact that Bedales, however pronounced its departures from the traditional pattern, was very much a 'public school' and therefore very English in the cast of thought that prevailed there. Marx would therefore have repelled not only, as at other schools, on account of his 'foreignness', but even more as standing for something which at Bedales aroused peculiar antipathy, namely a dogmatic creed. Marx's precise and uncompromising doctrines would have been almost as shocking as the

ALICE MARY KNEWSTUB AND HER MOTHER, BY WALTER JOHN KNEWSTUB

ALICE MARY ROTHENSTEIN, 1900, BY AUGUSTUS JOHN

WILLIAM ROTHENSTEIN, 1897, BY SARGENT

decrees of the Council of Trent. In practice no shock was suffered, as no such dogmas, at least in my hearing, were ever discussed: they were tacitly deemed to lie outside the boundaries of the area of speculation of reasonable men. According to the generally accepted view, any exactly defined belief was apt, by its very nature, to be discounted as an expression of narrowmindedness; likewise anything ecclesiastical as belonging to an order which a progressive society had left behind. (I would wish at this point to make clear that these observations relate to the period of the First World War. Today the leaders of thought at Bedales may, for aught I know, be Marxists and Ultramontanes, but I do not know, for I have never been back.) This climate of thought and feeling, most positive then among certain of the older boys, was not, I take it, so very remote from that at other public schools, except for the simple lifery and the absence of political Toryism and of conformity, even nominal, to the Church of England.

But already in my day there had come to be a distinction between the sandalled, vegetarian spartans and the main body of the school, which was far less unconventional both in belief and conduct. The old 'activists' won recruits from time to time among their juniors, usually from boys and girls from the wealthier, more conventional homes, to whom the high idealism that existed at Bedales made a particular appeal. In spite of the influence of the 'activists' and the periodic adhesion to their number of these recuits, the general tendency of the school was in the direction of a closer approximation to the conditions that prevailed in other public schools. There was no abandonment of the founder's ideals, but they began to be given a more flexible interpretation; the carrot and the sandal were fast becoming anachronisms. From what I hear about developments at Bedales since my own time, I understand that this tendency has grown still more pronounced. If Bedales has gone a long way to meet the world it has also, in a modest way, modified it. Ideas and practices which seemed revolutionary or eccentric at the time of its foundation have won wide acceptance, and to an appreciable degree as a result of Bedales pioneering.

I was not a success at Bedales: I gained little in the course of my years there, and gave less. This was not chiefly due to defects in the school so much as the fact that it was not the right school for me nor I the right boy for it. When I arrived there its particular form of idealism was one which made no fresh appeal for me: I had already become familiar with it at King Alfred's—a preparatory school, in fact although not in intention, for Bedales. I had become familiar with it through my whole Hampstead environment. I trust that I will not be considered immodest if I say that I already possessed, in however rudimentary a form, some of the qualities which it was the mission of Bedales to implant. I was capable, for example, of forming independent opinions; I was fairly tolerant of the opinions of other people, fairly free from national and class prejudice, benevolently disposed towards my fellow men, ready to co-operate with them, and appreciative of fine craftsmanship. The possession of these qualities was not due to personal merit: it just so happened that they were qualities fairly common among those with whom I was brought up. But my shocking intellectual shortcomings Bedales was far from ideally equipped to remedy. I had no shadow of a notion how important it was to secure an education, nor had I the faintest inkling of how hard a struggle survival, let alone the most modest success, involved. The teaching at Bedales was better than it was at King Alfred's, though it was in general far from good. But except in such exact subjects as mathematics, in which my knowledge could be precisely rated—at nil, I was able to get along without public discredit. As at King Alfred's, curiosity and a seriousness of mind, a capacity for seeing subjects as a whole and with a certain detachment, even gained me, I believe, the reputation of a fairly intelligent boy. Competitive examinations and competitive ratings were out of harmony with the Bedales *ethos*; so I was never shown up—until I had my first contact with the world outside. Drawing—which I cultivated with ease, as well as some crafts and intellectually peripheral subjects, which were deemed to rank with such crucial subjects as science and languages, masked my ignorance of these. Whether the depths of my ignorance were suspected I do not know: what I do know is that I was never told that I was wasting my own time and the time of my teachers; and never warned that I would be wise to reflect and that unless I showed improvement I had better go elsewhere—preferably to a coach.

It would be wrong to suggest that my years at Bedales were wretched, but I was vaguely oppressed by a sense of something being fundamentally amiss—I had not the wit to see that the want of application on my own part and of critical firm direction on that of my teachers was making nonsense of my presence there. There were, on the contrary, many aspects of school life that I enjoyed. First my friends, among others Malcolm MacDonald, Harry Carter, Basil Ivory, Peter Mrosovsky, and, of course, Tom Rowat. Within our circle was cultivated a lively and sophisticated sense of humour, exercised largely at the expense of the staff, which included targets by which the most lethargic sense of humour would have been tempted. One of our favourite targets was one of the best-liked masters in the school, Joseph Wicksteed, son of the authority on Blake and no mean authority in his own right. He was an ardent pacifist, yet because he invariably wore the khaki uniform in which he had performed some army welfare or educational service, he appeared as a comically martial figure. Driven by the housing shortage to extreme expedients, he bought two railway-carriages which, placed side by side, served as a dwelling for his family and himself. Its appellation was changed in the course of time—whether by him or by us I cannot now remember—from 'a couple of railway-carriages on the hill' to 'Froxfield Court'. It was, I recall, his disapproval of banks that accounted for the large accumulations of pound notes that used to flutter floorwards whenever a cushion was disturbed. A class taken by Wicksteed, whatever its ostensible subject, was apt to become a lament that the early Protestants, to the lasting detriment of their religion, hearkened to the equivocal voices of Luther and Calvin, to the neglect of Zwingli's. 'And more's the pity,' he would conclude. All this made life lively and eventful. Then there was the surrounding country, which we were encouraged to explore. In front, seawards, were the South Downs, the great smooth dome of Butser Hill—a calm presence always felt—their most prominent feature. Behind, a wooded hillside rose up steeply. The main school building itself, a great square stucco-faced block, built in a species of suburban-Edwardian-institutional style, was far from beautiful, yet pleasant enough to live in. The adjacent Hall, where all public functions took place, from the very secular religious services, about which I shall say something later on, to variety shows staged by the boys and girls, was a fine place, built of oak and red brick, in the arts-and-crafts style with which at home in the Cotswolds I had already become familiar, with something of the look of an urbanized barn.

It may be considered singular, at least by those who do not know

Bedales, that I do not include among the pleasures of life the presence of the girls.

The girls at Bedales lived in conditions very different from those prevailing, for example, at co-educational American schools and universities. At such institutions girls are enrolled as a matter of course. At Bedales it was otherwise. Their presence was an audacious experiment, and the school authorities were under a particularly heavy responsibility towards the girls and their parents. Moreover a baby would not only have been a tragedy for the girl concerned and her family, but it might have imperilled, or possibly even have ended, the whole Bedales experiment. That the authorities should have taken strong precautions against relationships which might have resulted in illegitimate births and other undesirable consequences was entirely understandable, but, speaking for myself, the safeguards imposed were destructive of almost all the pleasure that I might otherwise have taken in the proximity of the girls. I speak for myself only, because there was singularly little discussion among the boys about the girls, but I suspect that my own feelings were fairly widely shared. The principal safeguard was the fostering of an ideal of wholesome comradeship which involved the stigmatization of sex, or even romance, as 'silliness'. 'Unsuitable' couples, that is to say couples one or both of whom were suspected of being in any degree inflammable in temperament, were warned against or reprimanded for 'silliness'. Other measures were also taken, the withholding, for instance, of chits permitting certain boys and girls to go out of the grounds at the same time when it was suspected that they might meet. Moreover it was generally believed that boys or girls considered to be prone to serious or persistent 'silliness' were discreetly got rid of as 'unsuitable', although without access to records this would be difficult to confirm. However justified such measures might have been, their effect, so far as I was concerned, was to make my relationship with the girls constrained and uneasy, and it was with surprise that I discovered, during the holidays, that my relations with girls from conventional schools, however strict, were by comparison natural and relaxed. But in our remote corner of Gloucestershire girls, or for that matter boys of my own age, were very few. I was stirred and troubled by the proximity of girls and wished ardently to become friends with one or another of those for whom I formed romantic but remote attachments. I was myself, I believe, at one time regarded as 'silliness' prone, yet the excitement even of holding for an instant the hand of one of the objects of my successive attachments would have been unbearably intense. During all my years at Bedales I never made a single physical approach, even of the most modest kind, to any girl. I was at that time little troubled by sensual imaginings, and an odd circumstance quelled somewhat even the faint stirrings I experienced. I swam comparatively well and I was accordingly invited from time to time, with one or two other boys, to coach the girls for competitions by demonstrating the crawl and other racing strokes, timing their 'lengths' and the like. The spectacle of heavy bosoms, unmuscled bellies and pendulous buttocks of girls whose figures had seemed beneath their tunics so reticent and trim came as a shock to my susceptibilities. My ideas about the configuration of women derived, probably, from statues and paintings, and the difference between them and the ungainly adolescent bodies which emerged from the swimming-bath was so startling that on going back to our own changing room one afternoon I looked with relief faintly touched with desire at the slim bodies of the bathing boys, by comparison so taut and controlled. Bedales, so far as I am aware, was free from homosexuality, and I myself was ignorant of its very existence, yet that afternoon I had a momentary insight into the homosexual impulse. Provided that a boy and girl had no perceptible trace of romantic feelings for one another, or of any intention of forming a close friendship, however free from emotional overtones, they could associate freely, but the practice of the authorities of surrounding with an atmosphere of constraint couples who wished to be friends, romantically or 'platonically', meant that boys and girls could associate freely only, as a rule, with those of the other sex to whom they were emotionally indifferent. The situation was complicated by surprising exceptions: certain couples, whose intentions were suspect according to common report, were permitted, even encouraged, to spend much time in one another's company. Were these exceptions, we wondered, the result of errors of judgment? Or was it that a few 'show' couples, exemplifying the 'wholesome comradeship' officially inculcated, were considered desirable by the school authorities? Here again, we had no means of finding answers to these questions. However devious, the safeguards were, in a negative sense, effective. During my years at Bedales no scandal resulted from the association of boys with girls.

It remains to say something of the remarkable man whose convictions brought Bedales into being: John Haden Badley. He was born in 1865, educated at Rugby and Cambridge, and came under the influence of progressive educationalists such as Montessori and Frobel and of Fabian Socialism. He came to regard education as 'not concerned primarily with intellectual development . . . with the exercise of memory or reasoning powers, but with the development of the creative intelligence . . . the formation of interests, purposes and ideals.'[1] It is not to my purpose to join issue with my old schoolmaster upon the theory of education, but his approach seems to me to have a grave defect. All education must have a medium. Neither 'creative interests' nor 'purposes' nor even 'ideals' can be taught directly, *in vacuo*, so to say. As well teach chemistry without a lab. or painting without paint. It is my conviction that Mr. Badley's desiderata can be taught primarily through the enlightenment and the disciplining of the intellect, and that this can be best done through the medium of such traditional subjects as mathematics, history, science, languages and the like. Of course the traditional subjects can be taught in a deadening fashion, but as soon as I left Bedales I discovered that many of the friends I made from Westminster and Winchester had fulfilled Mr. Badley's aim through an application to such subjects which combined extreme rigour with intelligence and that, in particular, 'creativity' seemed to be fostered with particular success by the highly traditional curriculum of Eton.

Mr. Badley was an austere, spare man, bearded, a reincarnation of an Old Testament Prophet, tempered by Dr. Arnold's Rugby. He was aloof and withdrawn and abrupt and sparing of words, yet, in his rubber-soled shoes, silently omnipresent; an awe-inspiring figure, the loftiness of whose motives nobody doubted. He was, however, a poor judge of men, and boys, and chiefly through a propensity for judging them through their words rather than their acts: it was evident that someone who subscribed to high ideals was likely to find favour with him. Nevertheless he drew to himself many, both among staff and boys and girls, who ardently shared his own wholly disinterested dedication to his ideals. I write of him in the past tense, for nearly half a century has passed since I last saw him, but he is alive and flourishing, and to judge from photographs that have appeared in the press in connection with his hundredth birthday

---

[1] *Bedales—A Pioneer School*, by J. H. Badley, 1923, p. 201.

the austere, authoritative head and the spare, upright figure have changed little.

My school life was not eventful, but it was marked by one very curious incident, of which my account, in the absence of access to the records, must remain incomplete. One night I was woken up and told to go to the Senior Library where some of the prefects were assembled. I was surprised, for no such thing had happened to me before, nor, so far as I was aware, to anyone else. I was invited to relate what I knew of the circumstances in which a grey suit belonging to a boy named Budgett had been damaged. In a changing-room that afternoon, Budgett, who was a friend of mine, held up a grey suit, which had been hanging there while he was out on the playing fields. The suit had received a series of cuts across the elbows and knees. We all considered this odd, but I certainly gave the incident little further thought. I had no sooner expressed my surprise at being questioned about it than I suddenly understood, and with some trepidation, the reason why. The questioning prefect went on to ask me whether it was not a fact that I had borrowed a knife only half an hour or so before the finding of the suit. This was indeed the case: I had received a parcel tied with thick string and I had visited all four changing rooms before I was able to borrow a knife. Next night the same thing happened: I was informed with a hint of menace that boy after boy, on being questioned, had admitted to hearing me ask for the loan of a knife. Had I been more experienced, I would have found reassurance in the fact that only just before the discovery of the slashing these attempts had been so openly made, but as it was, after the questioning was repeated on successive nights, I became greatly disturbed, more especially as I had not long since egregiously broken rules and been detected. With Malcolm MacDonald I had climbed out of the school at night and walked for miles through the country. Examination by the Headmaster elicited the fact that this was not a first offence. I had, moreover, played an unkind practical joke that had rightly earned me a reprimand. At Bedales we slept in dormitories with about five to seven beds and a few changes were usually made at the beginning of each term. On the first night of the term when these events occurred I dismantled, while he was absent taking a bath, the bed and hid the possessions, in fact eliminated all traces of the presence of an unpopular boy who had just been placed in our dormitory. When he returned, lights had been put out; we

all feigned sleep, and in answer to his complaints we told him that he
was in error and it was *last* term that he had slept in this dormitory
but this term he had been moved to another. The poor boy wandered
about for a time feeling that he had no place of his own in an
unfriendly world. Concerned, then, at being in some deserved
official disfavour, I went one evening to the house of a member of
the staff, the physical training instructor, R. E. Roper, an eagle-like
man, widely respected throughout the school for his physical prow-
ess, his thorough knowledge of several subjects in addition to that
which he taught, and his invariable and imperturbable calm. He was
a particular friend of mine, but I had never before sought his advice
or indeed that of any other master. He listened without comment to
my account of what had taken place. Then he opened a large note-
book and proceeded to question me, searchingly and in the utmost
detail, noting down the substance of my replies. 'I don't know
whether you're aware,' he said, 'that people, innocent people, can
become very, very tired from being questioned, and eventually the
temptation to confess can become overpowering. If the questioning
goes on long enough, they are tempted to see in confession the only
possibility of relief. Any donkey examining the facts could see that
you couldn't have done this. You had no motive; you weren't alone
with the wretched suit, the facts simply don't add up to that—no,
there's no case, but hang on, however tired you get, and never admit
you did it.' But nothing I could say could satisfy my questioners.
Soon after the holidays began my father received a cryptic letter
from Mr. Badley suggesting, in effect, that I should not return to
Bedales. Shortly afterwards this was followed by a second, saying
that the culprit had been detected and was leaving the school for
good, expressing regret and urging my return. I did return, not
without indignant feelings, and was shortly afterwards appointed a
prefect. I never discovered who the culprit was, nor was any allusion
ever made to the incident or to my nightly interrogations.

My time at Bedales was not entirely wasted, and looking back it
seems to me that I drew some benefit from my growing sense of disharmony with my surroundings. It would not be easy to define the
causes of this disharmony. Perhaps the attitude of the authorities
towards the relations between the boys and the girls provides as apt
an illustration as any. It was perfectly clear to me that, however
tentative my own feelings, they were the first faint stirrings of the

impulse of which love, passion, marriage, procreation could be the consequences, and that to describe an impulse so momentous as 'silliness' was itself a text-book example of silliness. Had it been stigmatized instead as 'sinful', I would at least have understood what was meant. That would have had some meaning, but the term 'sinful', I began to apprehend, would have been repugnant to the Bedales cast of thought. To call a misdemeanour a 'sin' would have savoured of an appeal to a dogmatic system; a synonym for ossification; it might have provoked discussion involving clear-cut definitions; so a term empty of meaning—in the context at least—was understandably used instead. I became vaguely but increasingly uneasy at the idea of depending, to the extent to which we seemed to depend at Bedales, upon a diffused sentiment of tolerance and 'fair play', a sentiment which was, so to say, itself the law, instead of being the expression of some sort of clearly formulated and generally accepted set of principles. While I was being interrogated by the prefects, for instance, I felt suddenly frightened by the sense that, once the sentiment of tolerance and 'fair play' evaporated, I was left without protection. I had already come to feel that sentiments, however high-minded, were not enough, and I had begun to be dimly aware of my need of a firmly based system of ideas of wide application. I had no distinct idea of how to set about discovering such a system, and in any case I was not at first at all deeply in earnest. I read the lives of some of the great lawgivers—eleven lives of Napoleon, I remember, in one term—but while this fostered in me the beginnings of a sense of history, it brought me no nearer to a solution of my problem, or even to an understanding of its nature.

It was a recurrent event which, however improbably, brought my problem into focus. At Bedales the sermons after the undenominational service on Sunday evenings in Hall were not preached by clergymen but by members of the staff in rotation. It must have been some two or three years after I had been at Bedales that these sermons began, although in a manner remote from the preachers' intentions, to turn my thoughts towards religion.

When I was fourteen or fifteen years old thoughts about God, which before then passed but fleetingly and seldom through my mind, began to find there a securer lodgment. I do, however, recollect, many years before that, the occasion when I first consciously heard his Name. One morning when I was quite small, aged five or six perhaps, my father summoned me to the drawing-room and left me alone with a man dressed in black, who seemed to me to be very old. Presently he took me upon his knee (I can still feel its boniness and my discomfort at being perched on a precarious and unfamiliar place) and spoke to me very gently and simply of God, of his creation of the world and his love for it, and of the infinity of his love and his wisdom. The being whose existence was then revealed to me appeared too singular and vast and remote to engage even a particle of my understanding, but I was moved to a vague awe and wonder. The man in black was the Reverend Henry Woods, Master of the Temple Church and a close friend of my parents, whom they had asked to give me this instruction which they them-selves might have found difficulty in imparting, seeing that neither held anything approaching religious convictions of a kind expressible in dogmatic terms, which was in part due to their both happening to be the children of parents differing in religion.

The sense of awe and wonder implanted in me by Dr. Woods was sensibly strengthened during our summer visits to Normandy. My sisters and I made friends with several of the children of the local fishermen and farmers and sometimes accompanied them to Mass at the church at Vattetot: here, when the bells were rung and we knelt down, I apprehended that what was taking place had to do with the ineffable Father of the world. These, however, were but impressions passively received, and it was not, as I say, until I was fourteen or fifteen years old that I was occupied, in any positive sense, with reflections upon the nature of God. The occasions, and later on the strong stimulant, of such reflections were the weekly sermons I heard at school.

The tolerance, the goodwill, the accessibility to new ideas and the sense of social responsibility which the speakers for the most part displayed made at first a most favourable impression upon me, which, before long, however, gave way before a contrary one, namely, that the speakers were persistently evading a fundamental question. The name of God was of fairly frequent occurrence in their discourses, and there was even a tacit assumption that his existence was of cardinal importance in the universal scheme of things; yet time after time when the speakers' arguments called, however imperatively, for some reference to God's nature, even the loosest definitions were avoided. I would have listened with sympathetic interest to a professed atheist explaining why he believed there was no God, or to an agnostic frankly contending that it was not possible for human beings to know anything about the mysterious powers which con-controlled the universe. As it was I apostrophized them, silently and resentfully, as I listened: 'If you don't believe that God exists, or if you know nothing about his nature, why refer at all to a being whose very existence seems to make nonsense of a purely rationalist explanation of things, based upon the most exact knowledge available to us, namely the findings of science? Conversely, if anything definite is known about a being who, if he does exist, is the creator and ruler of the universe, is not such knowledge of incalculable importance? But evasion of the issue can only obscure both reason and faith.'

Repeated mention by the preachers of a God lacking personality, the mere shadowy emanation perhaps of the spirit of man, about whom nothing appeared to be known except that his heart was very much, so to speak, in the right place, prejudiced me, for a time, in favour of a universe without a God. I used therefore to envisage a universe which had come into existence simply by chance, or else in response to some undiscoverable laws, and upon an infinitesimal fragment of which we human beings found ourselves—a slowly cooling fragment miraculously complex and beautiful. The human race itself must in a few million years, therefore, be extinguished by the cold. Our first consideration, it seemed to me, should be to experience, to the fullest extent which our understanding and our senses allowed, the brief moments of our conscious existence, and to face, with the composure recommended by the ancient philosophers, the near prospect of our own final dissolution, and, more distantly, that of an ice-gripped and silent universe, from which the last vestige of man and his works should have disappeared.

There is something that I still find credible and even attractive in such a universe as this, in the inscrutable impersonality of its design, in the ultimate self-dependence, the disinterested love of experience and knowledge and a kind of *gravitas* which its acceptance would engender in the choicest spirits among its inhabitants.

The longer, however, that I pondered this interpretation of the world, the more difficulty I had in reconciling the intense purposefulness of every manifestation of life, even the minutest and least active, with an ultimate lack of purpose. I was driven therefore to reflect upon the purposes of living. I had an intuitive sense that in the fulfilment of the common ambitions, fame, love and wealth—intoxicating though I found the very notion of them—there was to be found no entire or enduring satisfaction. Upon what this intuition rested I had no notion. If one enjoying these blessings should yet remain unsatisfied, what, in Heaven's name, I asked myself, could he want? While I was fitfully occupied with the problem of the meaning of life the school curriculum once again brought me enlightenment, although hardly in accordance with the intentions of those who had devised it. There was a Scripture class taken by the Headmaster, who took us through St. Luke and the Acts, verse by verse, and my interest was so roused by his stringent, vivid comments that I was led to read the other Gospels, particularly St. John. My attention became fixed upon one matter which, in my earlier and more casual reading, I had overlooked or else discounted, namely the frequency and the distinctness with which Jesus claimed to be, in a quite special sense, the Son of God and a sharer in his Divinity. Here was a positive piece of information about the Being habitually spoken of with such exasperating vagueness in the Sunday evening sermons. I was persuaded, however, by the arguments propounded in Bernard Shaw's *Preface* to *Androcles and the Lion* that Jesus' conviction of his Divinity was a delusion. I am grateful to the providence which placed in my hands at that particular moment this searching and scintillating essay.

Because I have recalled at some length my early religious preoccupations, the impression may have been given that I was religiously disposed to an exceptional degree. Such an impression would be very misleading, for my interest in religion up this time was casual and intermittent, and vitiated by a suspicion that it was an unexciting subject. The *Preface* to *Androcles* killed that suspicion with a single flashing stroke: before I had read more than a few pages I knew that the relation of man to his Creator—supposing there to be a Creator—ought to be man's ultimate preoccupation. Although its immediate effect was to cause me to reject the notion of the divinity of Christ, this essay brought his personality before me with thrilling vividness. After reading Shaw, Christ was never again for me an archaic or a legendary figure, still less the Pale Galilean: but a complex, enigmatic, an overwhelming, endlessly surprising personality. I attended the Headmaster's Scripture class with enhanced attention. The same term we happened to be taking *Hamlet* and I fell to comparing Shakespeare with the Four Evangelists. Shakespeare's utterance is so god-like that there are times when it is difficult to remember that he was a man. The Four Evangelists in comparison with Shakespeare were quite ordinary men; only one of them could be said to have possessed unusual literary talent. Yet the supreme creation of a unique poetic genius does not compare, in subtlety, in consistency, in majesty, even in poetic quality, with the figure which emerges from the attempts at biography of an imaginative fisherman with a sense of metaphysics, of a cultivated and sympathetic doctor, of a publican and a terse and competent reporter. The same transcendency marks the central figure in all four Gospels, widely though the authors of these differ in outlook and in literary attainment. Him I therefore began to regard with a new reverence; and presently with something more than reverence. Eventually the time came when I was not longer able—Shaw's persuasive arguments notwithstanding —to believe that a Being of such transcendent wisdom could be subject to a delusion, or that a Being of such transcendent moral force could mislead his disciples and, through them, a great part of mankind. Jesus' claim to be God is stated in terms so specific that they must be rejected or accepted: it cannot be ignored:

'And Simon Peter answered and said, Thou art the Christ—the son of the living God. And Jesus answered and said unto him, Blessed art thou Simon Bar-Jonah: for flesh and blood hath not revealed it unto thee, but my Father which is in heaven' (Matthew xvi, 16).

'Have I been so long time with you, and yet hast thou not known me, Philip? He that hath seen me hath seen the Father, and how sayest thou then, Shew us the Father?' (John xiv, 9).

'And now, O Father, glorify thou me, with thine own self, with the glory which I had with thee before the world was' (John xvii, 5).

'Verily, verily, I say unto you, Before Abraham was, I am' (John viii, 38).

I now therefore accepted the Divinity of Christ but I did not know what was required of me on this account. It was plain that Jesus had ordained the establishment of a Church, yet I myself, although baptized into the Church of England, was a member of none. I therefore looked about me in order to discover which 'branch' of the Christian Church, either historically or according to the spirit, was the Church of the Apostles. I had no inherited loyalties to guide me and no traditions, or, perhaps, too many, for ours is a family strangely various in religion. It included Protestants—we possess a copy of a book written by an ancestor from whom I inherit two Christian names, and entitled, *An Aunswere unto certayne assertions, tending to maintaine the Church of Rome to be the true and Catholique Church*, published in London 'at the three Cranes in the Vinetree' in 1597— Catholics, as well as members of the race to which belonged both the glory of giving birth to Christ and the responsibility for his rejection and death.

I saw three institutions which seemed to me to have special claims to be considered. The first of these was the Society of Friends. I had read some history and had formed the impression (which experience has confirmed) that the Quakers were the only Christian body to manifest consistently the Christian virtues in action, more especially charity and mercy. But it was, I reflected, a small, all but hereditary sect, drawn almost exclusively from the most temperate classes among the most law-respecting peoples: its members might be said to have been conceived in respectability. Up to this time I had sinned—I think I may fairly say—but mildly, but I was already aware that mine was a turbulent heart, and that sloth and pride and anger and ambition could exercise deadly power over my nature. So I decided that there was no place for me in this aristo-cracy of virtue.

The second of these institutions was the Church which had attempted, in its finest moments, to act as the conscience of the British body politic, the Church of England. I well knew of a defect in myself which gave me reason to mistrust a national Church. I was possessed by a love of my own country which could too easily degenerate into unworthy partisanship. I was accordingly wary of a Church which was largely identical with the nation and which might therefore sit in judgment in its own cause. Furthermore, in spite of the nobility of the language of its liturgy I had so often sat unmoved through Church of England services.

The third institution was the Roman Catholic Church. This, on account of its magnitude and continuity, I could hardly ignore, yet it provoked in me still more positive misgivings than the Anglican Church or the Society of Friends. Ever since the Reformation it seemed to have acted the part not only of the enemy of England, but (what would be worse) the enemy of human liberty. I had often heard it denounced as mercenary and corrupt and avid of power. I began to read such books about it as the school library possessed. As I read, two notions began to take hold of my imagination: namely that it was (whatever its imperfections) identical with the Church established by the Apostles; and that it was animated by some vital principle which I could not detect as being consistently present in other religious bodies, a principle that lent a note of urgency to its exhortations, a note of authority to its pronouncements and a note of passionate zeal to its servants. I speak advisedly of these notions as acting upon my imagination rather than upon my reason, for having access only to a very few of the relevant historical and theological works, and lacking the requisite capacity for research, the notions to which I have referred were derived from evidence that was pitiably insufficient. I now have less insubstantial reasons for believing them to be well founded, but that does not alter the fact of their being, at the time of which I write, wholly unjustifiable by me. By what mental processes did I form them? Looking back it seems odd that I formed them at all. I spoke to no one about any of these matters, and the books to which I had access, without being in any exceptional degree anti-Catholic, were not in the main of a kind to lend support to the ideas which took shape in my mind. I find it difficult to account for my conclusions without assuming that there existed in me an innate impulse towards Catholicism. But this remained a blind and unconscious impulse until one day, rummaging among some dis-carded books in a cellar at Far Oakridge, I picked up a volume—how clearly I can see it still!—bound in red paper and printed on whitish pulp, of Newman's *Apologia*. Casually I turned the pages, then suddenly I was aware that I was reading words which I had longed to hear, and I lay down on the floor and read on, oblivious of the hours.

It was as though, having followed hitherto an erratic path across fields, scrambling through hedges and over walls, I had come out upon a broad and frequented pilgrims' way, upon which I had as a companion a tall delicate-looking young Oxford don. Of course I was too ignorant to follow precisely the subtle and far-ranging argu-ments set forth in the *Apologia*, but what held and charmed and above all reassured me was the character of Newman's mind, its combination of smiling grace with an unyielding, or rather an almost

untempted, integrity. It was a mind with which, in spite of the
immeasurable disparity between it and my own, I was at once upon
familiar terms. I understood how it was in his day that light-hearted
Oxford undergraduates 'would drop their voices and whisper
"There's Newman", as, with head thrust forward and gaze fixed as
though at some vision seen only by himself, with swift noiseless
steps he glided by. Awe fell on them for a moment almost as if it had
been some apparition that had passed.'

In reading about Newman I learnt something about the tares
which our Lord warned us would grow up among the wheat. I
became aware in particular of the existence of a type of priestly
politician whose conception of human dignity is summed up in the
words of one of its most repulsive examples: 'What is the province
of the laity? To hunt, to shoot, to entertain. These matters they
understand, but to meddle in ecclesiastical matters they have no
right at all.' It was a type whose animosity Newman inevitably
incurred, and which persistently attempted to break his spirit and to
destroy his reputation. Had Newman in fact been discredited and
crushed, my own acceptance of the authority of the Church would,
at the very least, have been long delayed.

Far more important than my awareness of the tares, and even of
the loftiness and supple grace of Newman's mind, was the vision of
the Catholic Church itself which through him was revealed to me.
I was chilled by the crimes and perfidies and above all the complacent hardness of heart of which certain of the officials of the
Church were guilty, but I began to discern, far transcending these,
the sublime form of the Great Society itself, embracing both the
living and the dead, to which Christ had entrusted the salvation of
the world, and I began to understand something of the faith which
it taught—a faith revealed by him, and, for nearly two thousand
years, the subject of continuous elucidation, under grace, by an
unending succession of wise and learned minds, by Councils and
by popes; an immense yet minutely articulated structure, as luminous and tough as burnished bronze.

Before I came upon the *Apologia* I was, in everything pertaining
to religion, entirely alone. With my mother, whose Catholic mother
died too young to ensure her religious instruction and who had long
ceased to practise her religion, I do not believe that I ever spoke of
my changing attitude towards the Church; I had no Catholic friends

THE CHRISTENING PARTY, 1901, BY WILLIAM ROTHENSTEIN

THE AUTHOR WITH HIS MOTHER AT 26 CHURCH ROW, 1903
BY WILLIAM ROTHENSTEIN

of my own age; and I lacked the courage to speak to any of my parents' friends whom I knew to be Catholics, Eric Gill—at that time a recent convert, whose wood engravings had deepened my Catholic sympathies—Maurice Baring, Frederic Manning, the Michael Fields and others whose frequent presence served as reminders of my own solitary condition. But after I had come to know Newman I felt myself to be neither solitary nor far from the Church. I bought a primer with the aid of which I began to puzzle out the principal Catholic doctrines.

Once I was convinced that Christ, in claiming to be the Son of God, was neither deceived nor deceiving, the rest followed. The Church of Rome—whatever the shortcomings of many of its servants—was manifestly the Church of the Apostles, and all others in schism, in disregard of Christ's prayer that those who believed in him should be of one fold.

There were moments when the Incarnation seemed to me to be an event strange to the point of incredibility, and radically at variance with the whole or with any part of the majestic and intricate pattern of creation; but there was at last a time when I found it less incredible than the only alternative of which I was able to conceive: a world empty of meaning. There came therefore a day when, on my knees before a Catholic priest, in the crypt of Westminster Cathedral, I abjured my errors and entered what with Newman I had come to believe to be the One Fold of the Redeemer.

This transformation of my ideas was a fitful, gradual, and to a degree a secret process. My father had no dogmatic objections to Catholicism: I never knew an educated and, in a sense, religious man for whom doctrine of any sort meant so little—so little that he was only remotely conscious of its significance for many people as the necessary formulation of religious truth. What he intensely disliked was the propensity of English Catholics—far more pronounced then than it is today—to form a closed world within a world; the idea of my becoming a member of a society that might make me sectarian, cut off from the mainstream of national life, and above all from that upper-middle-class Liberal tradition distinguished by a combination of independence and rectitude—exemplified among his intimates by such men as Herbert Fisher and Sir Francis Darwin, A. E. Housman and J. L. Hammond. My reluctance to act contrary to his wishes in so crucial a matter so long as I was being maintained and educated at his expense delayed my reception into the Church for some time after I had become a Catholic by conviction. Catholicism became for me a second and almost secret life. At school I would walk down to the little copper-domed church in Petersfield; at Far Oakridge I would bicycle across the valley to the Dominican Priory at Woodchester, and I rarely passed through London without a visit to Westminster Cathedral. During all this time I was oppressed and, quite mistakenly as it seems to me now, humiliated by my inability to take Holy Communion.

I hope that this account of my religious life does not suggest that my becoming a Catholic was the consequence only of simple thirst after righteousness. I had indeed come to believe that Christ was God; I believed that, in spite of the knavery and folly of many of its servants throughout the ages, the Roman Catholic Church, as a matter of simple fact—in so far, that is, as a historical fact is ever simple—was the Church established by Christ. There were other elements in my conversion. I was confused and eventually repelled by the vague, well-intentioned Liberalism in which I grew up, in which all was flux and without substance; which offered no hard answers to hard questions. For a short time I even suffered, by way of a crude reaction against all this, from an enchantment with the extreme Right. In the absence of anything right enough for me at home, I became a subscriber to the *Action Française*. Nor did my religious preoccupation effect, I believe, any improvement in my conduct. At home I was apt to be sullen and unresponsive to my family's affection. And sex was thrusting its way, late but ominously, into the foreground of my consciousness—late because I was extremely unprecocious.

In one respect (but alas in one respect only) these memories of my years at school resemble the novels of Jane Austen: they have omitted any mention of the great war that formed their background. Oddly enough the First World War made curiously little impact on our lives, chiefly, I suppose, because we were most of us so very young before it began that, in spite of the tragedy which it brought to almost every home, and in spite of our absorbed interest in its course, it came to have for us a hideous normality. I remember very clearly both its beginning and its ending. The hot August morning in 1914 walking with my father through the Long Close, a field next to our house at Far Oakridge, and a maid running towards us with a newspaper. A cold afternoon in November 1918 at Bedales: a master stopping the game of association football to tell us that an armistice had been signed. Both scenes, in sunlit pasture and on bleak plateau of a playing field, are as clearly imprinted on my memory as though they happened yesterday. The two conspicuous differences between the two world wars were the relative danger to the soldier in the First, and the relative, indeed almost total, safety of civilians. The consciousness of death was something which even the least thoughtful among us rarely lost: the casualty lists gave us a recurrent sense that England was bleeding to death; but even those who reached measurable distance of military age seemed to have few personal apprehensions. What our generation felt about the danger just ahead resembled the feelings of people in general today about the thermo-nuclear bomb: a gloomy but almost impersonal fatalism. I had only one sight of the war itself. Among the visiting music masters was one entirely unlike any other member of the staff: small, cocky, kindly, and marked by a vulgarity of voice and manner that at Bedales was almost spectacular, and by a wonderful kindliness that was not quite so common as anyone who did not know the school very well might have supposed. One evening there was a concert in Hall, in which, in the role of flautist, I took some minor part. A number of eighteenth-century quartets and the like were played, and the audience had become delicately attuned to the rarefied atmosphere these performances induced, when the visiting master stepped on to the platform, holding a long brass horn, upon which, with enormous zest, he played a piece of extreme vulgarity in a manner that all but split the eardrums of everybody present. I had always liked him (he tried to teach me the flute) and now affection for him welled up within me. I congratulated him upon his performance; I was the only one who did so, and he at once asked me to high tea next day at his villa in Southsea. It was on the afternoon of my visit that I saw the extraordinary spectacle of a part of the Grand Fleet, immediately after the Battle of Jutland, lying off Portsmouth, the ships scarred and shattered right down to the waterline.

The remembrance of this spectacle evokes two trivial recollections: a picture in *The Illustrated London News* of a German trooptrain leaving for the Russian Front, with faces looking out of the windows: the nearest, the sad face of a man trapped, was the face of the German master at Bedales; the sight of a wonderfully handsome young man with golden hair, dressed in an open-necked shirt, shorts, and carrying a huge pack, hailing, then talking to my mother. One of my parents' intellectual friends, I thought, turning away to examine the blue cloisonné enamel lettering of the words 'Debenham & Freebody'. I was right: he was the poet so soon to lie in the corner of a foreign field that would be forever England.

An image that constantly occupied our minds was that of the vast theatre of action, 'The Western Front', the long wide swathe of pestiferous mud, blasted tree-stumps and barbed wire, lit up at night by Verey lights and starshells. The low mutter of the guns was just audible when the wind blew from the south. This image, formed out of press photographs, the paintings and drawings of the war artists, the poems of the war poets and the accounts of innumerable actors in this sombre performance, was barely escapable.

My father spent some time at the Front as an Official War Artist, and was caught up in the great retreat of March 1918, when we were long without news of him, an impassioned, almost an exalted, observer of a spectacle of the horror that war can inflict, both on man and on nature, without parallel in the history of the world. Yet even for those of us who never saw it it was as familiar as our own back yards; it remains in my own memory more indelibly than any scene of bomb devastation inflicted on London during the Second World War, of which I was a continuous witness.

Another great event seemed singularly near to us. This was the Russian Revolution. There were several Russian boys and at least one Russian girl at Bedales. From them, the children of aristocratic Liberals, were heard accounts of tyranny and corruption—in those days the Okrana, the secret police, had a sinister reputation. From the few Finns in the school—one of the Zilliacus brothers in particular—we used to hear grim accounts of Russian oppression. The October Revolution was accordingly greeted by most of us not as a victory of one political system over another, but as a victory of ordinary humanity over dark and cruel forces.

When a year after the armistice I left Bedales it was as though I had already left it, so far had I grown away from the ideas which guided it. I drove to the station in a cab shared with Malcolm MacDonald and Basil Ivory. 'There go the Army, the Church and the State,' someone shouted. Basil Ivory was destined for the Army and Malcolm MacDonald was inveterately a politician. When he and

I were up before the Headmaster after the discovery of our nocturnal cross-country walks, he managed the interview with so deft a blend of candour and contrition that he left the study in higher favour than ever, while I, who spoke too casually of our theft of two pieces of cold suet pudding from the school kitchens, observing merely that 'we were hungry after our long walk', left it with a black mark against me. He and I were constant companions, but at school there was something faintly ambiguous about his relationships, and I never felt sure of his friendship until after we had left. I still bear the mark of an encounter with him: he was boxing champion of a certain weight and I was challenger. We fought four savage rounds with the Headmaster as referee. Malcolm won on points, and I broke the base of my right thumb, for which the school doctor, insisting that my injury was nothing but a bruise, prescribed massage, and it is crooked still.

CHAPTER THREE

OXFORD

THE year following my departure from Bedales was among the unhappiest and most fruitless—unhappiest mainly because most fruitless—of my life. The cause of my unhappiness was academic failure. I sat for Responsions, the entrance examination for Oxford; I failed wretchedly, and in the most elementary subjects. I sat for a second time, and failed again. I had become listless at home, and out of harmony at Bedales, and now came the crushing realization that, after seven years at a school to which my father could only send me at heavy financial sacrifice, I was unable to meet even the minimal requirements for entering a university which had always tacitly admitted its quota of idle socialites and ignorant athletes. I, who envisaged my life as dedicated to some serious pursuit, was unable to scrape into Oxford with the most frivolous and stupid. When my mother met me at Chalford station after my second failure, I could not speak, and she tried to comfort me with words of loving irrelevance.

Early in 1920 my father was appointed Principal of the Royal College of Art, and we accordingly moved to London. I went to a crammer's in Earls Court, learning, along with a number of mostly conspicuously stupid young men, the elements of arithmetic, algebra, Greek, Latin grammar and the like. And, for the first time, I did learn them, and I passed Responsions. No winner of some coveted distinction could have been happier than I at the passing of this routine examination. This momentary happiness did not dissipate the crushing sense I suffered of my ill-preparedness for life in general and more particularly for life at Oxford. But unhappiness, like its opposite, is rarely unalloyed, and the latter part of my time at Far Oakridge was enlivened by the visits of friends, chiefly our parents' friends.

The attitude of my sisters, my brother and myself towards them, more especially towards those of them whose lives were given to

42

some imaginative or intellectual pursuit, was, perhaps, a singular one. My parents had always lived very near to the centre of the worlds of art and literature, and their successive homes were places in which writers and artists constantly foregathered. My father's boundless reverence for the creative faculty, his readiness to fight the battles of the artists and writers whom he admired, to lend them or give them money in times of need—however precarious his own situation—and to use his ever-growing influence in their support, and my mother's beauty and high spirits, drew into their circle an extraordinary variety of genius and talent. Its presence seemed to us unremarkable, and our interest was more readily aroused by those who led adventurous lives. But there was not one among them—with the exception of Yeats, whom I never came to know well enough—for whom I did not feel the most positive affection, and I believe the same was true of my sisters and my brother. They were men of compelling benevolence and charm. However little glamourized by those who followed intellectual or imaginative vocations, we all four of us drew, painted, acted and sang, which seemed to us as normal as playing games or going for walks. My elder sister was unusually well-read, especially in the classical English novelists, and I was myself not entirely ill-read in the same authors—Hardy, Meredith, Fielding, Thackeray and the like—as well as the historians and the poets. I came lately upon the following letter from Conrad which shows that I had not only read *Victory* but written to him about it:

28 August '17
Capel House,
Orlestone,
Nr. Ashford.

My dear John,
Thanks for your charming idea to write me about Victory. I am very pleased to hear that you like the book. I have a little weakness for it myself. Still nicer, if possible, are your friendly references to Borys.[1] I hope the time will come soon when you'll be able to renew your acquaintance and lay the foundation of a friendship which will carry on in the future the warm affection and the great regard I have for your Father. We had news from B lately. He is

[1] His son.

on the Ypres section of the front and very busy. We have heard he is going to be promoted lieutenant in a few days, which, no doubt, will please him, after 2 years of active service. Pray give our love to your Mother and Father.

Yours affectionately,

J. Conrad.

But I delighted in the conversation of Conrad because he talked about ships and the sea, of Tagore because he entered so fully into whatever happened to preoccupy my thoughts, of W. H. Hudson because of his stories of animals and birds, of Cyril Holland because of his vivid talk of army life and not because he was a son of Oscar Wilde. 'Distinction', by itself, in our parents' guests, was apt to prejudice us against them. Yeats, for instance, although he was good for an occasional ghost story, personified, as well as anyone, this unattractive, pure 'distinction', but I could not but be spellbound by his solemn, incantatory voice. I remember leaning out of my bedroom window on a fine night at Far Oakridge listening to his reading, to my parents and a party of their friends, seated on the terrace below, from his translation of Tagore's *Gitanjali*. The memory of Yeats' sonorous voice awakes reverberations in my inner ear of another and wilder sound, that of André Gide's playing of the piano. With Marc Allegret he came to stay not long after the end of the war. I can see him seated at the shabby upright piano in my sisters' schoolroom, his head thrown back, battering at the keyboard and ecstatically gesturing, intoxicated, obviously, by the storm of notes he raised. These performances contrasted with his conversation, which was penetrating and relaxed. And how well he knew how to listen, fixing each speaker intently with his keen brown eyes, as though he expected him to say something of consequence. For some reason I remember his clothes: black velvet jacket, red and yellow scarf round his neck, loose-fitting, buff-coloured Jaeger trousers. But how distressing to have seen and to have talked with so many of the possessors of the finest intellects and imaginations of the time before I was of an age or of a disposition to avail myself of the privilege, and to remember about them only what was superficial. It distresses me that I am able to recall, and so exactly, the faces of so many men and women whose achievements I admire, and so little else: the faces of Shaw, Gordon Craig, Ellen Terry (who wrote on a menu on the day of my birth ('long life to little John'), Augustus John, even the pale face with the dark heavy-pouched eyes, the black skull-cap, of a member of the Pre-Raphaelite Brotherhood, William Michael Rossetti; and how many more. I encountered some of them, fortunately for me, later on, when I had become more concerned with the essence and less with the incidental.

There was, however, one of these men whom, after years of friendship, I came to know intimately: this was Max Beerbohm. I cannot remember not knowing him: my earliest memories of him were connected with the Sunday luncheons at the Beerbohm house in Upper Berkeley Street presided over by 'Old Mrs. Beerbohm', Max's mother. This house put me in mind of that of my grandparents in Bradford: it had something of the same Victorian and faintly Germanic aura, but it was a livelier and more sophisticated place, frequented by people of the theatre, and Max's wild legendary brother Julius, about whom I recall fragments of a saga about his winning a big farm gambling at Dieppe, losing the particulars about it and journeying all over Northern France in an unsuccessful attempt to find it. But it was at Far Oakridge, soon after the beginning of the war, where Max and his first wife Florence came to stay for a weekend and remained for I forget how many years, that I came to know him well. He stayed, the perfect guest, first at my parents' house and later at a cottage called Winstons, in the village, which my parents later acquired. I came not only to know him but, in an auspicious way, his work. It was partly his amiability and partly his eagerness to 'try out' his work that led him to read aloud to us his essays as soon as they were completed and to show us his caricatures in progress. After dinner we would sit round the fire—Max needed a fire on all but the warmest evenings, and at Oakridge these were infrequent—and in his suave, slightly hesitant voice he would read out the essays published as *Seven Men*, or else he would show us the successive drawings of the series which he titled 'Rossetti and his Circle' (which, years afterwards, I was to persuade Hugh Walpole to bequeath to the Tate). I do not recall that any suggestions were ever made for the improvement of his prose, but with his drawings it was otherwise. He could be preternaturally observant and perceive revealing subtleties of feature and expression: yet he could on occasion overlook the obvious. He showed me a caricature of a 'cellist playing, and he was at first incredulous and then distressed when I

pointed out that he had represented the upper part of the instrument
as the larger.

Max was a man of rare worldly wisdom and he showed it in
nothing so much as in his attitude towards his own reputation. Like
most artists he was not immune from the noblest frailty, but regarded
injudicious praise as a far greater danger to reputation than denigra-
tion or even neglect. Most men desirous of fame willingly tolerate,
when they do not actively foster, over-praise, in the hope that some
of it will 'stick'. Max I have often heard discourage, with manifest
earnestness, critics whose flattering intentions he divined, so concerned was he that his reputation should never become inflated and
thus liable to unjust depreciation. Depreciation already begins,
however, to erode his reputation. During the memorial exhibition
held at the Leicester Galleries in 1957 I heard many younger friends
speak of him as a slight and affected figure, who seemed, moreover,
to exclude them from the little privileged world which he satirized.
As I write these words he has been dead only a few years, yet—in
spite of David Cecil's detailed and widely praised biography—none
of his generation has become so remote: that Max should have survived to witness (or to ignore) the rise of Tachism is as incongruous
as the survival of Holman Hunt until the issue of the First Futurist
Manifesto. The rediscovery of Max is inevitable; and if it comes
about sooner rather than later it is likely to be in some measure due
to the modesty of his own evaluation of his talents.

In our remote village he would dress as though for a stroll down
Bond Street, except that in winter for his daily expedition outdoors
Florence would cover his boots of glacé kid and his pearl grey spats
in a pair of woollen socks to prevent his slipping. His destination
was every day the same: the Nelson Inn, whither in homburg hat at
a delicately jaunty angle, long-waisted overcoat, and an ivory-topped
malacca cane in his hand, he would walk, as it were ceremonially,
to buy a packet of Goldflake cigarettes. I have much to be grateful
for to Max, but for nothing more than his serene confidence about
my own future at a time when there seemed to be little to justify
it.

Max was indeed a wonderful guest. (He used to say that people
were innately either guests or hosts, and that he was a guest.) He was
fascinated by the world, especially the 'great' world of politics and
society, but unlike many who share this fascination, it did not make

him restless; he seemed to have no strong inclination to re-enter its orbit. His precise and luminous recollections of its inhabitants were ever with him, and from an occasional weekend or dinner he would bring back new observations; he possessed in a supreme degree the artist's capacity for extracting the utmost from experiences that would provide little to less perceptive men. Although always prepared to talk about Henry James, Lord Balfour, Lord Curzon, Asquith or George Moore, he behaved towards those in whose company he found himself as though theirs was the company in which he were happiest. If conditions were not entirely to his liking he would mend them: if for instance there were an intrusion of fresh air he would choose the moment before the climax of some story he was telling to close the offending door or window. Such precautions taken, he would settle down again with an air of infinite contentment, as though ready to converse for ever. I doubt whether anybody was ever bored in his company.

In spite of his preternatural eye for weakness of any sort his outlook on the world was benevolent: many people moved him to ridicule, but few to dislike. Prominent among these few was H. G. Wells. I was unable to discover whether his dislike had a personal cause, or whether it was due to the conspicuous part that Wells played in bringing into being the egalitarian, utilitarian age that eventually made Max feel, except in the company of friends, an exile even in his own country. Whatever the cause it was a fierce dislike, and one that moved him to censure conduct on the part of Wells which in others he would have regarded with tolerance or even with affectionate comprehension. Not that he was incapable of criticising his friends. At Oakridge he once spoke to me with a severity worthy of my father himself about my father's, to his mind, excessive diversion of energy to farming and to village affairs.

Like Carlyle Max saw history as 'the essence of innumerable biographies'; he never envisaged the mass of mankind otherwise, I think, than as a grey, featureless setting for the achievements of individuals: philosophers, poets, artists, heroes, even of villains and fools on the grand scale, not excluding men who owed their significance to the offices they held, popes, kings and the like. Considering how wholeheartedly traditional his sympathies, his streak of republicanism, of positive anti-royalism, was unexpected: it was certainly not the product of any notion of constitutional reform, still less of radicalism; it was rather, I think, a vestige of Whiggism, according to which the monarchy was a constitutional convenience without mystical overtones. I wish I could recall his account of how he left the MS of his poem with the alternate refrain: 'The King is duller than the Queen', 'The Queen is duller than the King', in a taxi, and his description of the imagined arrival of someone from Scotland Yard with the recovered MS and the ensuing dialogue between stern interrogator and nervous author.

Another friend and neighbour of those days, who rented Winstons Cottage immediately before the Beerbohms moved into it, was John Drinkwater—a happier man then than he was to become when success—brought him by his play *Abraham Lincoln*, which he wrote at Winstons—involved him in problems which his essentially simple and direct nature was ill-equipped to resolve. Success diminished neither his innate kindliness nor his loyalty to his friends nor his high purpose as a writer. But the trappings of success, which Arnold Bennett enjoyed so zestfully as to make the world share his enjoyment, sat uneasily on John Drinkwater. He, of course, enjoyed the trappings, but he never reconciled the wearing of them with his high-mindedness, and when we met in the later years he seemed less happy and certainly less at ease. The poetic simplicity of the life he lead at Winstons with his first wife Kathleen—a life to which his nature seemed perfectly attuned—had gone. He was not a particularly visual man, but he decided that a successful dramatist ought to form a collection. But of what? Eventually he decided upon a species of salt-glaze, and whenever he acquired a piece—and he assembled a formidably large collection—he showed it to his friends, indicating with authority and pride its finer points. After his death when his effects were auctioned, my father said, 'I've left a small bid on one of those pots of John's: I never cared for them, but he was so proud of them and I thought we should keep one in his memory.' Next day the auctioneer informed him that his small bid had sufficed to purchase the entire collection, and I remember those pots standing in serried ranks on the upper shelves of store cupboards for years, until breakages and wedding presents reduced the collection to manageable proportions. But while at Oakridge he collected books, which he well understood, and he was happy in his steadily growing reputation as a poet. (What a poet he looked, with his pale, handsome face, set off by his hair, like blackbird's wings, and his blue shirt.)

I well remember his bringing the manuscript of *Lincoln* to our house one evening, and hearing him read it for the first time in his fine voice, just touched by sententiousness. My father's elder brother Charles, who was staying with us, was so impressed by *Lincoln* that he offered to guarantee its production, but in the event no such help was needed.

Several months of my last year in Gloucestershire were spent not at Far Oakridge but at a house some miles distant, which belonged to friends named Margaret and Claude Biddulph. This house was Rodmarton, a remarkable place which must have been among the last big country houses to be built in England. The Biddulphs had come to Gloucestershire intending to hunt, shoot and engage in politics in the Conservative interest. What it was that diverted them from this intention I am not certain. They did indeed hunt and shoot but from an early time during their life at Rodmarton these activities ceased to be more than incidental. The Biddulphs became the principal patrons of the diffused revival in the arts-and-crafts focused in the Cotswolds. Working under the impulse originally given by William Morris were a number of architects, cabinet makers, potters and other craftsmen who had settled in the Cotswolds, in particular at Sapperton, a village in our own immediate neighbourhood. The chief among them were Ernest Gimson, the brothers Ernest and Sidney Barnsley, and Alfred Powell. Although my father was sometimes aggrieved that Gimson should take all the best local craftsmen into his workshop, where they were employed in making austere-looking luxury furniture for the rich and thereby hindering their employment by more modest local patrons like himself, he admired, and even idealized, these men for the integrity of their work and the simplicity of their way of living, distinguished by the eschewing whenever possible of industrial products and the making of everything feasible at home. Most things in their houses, not only furniture but carpets, curtains, ironwork and even the bread, had a 'home-made' character (home-made, if not within the house, at least in a neighbour's). We all liked the Barnsleys in particular, and Sidney's son Edward, now a leading designer of handmade furniture, was my constant companion. I sometimes wondered whether the principles of our craftsmen-friends were quite so austere as my father liked to suppose. Staying, with its new owners, in the house of one of our craftsmen-friends immediately after his departure and happening to look down the wooded declivity behind it, I noticed something which glittered brightly through the undergrowth. Further scrutiny revealed another and yet another such point of light. Examination led to the surprising discovery that the whole bank was in fact an escarpment of empty tins. My father's incredulity turned slowly to amused distress as I told him of this discovery.

The Biddulphs came in contact with the Cotswold architect-craftsmen very early in their life in Gloucestershire, and I remember joining a bicycling expedition to Rodmarton, organized by my father, of almost all the craftsmen of Far Oakridge, and of the neighbouring villages of Oakridge Lynch, Waterlane and Bisley, to enable them to see the partly built house, designed by Ernest Barnsley. This expedition took place some six years before I went to stay at Rodmarton which had in the meanwhile grown into a great, and in our time, I fancy, a unique house. For it was surely the only great modern country house in which almost everything both of use and ornament that it was possible to make locally and by hand was so made. Almost everything needed for the building, the furnishing and the embellishment of Rodmarton was made either in the village of Rodmarton or in the neighbourhood, splendidly demonstrating what could be accomplished given energy, taste, patience and wealth. A hundred people doing as the Biddulphs did would have gone far to transform the face of rural England.

It was an exciting experience to stay in this house and to see well and often splendidly designed and fashioned objects that had been brought into existence instead of objects that had merely been moved out of the possession of one person and into that of another. Even more impressive than the intelligent employment of the best available craftsmen was the way in which Mrs. Biddulph induced the women of the village to make tapestries depicting the life of Rodmarton and the surrounding country. It was Mrs. Biddulph—austerely elegant, her benevolence intermittently masked by her caustic wit—who, presiding over house and village like the abbess of some great mediaeval religious house, was the animating and directing force. Her husband, I fancy, for all his liberal support of her innumerable projects, must often have contemplated with astonishment the unusual environment that was growing up about them, at the large areas of new oak panelling and furniture, at the richly coloured wall hangings, the ample vases embellished with their coats of arms, conjured up, so to speak, out of their own ground, or that of their near neighbours.

Mrs Biddulph, whose sharp-edged and uncompromising mind was ever probing after first causes, had already become critical of the easy-going, incurious Anglicanism of the time, and was drawn towards the Catholic Church, into which, however, she was not received until some years later. This disposition made her always enjoyable company especially sympathetic to me.

A melancholy event marked the end of my life in Gloucestershire and brought about a harsh solution of a domestic problem. We had owned for many years an Old Fashioned English Sheepdog, a huge, long-haired steel-grey creature gifted with unusual intelligence and a mild and affectionate disposition, and well-liked in the neighbourhood, about which he used to roam, without predatory intentions, but to satisfy a wide-ranging curiosity. His habit was to walk the roads, pausing at intervals to place his forepaws on the top of the stone wall, first on one verge and then on the other, in order to survey the landscape. One night he did not return, and in the morning I found him dead at the foot of one of these walls: someone had shot him in the face as he was making one of these habitual tours of inspection. The question, which had exercised us all, of how he would adapt himself to London life, was one we no longer had to ask.

In our part of the Cotswolds there was an undercurrent of madness and violence: we knew the daughter of a man hanged for murder: his father ill-treated his mother and he threatened to kill him unless he left her alone, and he carried out his threat. People, even children, used to jump down wells. So the murder of a dog would have seemed no great matter to certain of our neighbours.

There was one expression of the proneness to violence of the men of our village that I could not but find endearing. At the beginning of the war a woman in the neighbourhood had spread rumours that the concrete base in our garden for a projected summerhouse was intended for a gun emplacement which would command the vital mainline of railway across the valley below. It was a time when some people were easily excited to suspicion of bearers of German names. This rumour took some hold, especially among some of our middle-class neighbours from nearby villages. One night six or seven of the men, farm labourers and masons of our own village, asked to see my father. I can see them now, standing in the light of a green-shaded oil lamp. For a moment or two they said nothing in response to my father's greeting; they stood silent, and stirred uneasily. Then one of them said: 'We've all heard this talk about you, Sir, and that there concrete floor in your garden. It b'aint right and we don't like it. We know who's responsible, and if anything happens to you that person's house will burn. That's all; good night Sir, good night Mr. John,' they said, and out they went into the dark.

With the autumn of 1920 there came a complete transformation of my life. My home was now in London instead of Far Oakridge—for a year in a Gothic house by Waterhouse, then 18 (now 32) Sheffield Terrace, Campden Hill, and a year later at 13 Airlie Gardens, a great gaunt house a few yards distant—and I was at a university instead of at school.

The transformation was so complete that I find it difficult to discern with any degree of clarity my present identity in the aimlessly drifting schoolboy and the morose and solitary walker along the highroads of the Cotswolds. The self of the earlier years has for me that elusiveness which for students of English history seems to veil the personalities of those who flourished prior to the age of the Tudors.

There were, it seems to me, two causes for this change. I had suffered exceedingly from my failures to pass Responsions and from the searing recollection of the more radical failure which made them inevitable, and my belated 'success' in passing filled me with an exhilarating sense of having a second chance. The other and more radical cause was, quite simply, that the substitution of London and Oxford for Far Oakridge and Petersfield brought me into an environment where, solitary and insignificant though I was, I felt at home in a way I never had before.

But almost before I had time to establish myself in my new environments I suffered a loss that for a long time cast a dark shadow over my life. Tom Rowat's mother wrote to tell me that while supervising the unloading of his regiment's equipment from a ship at Alexandria a cable had snapped and he had been killed by the consequent fall of a car. His mother's letter was followed by letters from Tom himself—posted at various Mediterranean ports on his journey to Egypt. This boy, so far my superior in almost every attribute, gave me a devotion which I valued the more deeply because I was aware how little—except for my heartfelt reciprocation of it—I

THE AUTHOR WITH HIS FATHER

FAMILY WALK AT THROUGHAM, 1908, BY ALBERT RUTHERSTON

deserved it. How bitterly I mourned his gaiety, his courage, his magnanimity, above all his total superiority to mean or petty motives. He was free from them himself and, although extremely unsuspicious, he had the quick apprehension of evil that belongs to the very good—as also to the very bad. These qualities and others were mourned by a circle of intimate friends of which Tom and his beautiful sister Phillis were the centre. It was with the Rowats during school holidays that I first became familiar with night life. We used to go dancing at Rector's, or else at Murray's or Skindle's at Maidenhead. Phillis used frequently to visit such places from the age of sixteen, and when her mother's friends hinted their disapproval Mrs. Rowat merely smiled and said nothing, assured that no harm could come to Phillis unless Phillis willed it, and that she did not will it. And I am sure that nothing harmed her, unless perhaps this addiction made her restless, for in later life she fell into a habit of too frequent marriage—and the habit grew upon her. Once, many years later, after accepting the proposal of some undesirable, she suggested vaguely to her perturbed solicitors that he might be 'good with her boys'. They shook their heads and objected that if they had been aware that this was her motive for remarriage they would have suggested the name of a suitable tutor.

Oxford at first was something of a shock. Not having been at one of the larger public schools I had little notion of what to expect. During the weeks before I went up I fed my romantic imaginings of Oxford with poetry. Snatches of it caught, but only precariously retained by my wretched memory, ran constantly in my head, until I longed to live in the place which had inspired such lines as

> 'And the tired men and dogs all gone to rest,
> And only the white sheep are sometimes seen.
> Cross and re-cross the strips of moon-blanched green.'

or

> 'Thee, at the ferry, Oxford riders blithe,
> Returning home on summer nights, have met
> Crossing the stripling Thames at Bablockhithe,
> Trailing in the cool stream thy fingers wet,
> As the slow punt swings round:
> And leaning backwards in a pensive dream,
> And fostering in thy lap a heap of flowers
> Plucked in shy fields . . .'

The imagined idyll of life beneath the dreaming spires, the life which Thomas More, Christopher Wren, Pitt, Dr. Johnson, Fox, Shelley and Newman had shared and which Matthew Arnold and a hundred other poets had celebrated, was within the first weeks of my taking up residence in Worcester College violently shattered. First there was an occasion when the freshmen were entertained by their seniors to a dinner in Hall for the purpose of making them drunk. If such were its purpose—and the insistent character of the hospitality offered us permitted no other interpretation—it was largely successful. What shocked me most were the incurious glances of passing dons at the callow victims of drunkenness lying or reeling about the cloister. A little while later some success on river or playing field was the occasion of a celebration by some section of the athletic fraternity—the 'hearties' as they were called— which caused me to open my eyes wider still. After their dinner the 'hearties' debouched into the quad, some falling down drunk and others baying for the blood—or rather for the furniture—of unpopular members of the College. Soon there was heard the sound of furniture sent crashing from windows, shortly followed by the glow of the flames as the shattered fragments were ignited. I happened to be sitting drinking port in the rooms of a fellow freshman who had made known with an incautious precipitancy his socialist convictions, and whose aristocratic appearance and connections seemed to aggravate this offence. Presently there were raised hostile shouts beneath his windows, then heavy footsteps sounded on the stairs. In burst a group of 'hearties', very drunk, with evidently aggressive intentions towards my host. Some laid hands on his furniture, while others muttered that he should be taken into the quad and 'debagged', and they prepared to carry out the sentence. It so happened that I was acquainted with one of the raiders. I had come up punctually at the beginning of term and a representative of some games committee called on me to ask what games I intended to play and in particular whether I would play in a Rugby football match that very afternoon. They were, he explained, in difficulties; they were unable to complete the team as most members of the College had not yet come up. I told him that I intended to play no games at all and that in regard to his particular invitation I had been at a school where only Association football was played. He proposed that I should nevertheless be coached and join the team. This I agreed to do, but subject to a strict condition, namely that I should never again be asked to participate in any athletic activity whatever. To this condition he agreed and I was intensively coached, and I represented my College in a game I had never played before. I was no doubt quite ineffectual, but my willingness to play was welcomed with a disproportionate cordiality. My acquaintance was the representative of the games committee and to him I was able to appeal with success against violence being offered my host. Honour was satisfied after one or two insignificant objects had been flung from the window, and we were left in peace. When returning to my rooms I was once again shocked by the indifference of occasionally passing dons to this scene of drunken violence and destruction.

My susceptibilities about the indifference of the dons arose from my failure to comprehend the simple fact that I was no longer at school but at a university where, though there were various rules in force, undergraduates were treated as responsible adults, both as regards their habits of study and of living, and where certain manifestations of disorder, sanctified by tradition, such as those which followed dinners held in celebration of success on river or playing-field, were tacitly tolerated. Had these same members of the College behaved in similar fashion during the morning, they would without a doubt have been suspected of criminal lunacy and 'sent down' within the day. In any case the early 'twenties was a time when violence was more common than at others: Oxford was full of men who had been taught and who had practised violence during the preceding years of war, who had forgotten the disciplines of school and who experienced recurrent moments of fierce exaltation which arose from the realization that their ordeal was over and they had come out of it alive. At Oxford, at Worcester, during my time at all events, it was customary to tolerate internal disorders, but I had the feeling at times that interference might have inflamed yet further already ugly situations. Violence of the kind I have described abated in later years when the tough and overwrought war generation had gone down, and the excess of those wanting to come to Oxford over the available places had strengthened the hand of authority. Although at Worcester outbreaks of destructive violence were not infrequent, they were more alarming than dangerous. Nobody that I heard of was ever hurt, nor was there, I believe, any personal malice behind them. The rioters, breaking rigorous training, perhaps

reacted to the effects of alcohol more violently than others; needed,
so to speak, lightning conductors for their feelings, which led them
to seek out 'socialists' and other eccentrics. There was no question
of the systematic persecution of socialists—Kenneth Lindsay, for
instance, Socialist President of the Union, was a particularly well-
liked member of the College. This loutish thuggery made me wonder
what Flecker could have been thinking of when he wrote of Oxford's

'Fair and floral air and the love that lingers there.'

If my dream was shattered, life in the meanwhile was more
interesting than I had ever known it. One of the chief experiences of
my first year was one which I only intermittently enjoyed but for
which I have been grateful since. The College was crowded and
freshmen had to share sets of rooms which their predecessors had
occupied alone. I accordingly found myself sharing the first-floor set
(consisting of a large sitting-room and two bedrooms) in the Queen
Anne Wing, next to the Provost's Lodge, with an Anglo-Russian
some six years my senior named William Gerhardi. Older even than
most of the other undergraduates who had served in the war,
Gerhardi was intellectually mature beyond his years. I found myself,
an ill-educated, largely country-bred boy from a small school, in
intimate daily contact with a mind of extreme acutness and of a
highly critical turn. In spite of his mainly British ancestry, Gerhardi
had the characteristic Russian urge to talk constantly about his
fundamental beliefs and the most intimate aspects of his personal
conduct. But his talk had nothing of the characteristic Russian
idealism and largeness; it was as though conversations from Tolstoy,
Turgenev and Dostoievski were parodied by some cynical member
of the Goncourt circle. But Gerhardi carried his cynicism gaily; few
people I have ever known have an acuter sense of the absurd, of the
difference between the realities of life and the obscuring cant. He had
recently been attached to Admiral Kolchak's staff during the Allied
intervention in Siberia, and the tragi-comic aspects of it were a
constant source of inventive reminiscence, which crystallized in his
first novel *Futility* (which I believe I titled) and on which he was
then engaged. He was also preparing a B.Litt. thesis on Chekhov, a
writer whose outlook contributed much to the formation of his own.
We got along harmoniously enough, although there were times when
I resented the midday emergence into our common sitting-room of

this tall, nervously pacing being with the pale flat face, the high veined forehead, the pale protruding eyes, the sensual mouth, red as though made up, whom sleep had charged with desire for aggressive argument, about politics or literature, but more often about sex or religion, which I regarded as private matters. This view of them he ridiculed, forced me to declare myself, assailed any conclusions I had reached, and in general, by his unkind and disillusioned probing, compelled me, as no one had before, to think clearly and independently. My subsequent gratitude far out-weighed the exasperation which his procedures sometimes provoked: it was, in fact, largely through my intimacy with him that I began to be intellectually mature. Association with Gerhardi was a rigorous discipline, for he talked almost continuously and scarcely ever went out.

For several years we kept in touch by an occasional exchange of letters. The three which follow, written when he was beginning to win success as a writer, precisely recall his conversation as well as his own nomadic way of life, also led by certain characters in his novels.

> Baronial Castle,
> Bolton.

(1923: undated)

My dear John O'London,

This is a new name for you. Don't you like it? . . . It is a revenge for your not writing to me for so long. I was awfully, awfully glad to get your letter. I have been languishing in these aristocratic surroundings trying to get myself to finish my Chekhov book. But it's only at Oxford that I ever could work. How I miss it—the playing fields (have we beaten Oriel?), the rough and bracing athletic life that I used to lead at Worcester. I play soccer in my dreams, I live through that glorious moment when I scored that goal, do you remember? (We were playing Hertford and I was goal-keeper.) Oh, for a round of hockey. (I hope a 'round' is the correct technical expression.) And *how are* we doing on the river? I have been looking through the papers to find news about the Eights—but as usual, poor Alexander[1] was disapp.

How is your hair? I suppose by now you have gone bald. My own hair, on the contrary, is flourishing. Such a mop! It begins

---

[1] His second christian name.

just above the brows, it's all curly, too, and I look the poet that I am. In order to harmonise my personal appearance with my books, which are all of the good, clean-limbed variety, I have conceived a way of drawing in my lips when I am being photographed, the result being a kind of hardy, sea-wolf, Admiral Jellicoe expression, like this . . .

Please bear this in mind if you ever think of caricaturing me again.

I had a letter from Bantock,[1] who asks me for a copy of *Futil.* I shall write to say that I must consult you on the subject. He signs himself:

'Raymond Bantock,
Celebrated Poet and Playwright.'

I am *very* honoured to think that your father has read my book as I always felt by what you said about him that he was a good judge of literature. Perhaps some day—who knows?—you too will read it. I haven't abandoned all hope, anyway, though it's an ambitious expectation! As for Wells—Ah! I don't expect he will ever read it now. My publisher sent free copies to Shaw, Wells, and Bennett, among others. But not one of them has even acknowledged the book.[2] But I have had letters from J. C. Squire (inviting me to contribute to the London Mercury), from Michael Sadleir (inquiring on behalf of Constable, of which he is a Director, if they may become my future publishers), from Middleton Murry, Mrs. Edith Wharton (who is arranging for a French translation of *Futil*), Aylmer Maude, Mrs. Constance Garnett, O'Donovan, Lady Russell and Katherine Mansfield (the last three writing to C.-S.[3]), Arnold Bax, the composer, three American publishers, photographers, etc., and Rebecca West has sent me a message, through Mary Somerville, that my book is the best of the year. The book is to be published separately in New York, by Duffield. I have had good reviews, and, by the way, the Spectator has mentioned me three times. To whom have I to attribute this honour? Is it John Strachey?

---

[1] A fellow undergraduate; son of the composer, Sir Granville Bantock.
[2] Wells afterwards wrote in *The Adelphi*, 'Why was there no shouting about Gerhardi's *Futility*, shouting to reach the suburbs and country towns? . . . A wonderful book!' It also won the praise of Bennett and Shaw.
[3] Cobden-Sanderson, his publisher.

But life is drab. I was so glad to read that Sir Almerick's conviction had been quashed. It was a damned shame to convict him at all. What is the world coming to? I am going to London on Saturday for a few days—hm-hm! By the way, could you, if you write to me again, tell me what are the next few degree-days; I should like to come up before Christmas, and get it over. Or is that too much to ask? If you refuse, I shall have to write to Allison[1]—my only other friend at Oxford. Are you editing any reviews this year? Are you in your old rooms? I am going to live in Paris soon. Are you writing anything? Give my love to Henderson.[2] Are my books in any shops at Oxford?

Yours ever,
William Baronio[3]

How I miss the intellectual stimulus of Pot. Tell him to beware of Hyde Park.

> Villa Edelweiss,
> Mühlau,
> Bei Innsbruck,
> Tirol.

August 23, 1923

Ah, well, Johnnie, I have no proper writing-paper on which to write—nothing so beautiful as yours. I love the shape and colour of it. It just happens that Mrs. Wharton's is exactly the same, & it isn't long since I wrote to her to tell her that I loved her jolly writing-paper! Thank you for reading *Futility* & for what you say about it. Oh yes, we are great men—I mean I and you. Have you read the June & July numbers of the *Adelphi*, in which your friend (& 'my contemporary') H. G. Wells refers to 'Us'—(to use the first person plural à la Nicholas II)? There is no one I wished so much to read my books as H. G. Wells—I hear on all sides my wish has been fulfilled?

You ask me when I am coming to London. Why should I come to London? Why should I ever come to London again? I am perfectly happy where I am. You will imply from my address that

[1] Our 'Scout'.
[2] Gavin Henderson, afterwards Lord Faringdon, a fellow undergraduate.
[3] 'Baron' was our nickname for him.

I have bought a villa. Alas! not yet. This is a *pension*, and we have the whole southern portion of the second floor, with a magnificent balcony, overlooking a view which it is hard to beat! I have my father & mother & aunt here. We have left Bolton for evermore. Nothing will ever induce me to go back there, & so you may cancel my address there. Tomorrow my sister (whose photograph I had on my chimney-piece) is arriving with her husband—a Frenchman —& they will spend a month or more with us. The society here is very 'mixed' & peculiarly interesting for my purposes. There is a famous English society beauty, now in her sixties, a fabulous Russian princess, a fat old Swiss shopkeeper who sleeps with a fresh woman each night, & when asked by me how he liked her invariably replies: 'Prima Qualität'. He speaks a strange mixture of German & Swiss-German & he often 'orders' women for my use— as though it were cabs! But compared with him I am fastidious, & I have turned down every one of his 'orders'.

And now what of Oscar? What of Oscar Wilde? I believe that the messages are genuine, don't you? I believe in spiritualism of a sort because, to my mind, we have not sufficient data not to believe in it. It is more likely than not that the incredible should happen because, when all is said, all life is a miracle. It would be incredible, since life is a miracle, that only the credible things should happen. It would not be quite up to the standard of miraculous life, don't you see? However . . . However . . .

What a novel I am writing just now! I have altered the name & have called it 'About Love'. It is enormously rich, full of moods as varied as life itself. But I am beginning to boast. You will begin to wonder what has happened to my well-known modesty.

So you have left Oxford at last. What are you doing? Have you begun to write *seriously* yet? Have you settled down to a novel or, let us say, a 4-act drama? John: there is only one piece of literary advice of any use to any one, & that is this: don't write as you think you are expected to: write just as *you* feel life. That is to say, if you deal with an unfamiliar subject—say the sea—don't weary yourself about finding out about the technical side of, let us say, navigation, but write of ships & so forth just as they happen to have impressed you and—chiefest of all—*not unless they have impressed you*. If I see a garden full of beautiful flowers, if I have been stirred by the sight (I may be ignorant of the name of the flowers), I am merely concerned with *communicating* to the reader my particular emotion, & only *indirectly* the visible effect of the whole. However . . .

Do you see Strachey & Sackville-West? The last-named was writing a novel when I last saw him in Oxford—a finely spun web, à la Marcel Proust. Marcel Proust, by the way, is a jolly good writer. Have you read *Du Côté de chez Swann*?

My mother was delighted that you should remember her. Please give my kind regards to your own Mother & Father, but don't show this letter to anyone young, or they may think I am a bad man.

Yours ever,
William

I have just received a letter from our friend Mary Somerville. She said she would run me out in her little car to see the beautiful Julien[1] when I am next in Oxford! I think I must come to England now. I envy your being in London now: you will be able to see the Moscow Art Players.

Hotel Schönruh,
Amras
bei Innsbruck,
Tirol (Austria).

About the 4th or so of September 1924.

My dear John Rothenstein,
How are you? Why don't you write to me? What are you doing? Are you, with the rest of us, pledged for life to literature? I scan the publishers' announcements in the hope of finding mention of a masterpiece from your delicate pen—but I scan in vain! Why so?

Do you ever see any of our friends? Pot, for instance? Of all men at Oxford with whom I came in contact Pot has made the richest impression on my mind. And I know you share my enthusiasm for his intellectual, spiritual & other gifts.

How are you? I often think of you—of the time when we were together. In spite of all your misdeeds I like you very much—for

---

[1] Julian, daughter of Philip and Lady Ottoline Morrell.

your delicate humour. You ought to write not as you wrote but
as you spoke to me at breakfast—delicately, humorously.

I am awfully well & happier than I have ever been. I've just
finished my second novel—very long, 150,000 words.[1] It may still
appear in *Harper's* serially but they can't begin with it till June
1925, & unless Curtis Brown find another magazine for it, I will
let it come out as a book forthwith. It's good, I think, though not
on a level with that well-known masterpiece of mine called *Tact*,
of which you are so ardent an admirer! Strachey wrote to me some
weeks ago to ask me if I had any short stories for him. I daresay
he is still under the spell of 'Tact' & so craves for some more stuff
of the same kind! You must read my 'Polygots' when it comes out,
because the heroine of it is our friend Teresa—oh, the darling!
She is still in Melbourne, never writes—only cables. I've grown
much better looking and am surprisingly successful—I never used
to be conspicuously, before—with girls & women.

I want to go to Vienna for the winter, but if you write to me
here the letter will be forwarded without fail. When I'm rich I
want to buy a little spot in Southern France, somewhere round
about Toulon & build a little house, & you will come & stay with
me, won't you.

> Do you read the Adelphi? I do. It's good. Very.
> Yours,
> William G.

During my first year I worked steadily—I was reading Modern
History—and passed Moderations without difficulty . Early in my
second year my life, and alas my work, underwent a radical change.
Hitherto I had lived quietly, making a few friends within the College
and a rather larger number outside, without finding my way into any
particular circle. The ease with which I passed Moderations,
together with a surging zest for living, made me forgetful of how
bitter were the fruits of idleness. I moved into a beautiful set of
rooms of my own, said to have been occupied in former times by De
Quincy, on the mediaeval side of the quadrangle. At least it was
potentially beautiful, but its fine eighteenth-century panelling was
covered with khaki-coloured paint and the rest of the woodwork with
chocolate. I had it all scraped and painted gleaming white and hung

[1] *The Polyglots.*

with drawings by my father, Augustus John, Max and other contemporaries, some eighteenth century engravings and a Goya
etching. Of the drawings I collected at Oxford one which I particularly valued arrived by post from Italy at the beginning of my
third year. It was Max's first illustration to *Zuleika Dobson*, made
specially for me, and round it he had written a letter. 'Rapallo, Oct.
1922, My dear John,' it ran, 'As you are at Oxford (which is the next
best place to Rapallo), and as the Duke of Dorset and Miss Z. Dobson and the daughter of the Duke's landlady were there before you,
perhaps it might amuse you to have this sketch. I call it a sketch, but
it is really a cartoon for a fresco—which sounds much grander and is
the title to use in speaking of it—if you ever do speak of it. On the
walls of the little house where Florence and I live I have recently
done two frescoes on eligible blank architectural spaces that seemed
to be crying aloud for something upon them. Not frescoes in the
strict sense—not things painted on wet plaster which is added on in
bits while the master feverishly works. But mural paintings done in
tempera and Indian ink on plaster that has been laid on by a local
workman and has since dried. The design that I send you will be
"executed" at just double this size, and in a simpler, flatter more
mural fashion—the figures all white, with just slight modelling,
against the sort of modelling that you here perceive. You must make
your family bring you out here to see the enlarged version, and to see
Florence and me. *We* are just exactly the same as ever; but I suppose
you are alarmingly different, with an Oxford manner that would
frighten us both out of our wits. Knowing, however, that behind the
manner was our well-remembered young friend all the time, we
should be able to control our tremors and cope with you very
happily. Yours ever, Max Beerbohm.' Another 'Max' which also
arrived by post was a caricature of myself—a twenty-first birthday
present. This particular combination of drawings and engravings
with a white background, conservative, indeed timid, according to
the taste of today, in contrast to the prevailing backgrounds of khaki
and chocolate in the rooms of fellow undergraduates, the photographs of crews and teams, surmounted by school or College arms,
the family photographs and the occasional hunting print, made my
rooms as conspicuous as a white whale. They caused a mild ripple
of interest throughout the College; it even began to be whispered
that I must be a homosexual. Although I went to much trouble to

make my surroundings reflect my taste, without other motive than delight in the possession of rooms of my own and of exceptional beauty, they became a setting, almost as soon as they were ready, for an entirely altered way of life. I saw less—though I did not value less —the friends of my first year: Malcolm MacDonald, Harry Carter, also a Bedales friend with whom my relations became closer after we had left Oxford, and Philip Hendy, in whom I detected no flicker of interest in the visual arts nor anything of the seriousness of purpose or the courageous independence of outlook that were to make him, a quarter of a century later, an outstanding Director of the National Gallery. He shared rooms in Christ Church with Robert Bevan, son of the humane painter of gaunt urban horses who was Gauguin's friend. I was as surprised, when I heard a few years later that Philip Hendy had gone into the Wallace Collection, as I was at the entry into Parliament of Anthony Eden, whose interests at Oxford appeared predominantly aesthetic. Philip—who looked, someone said, as a Spanish nobleman might hope to look—and Bobbie always gave a warm welcome to their friends who came to enjoy their genial, somewhat rowdy company.

Another friend of my freshman year—friend is not quite the proper word, although he was more friend than acquaintance— was Lawrence of Arabia. A few months before I went up to Oxford I returned late to lunch at my parents' house in Sheffield Terrace to find a man in Oriental dress seated at the table. The sight affected me as in no way unusual, since my father's interest in India brought him a long succession of Indian visitors. A second glance showed me that this particular guest was not an Indian: from beneath a white Arab burnous, surmounted by a heavy gold circlet, I saw a young pink face. The sand-coloured eyebrows knit abruptly together as the large blue-grey eyes focused on me. Before the introductory words 'Colonel Lawrence' were pronounced I had time to hope that this might be the man whose campaign in Arabia was being talked about as one of spectacular audacity and skill.

As he half rose from the table I was surprised at the smallness of his stature and the diffident gentleness of his handshake, at how little, in fact, he conformed to the popular image of the soldier.

Lawrence was wearing Arab dress because my father was painting a portrait of him (now in the National Museum in Belgrade), the only full-length, I believe, he ever sat for.

The features that I most clearly recall were his eyes: wide and far-focused as a sailor's, yet evasive and downward looking, occasionally giving you a direct glance, which would be friendly, quizzical but keenly observant. The eyes would dilate suddenly if he saw a painting or a drawing he liked, and he would look at you to see whether you shared his preference.

When I asked him a question about his campaign in Arabia (which at that time was not yet history), he replied, 'There are so many more interesting things to talk about', and he asked me probing questions about the younger painters and writers. On our doorstep as he was leaving he said, 'When you go up to Oxford, however much you enjoy University life, there'll probably be times when you'll have had enough, and need to escape. If you ever want a place where you can be quiet, come along to my rooms at All Souls. Don't let me know in advance; don't knock; just walk in.'

Although he had discouraged my questions about the Arabian campaign, he did not forget my disappointment at his evasion, for when he next called, a week or two later, at my parents' house, he brought with him a copy of a red-covered publication which he placed in my hands, saying 'this contains all that's worth telling about my part in the Arabian campaign. The legend is nonsense. Keep it if you care to.' The journal was a copy of *The Army Quarterly*, to which he had contributed an article entitled 'The Evolution of a Revolt'. It was signed 'T. E. Lawrence (late Lieutenant-Colonel, General Staff, E. E. F.)'.

On his second visit as on the first he pressed me to speak of the younger painters whose work I knew. How voracious was his interest in painting may be judged from his eagerness to exchange for his own acute and informed observation opinions such as my own, based upon slight information and less thought. His clearly marked preference was for an art, in the words of the philosopher T. E. Hulme, 'where everything tends to be angular, where curves tend to be hard and geometrical, where the presentation of the human body is . . . distorted to fit into stiff lines and cubical shapes', that is to say the art of such men as Wyndham Lewis, the Epstein of 'The Rock Drill', Wadsworth and Roberts.

One midday at Oxford, walking along the High Street, I turned without premeditation into All Souls. Lawrence's rooms were empty, but a moment later there was a light footfall outside, and Lawrence

was there. He never allowed more than an instant for conventional
greetings but engaged immediately upon some subject worth discussion. 'You should read, if you don't already know it,' he said on
this occasion, '*Sons and Lovers*, by a certain D. H. Lawrence (no
relation of mine) whom I place among the great writers.' I had
never heard of D. H. Lawrence, but immediately read the book. He
asked me to stay to lunch. The sitting room was a fine one, a warm
fire blazed in the grate, the lunch was good, yet it seemed to me that
he had little need for any such things, and that had we been sitting
instead out on Boars Hill in a drizzle, eating bread and cheese, he
would not have been conscious of the difference. He showed a simple
gratitude to All Souls for the security and comfort it afforded at a
time when he had need of a measure of security. But I sensed something the contrary of possessive in his attitude towards his Fellow-
ship—he seemed to regard it as another might a sunny spring
day, as something that comes by chance, belongs to nobody, to be
enjoyed while it lasts without thought for the morrow. The only
objects which seemed to evoke any sense of possession were his
books: first editions, editions with fine bindings; the room fairly
gleamed with vellum spines.

In spite of his habitual avoidance of looking his companions
directly in the eyes, Lawrence's was a sharply probing presence: he
wished to discover the points where they were weak and those where
they were strong, more especially whether men were disposed—I say
men rather than people, because although he had a few women friends
I do not recall his ever discussing a woman—towards austerity.

One day he began, 'I think Jews in one respect are prone to
extremes: they incline either to excessive self-indulgence or to the
most rigorous austerity. You've some Jewish blood. In which direction does it affect you?' In a moment we were deep in the whole
question of the polarity of discipline and excess—a question to
which he often adverted. Austerity for him seemed to hold a persistent fascination. Also courage: he confessed on several occasions
how frightened he had been in his Arabian campaign when he had to
lead attacks in person in order to foster morale and win confidence in
his leadership. It has been said and written of him that he was con-
ceited. Even had he not had the wit to see that he was the possessor
of a combination of talents of the rarest order, he could hardly have
overlooked the admiring curiosity, the adulation even, which he

evoked. That he was aware of being an exceptional man was obvious, but never in the course of many meetings did I hear a remark or perceive a gesture expressive of conceit. He seemed to me, on the contrary, a modest, even a humble man, revering great achievement, conscious of possessing talents sufficient to enable him to do great things himself, yet not knowing to what end to use them. Action? No theatre of action tempted him—the land of the Arabs whom he considered to have been betrayed least of any. Literature? He did not believe he had talent to write anything that would satisfy the rigorous standards he set himself. Lawrence was a dedicated man without a cause, and when I met him during the few years between his leaving Oxford and his death he appeared to have become careless of himself; and when I heard of the manner of his death it seemed to me to be the consequence of the indifference he had come to feel for a being for whom he had been able to discover no use at all commensurate either with his powers or his desire for self-dedication.

On another visit he spoke bitterly about the Peace Treaty as it affected the Arabs, and of his sense of having been the instrument of the betrayal of hopes of independence that he had been permitted, even encouraged, to foster in them. Turning to a bookshelf he took down one of his vellum-bound books and wrote a few words on the fly-leaf. The book was *Fleurs du Mal*; the inscription ran: 'To J. M. Rothenstein from T. E. Lawrence, Dec. 1920. I want to get rid of this: it's v. g. and was the one bright spot of the Peace Conference to me: but let's forget that:—we grew a much worse crop than we dreamed of.' It was a subject he reverted to several times that winter, and always in anger.

Lawrence's life at Oxford was secluded. From the one occasion when I was his guest for lunch in Hall I gathered that he was on friendly terms with the resident Fellows of All Souls (though the visitors to be met with in his rooms were soldiers, poets, artists and Civil Servants rather than dons), but otherwise his Oxford life seemed to be lived remote from the University. Considering that he was a Fellow of one college and had been an undergraduate of two others and that he had become so illustrious a figure in the world, there was something extraordinary about the extent to which he contrived to escape notice. I never saw him in the street or met him outside All Souls, except for one occasion when he arrived, to my immense pleasure, unannounced in my rooms at Worcester. I do not recall ever hearing of his visiting anybody's house except that of the archaeologist, David Hogarth, one of his few close friends. In fact the University seemed virtually unaware of his presence; when he was spoken of it was as someone legendary. Sensing half-consciously his wish for seclusion, I do not believe I mentioned my visits to his rooms to any of my friends.

Lawrence's statement on our second meeting, that his article in *The Army Quarterly* contained all that was worth telling about his campaign, was evidently not literally meant, for he was engaged at this time on his *Seven Pillars of Wisdom*. The writing of it seemed to give him little satisfaction, for he spoke critically of his prose as 'contrived' and without natural style. He showed no reluctance (as he had at my parents' house) to talk about the war in Arabia. Surprisingly he said that he had been able to apply many lessons learnt from his study of the campaigns of Turenne and Saxe. Both commanders he considered to be underestimated: historians, he thought, had been led by the many-sided genius, overwhelming success and dramatic destiny of Napoleon to overestimate his purely military capacities. 'Napoleon often gained his objectives,' he said, 'at disproportionate cost—one of the principal arts of war is the knowledge of how to avoid casualties—on one's own side, of course.' The only aspect of his own successful campaign I heard him allude to with satisfaction was the smallness of its cost in human life. Of Allenby, his chief, he invariably spoke with admiration, in particular for his respect for the lives of the men under his command. Although I listened with absorbed attention to his talk about his campaign, the deficiency of my own military knowledge prevented me from eliciting his best. One day he invited to lunch with him at All Souls Field-Marshal Sir William Robertson, Geoffrey Dawson, Editor of *The Times*, my father and myself. Lawrence made some statement about the conduct of war—I forget what it was—which Robertson (with Dawson's support) challenged, and hammered with well-aimed blows. Robertson's arguments were based upon intuition and experience and were of an impressive simplicity. The tactics Lawrence employed to meet this attack were not unlike those he developed in his struggle with the Turks: he did not resist—he asked questions, drawing his opponent on into unfamiliar regions of psychology and history, then, with audacious generalities, he forced him to pause to reconsider the premises on which his attack was based. It was an

THE PRINCESS BADROULBADOUR (THE AUTHOR AND HIS SISTERS), 1908,
BY WILLIAM ROTHENSTEIN

THE AUTHOR *aet.* 9

FAMILY GROUP AT ILES FARM

extraordinary exercise in dialectic skill, innocent of craft or undue exploitation of his special fields of knowledge. Robertson showed him a deference that was an expression of something more than courtesy: it was the tribute of a great professional to an amateur of genius.

My increasing absorption in other interests diminished the number of my visits to All Souls. The merest scraps of his conversation are all that my memory retains of my last visits: how humiliating it was to be mistaken for an Arab, as he was more than once, by British officers; out of what a popular Egyptian cigarette was made (he himself used for a time to smoke cigarettes filled with herbs); about the theft, on Reading station, of the first draft of *The Seven Pillars of Wisdom*; and of the astonishment caused at All Souls by an unheralded visit by King Feisal. We continued to meet from time to time during vacations at my parents' house. Here our interchanges were less intimate and sustained than those at All Souls, but I recollect his meetings (for the first time) with two men for whom he had an ardent admiration—and the more clearly perhaps because both meetings took a curiously similar course. These men were W. H. Hudson and Frederic Manning. Lawrence, being as elusive as he was legendary, was assiduously courted and had come quite justifiably to assume that people in general and writers and artists in particular would eagerly welcome the chance of meeting him. Again and again I noticed that when people unlikely to arouse his interest made overtures he, on his side, always with courtesy, would confine the resulting encounters within the narrowest limits. In writers and artists, on the contrary, his own interest was perennial and he was disposed to idealize them, although increased knowledge served as a corrective. It so happened that on successive or proximate Sunday evenings at my parents' the two men in question were present. Lawrence made no secret of his eagerness to meet them. Neither of them showed, however, the slightest interest in *him*. Hudson had grown suddenly old and was enclosed in melancholy because his splendid sight and hearing were failing him at last—a failure he had anticipated with particular dread. Although his devotion to his few friends and to places long known to him was undiminished, for new interests he had little room or none. Fred Manning had spent most of his life—except for the relatively brief but fruitful period on the Western Front, which resulted in his remarkable book *Her Privates We*—in a small circle of intimates on whom he lavished his dry wit, his learning, his affection and his letters, of which the calligraphy was worthy of the contents. Outside this circle he ventured with fastidious circumspection. The same scene was enacted on Lawrence's encounters with both: he, the all but invariably pursued, became the pursuer. In neither case did he at first perceive, in face of their indifference, that his identity was already known, and he related, one after another, dramatic incidents about fighting in Arabia and peace-making at Versailles. Neither man showed more than a perfunctory interest, but Lawrence betrayed no trace of pique. Later he came to know both men, and after Manning's death Lawrence wrote to my father that life seemed scarcely worth living on account of it. Within a few weeks he himself was dead.

After Oxford we exchanged an occasional letter and met rarely. I had occasion to ask him, in connection with a catalogue of my father's portrait drawings I was compiling, whether he was, in fact, as had been widely reported, a Prince of Mecca. My enquiry drew the following reply:

> 338171 A. A. II Shaw,
> Hut 105,
> R.A.F. Cadet College,
> Cranwell,
> Lincs.
> 1.X.25

Dear Rothenstein,

Letters take so long to sink through the various layers of my disguises. I only got yours yesterday.

The description of me isn't very accurate, I'm afraid. Who's Who took it from the Strand Magazine, despite my protests. I'm not C.B. nor D.S.O.: nor is 'Arabic scholar' proper of one who never learnt to read or write that very difficult, and for me un-attainable, language. 'Fellow of All Souls 1919–1925' is accurate. Prince of Mecca I never was. It is a territorial title, at present held by Ibn Saud, chief of the Wahabi heresy. He took it from King Hussein, the late King of Mecca: but Hussein didn't love me & never gave me anything at all! The title Prince of Mecca was conferred on me first in the Strand Magazine, by an American Journalist, called Thomas. . . .

As for suggesting another description of myself! Heavens. I'm now in the ranks of the Air Force: but that hardly concerns iconography. I've never been anything in particular. 'Late Lieut. Col.' would be strict truth. 'Senior Demy of Magdalen College Oxford!' 'Scholar of Jesus?' 'B.A. ?'

I'm glad I haven't got your job. One of your father's representations was my head: a simple thing to do. The other was all myself, in Meccan clothes. Are you cataloguing everything? What a flood.

Sorry for my delay

Yours ever

T.E.S.

Richard Aldington, in his book *Lawrence of Arabia, a Biographical Enquiry* (1955), wrote of the title 'Prince of Mecca' . . . 'there seems a strong probability that Lawrence conferred it on himself.' The letter quoted above well illustrates the contrarieties of Lawrence's temperament, for he emphatically disclaimed the title—a title, or one very similar, which was in fact conferred upon him, and he wore the insignia in the presence of Feisal, which would have made him ridiculous had it not been properly conferred.

But each of our contacts brought the assurance that his friendliness, however detached and astringent, had not diminished. When for instance my father sent him a copy of my novel *Morning Sorrow*, in spite of its immaturity, he read it twice, and wrote a detailed, careful criticism of it and made suggestions for the revision of a number of passages, as well as a letter about it to my father.

The sombre presence of the unemployed, the General Strike, the Depression and other symptoms of the malfunctioning of the economic system caused a number of my contemporaries to speculate upon whether a form of government in which greater power was concentrated in one man's hands might not be able to deal more effectively with the menacing problems which beset our society than the prevailing democratic system. In the course of such speculations the name of Lawrence was on several occasions mentioned as the person to whose hands such power might most rewardingly be entrusted. Happening to see Bernard Shaw soon after Lawrence's death—I used occasionally to talk with Shaw while he sat to my father for portraits, in order to keep his expression animated—I asked him how he thought he would have used such power. Knowing Shaw's admiration for Lawrence and the attraction which the idea of dictatorship held for him (more freely expressed in conversation than writing) I was surprised at his response: 'Lawrence,' he said, 'was a brilliant boy, a boy of quite astonishing brilliance to be sure, but he was not fitted to exercise supreme power because he never made up his mind about the two crucial questions, about government and religion.' Today I agree with Shaw, but at the time I argued that, as Lawrence himself used to remark, leadership, particularly in England, was determined by character rather than intellect, and who was more courageous, freer from self-interest, more responsive to what was fine in thought and action than he—or more intelligent?

*

One, perhaps the most influential, of the circumstances which made for the radical change in my way of living noted earlier in this chapter was a friendship that began with my receipt of a note, on Madgalen writing-paper, of which I was at first unable to make out anything at all and which I supposed to be written in some foreign language—signed, apparently, 'Job Stocking'. Upon close scrutiny I perceived that English was, in fact, the language of the note, and I could even make out the words 'Know my cousin Tulla . . . lunch Friday one.' But the list in the Porter's Lodge of members of the University in residence made no mention of any Stocking. In my perplexity I consulted the Porter's Lodge at Magdalen, and it appeared that the name of my unknown correspondent was not Stocking but Strachey. At the lunch I met an old friend from Bedales days, Julia—the 'Tulla' of the note—Strachey, cousin of my host John Strachey. He and I became friends at once, and there must have been few weeks during our two remaining years at Oxford when we did not dine together at least once.

John Strachey was tall and he had inherited the conspicuously Latin looks of a Portuguese ancestor. In speech and gesture he was deliberate and slow. His powerful intelligence was of an extraordinary range, but it was part of the charm of this formidable being that he entered so zestfully into the smallest concerns of his friends, above all their jokes, for his sense of humour was highly developed. The conclusions of his small-grinding reason he followed unmindful of the consequences, so that never, either as a youthful Tory, or later as a mature Socialist, was he ever regarded as remotely 'safe'. Many people are mistrusted for their duplicity: the mistrust that John was apt to rouse was solely due to his combination of intellectual power with independence. Political associates were often disconcerted by his capacity for seeing a problem in all its aspects, which bred a detachment that they were inclined to regard as more proper to a historian than to a politician. In those days he had not yet set foot on the path that led to learned commentaries on Marx and to portfolios for Food and War in Labour Governments; on the contrary he was a Tory, and in his manner almost aggressively 'public school'. But he was also an original, contemptuous of public opinion. One afternoon that summer I went to meet him at some cricket ground where he was playing for his College. As I arrived he went in to bat, a huge French peasant straw hat on his head, profusely ornamented with trailing pink ribbons. The contrast between exotic headgear and the College caps of the other players was startling. 'Just look at what that bastard Strachey's got on his head,' snarled one spectator. With such deliberation did he face the bowling that he seemed to be moving as though in a slow-motion film, but he knocked up ninety runs. It was through John Strachey that I met a number of those whose friendship I valued most. When I was sitting in his rooms in Magdalen New Buildings, an angular, loose-limbed young man with a face like a gaunt gothic carving, whose movements were disconcertingly un-coordinated, came in, uttered a few words so rapidly that I was unable to catch them, and walked out. 'That,' John explained, 'was David Cecil: a very remarkable mind, but he's a Christian.' 'A Christian?' I enquired. 'Yes,' John explained in his preternaturally slow drawl, 'you see he believes in the authenticity of a few passages in St. John's Gospel.'

John Strachey was the son of St. Loe Strachey, editor and proprietor of *The Spectator*; he had been at Eton and had come to Oxford with connections far-reaching and distinguished. Among his friends who shortly became mine were besides David Cecil, Lord Balniel, Edward Sackville-West, Robert Boothby, Roger Senhouse, St. Joseph Brewer, Richard Hughes, Adrian Stokes, and a strange doomed figure, Thomas Darlow. In a matter of weeks I found myself a member of an intellectual and social group whose members regarded themselves as belonging to the University rather than to any particular college; strictly college connections they tended, in fact, quietly but firmly to ignore. In so far as it had a centre, this was the Gridiron Club, 'The Grid'—although not all those just named were members of it—which had its premises on the first floor above the Midland Bank at Carfax. Another characteristic of this group was that the members of it used no slang expressions whatever and few abbreviations; the patois that featured in 'Oxford' novels they would barely have understood.

About the same time another avenue into this larger University world opened out from an unexpected point of departure. During my first year I noticed—I could indeed hardly have failed to notice—a man with an insolent face, with wide, slightly protuberant blue eyes and a sensual mouth, a loud voice that sometimes ascended to a scream, and fashionable clothes. His rooms were a few staircases away from Gerhardi's and mine. His looks slightly repelled me; he was generally regarded in College with dislike—a dislike which I was foolish enough unreflectingly to share. Athole Hay, for this was his name, made several friendly but tentative advances towards me, which I had discouraged. One afternoon, after declining an invitation to lunch with him, we met face to face in the College gardens. 'I'm sorry you didn't come to lunch today; I had several people who'd have liked to meet you.' Upon my enquiring who they were he recited the names of some marquesses, earls, a vicomte and a baronet. I must, I suppose, have made a priggish gesture indicating that there was something snobbish about such all but exclusive foregathering with members of the peerage. At all events he replied, with perfect good nature, 'But not to be a snob is surely to be content with low company.' I liked his candour, his good nature and his assured cordiality untinged by ingratiation. That afternoon I tacitly accepted his advances and before long we became warm friends, although it was not until years later that I came fully to appreciate what a rare being he was. Through Athole Hay I was brought in touch with the more purely social life of Oxford, with 'Chips' Channon, a Chicagoan who already had a wide acquaintance among crowned heads and heads until lately crowned; but, socially adept as he was, Chips was a worker, although, I think, he kept very quiet about his reading. He shared with Francis Stonor a fine house in Broad Street occupied not long before by W. B. Yeats. One day I was summoned to the telephone—in those days rather a portentous event—by Chips to tell me that Athole had been injured, and that he was coming round to Worcester straight away, and to suggest that I should join him in Athole's rooms. Athole was in bed, his head almost totally swathed in bandages through which blood was seeping fast. Very quietly we asked what had happened. His mouth moved; he seemed too weak for speech. Suddenly he screamed out, 'It's my own fault, all my own fault. I'd never been to see my tutor, and thought I ought to go at least once. On my way I caught my head on the top of a wicket gate. It's taught me a lesson; I shall never be so stupid as to try to see my tutor again.' Nobody I knew so entirely ignored his academic studies, but he claimed to be devoting his energies instead to the writing of a book. When I asked to see the manuscript he pointed to a disordered heap of scraps of tattered paper on a bedside table, from which he absently selected from time to time a sheet to twist into a spill for lighting a cigarette. He was exceptionally intelligent, yet it did not, until many years later, occur to him to do anything beyond living a civilized, idle life.

He was often exploited by those who wished to profit by his social connections, his money or his intellectual capacities. His shrewdness enabled him to gauge these intentions with a precision which they would have found disconcerting had they been able to read his mind as well as he read theirs, but he was too little self-protective and too contemptuous of spongers to give himself the trouble of resisting their importunities. Athole was more indifferent to the solicitations of ambition, less competitive, less disposed to take even the most elementary precautions to ensure his own well-being, than any man of talent that I had ever known. One morning in the summer of 1923, just before I was due to sit for 'Schools', my final examinations, I was in bed, suffering from influenza. Athole walked in, settled himself down and began to talk. My mind was somewhat occupied with my impending ordeal, and I exclaimed suddenly 'Athole! Surely you ought to be taking your own first paper at this very moment'. 'When I went to the Examination Schools this morning,' he answered, 'they wouldn't let me in. They told me I was improperly dressed. I contested that; I pointed out that I was wearing the required black suit and white tie.' (He was dressed for riding in black jacket and white stock.) 'But it doesn't matter; I'm going to ride out to Cumnor, so I couldn't have stayed long. In any case I'd much rather be sitting here talking to you than taking an examination.' I delighted in a man who attached so little importance to gathering the fruits of three years' work, however desultory. For him the work itself was what counted, and if this were indifferent, how much the more ignoble to strive to transmute it into a degree. I delighted, too, in his total loyalty to his friends before the world, however severely he could on occasion upbraid them in private for their faults.

The early 'twenties at Oxford was a time when not only pronounced character but eccentricity flourished richly. Richard Hughes, the sardonic future author of *High Wind in Jamaica* and a number of fine poems, disturbed his friends by sleeping in the open in inclement weather. Upon my once expressing their anxieties he replied, 'If you sleep outdoors in the rain, and you are nervous about what may result, you will contract rheumatism, pneumonia and I know not what else; but if you sleep outdoors in no matter what conditions, with the right disposition of mind, that is to say, with confidence, nothing will harm you.' Another friend, Jeffrey Prendergast, reflected in its most uncompromising form the cult of the effeminate by which only a minority of the circle in which I came to move was entirely unaffected. Calling at his rooms in Balliol I found him slumped at a table, his face drawn with misery. 'What is wrong, Prendie?' I asked. 'I don't know what to do, John; you see,' he said giving me a tragic look, '*I've lost all my allure.*' Walking out in the street Prendie might be seen pulling behind him on a string his white woollen lamb on wheels. This cult of the effeminate did not necessarily denote effeminacy in the generally accepted sense, nor even homosexuality, ubiquitous though this was. During the Second World War, for instance, I met Prendie in a café in London, and having known him well it was perceptible to me that there was tension beneath his affectionate amiability. And not without cause. I discovered that he was to be 'dropped' that night, with nothing but a machine-gun and iron rations, over occupied Yugoslavia. And another and more intimate friend carried for a time a small green leather bag upon his wrist which contained powder and puff. He afterwards played a distinguished part in the history of the armed forces. Although the cult blossomed in the prevailing homosexual climate—it would hardly have been conceivable without it—it must be made perfectly clear that most of those who affected it were not themselves homosexuals. It was the product of several causes, not the least of which was the defiant assertion of the dandified intellectual (or 'aesthete' as he was called) in the face of the formerly hectoring athlete, or 'hearty'. But whatever the personal predilections of the members of the little world of which I am writing, it can scarcely be denied that its 'tone' was predominantly homosexual. For most of us women were remote, improbable creatures, which neither the University's traditions, nor its regulations, nor the predilections of many of us, encouraged us to give attention to, much less to associate with. There was no hostility to women undergraduates, but they were considered peripheral, if not irrelevant, to Oxford life, and even faintly funny. I recall an ill-natured joke played upon them that would be unthinkable now. Walking one morning across Radcliffe Square I noticed a number of young women in academic dress who had evidently just come out of the Camera, and who were wheeling their bicylces away. Why did many of them look hurt and angry, and why were a few others in tears? And why were none riding? A thin horizontal silver gleam between a saddle and a pair of handlebars supplied the answer: while the young women were pursuing their studies, someone had wired up every one of their mounts. Some of us occasionally entertained to tea women members of the University whom we already knew, mostly dullish daughters of parental friends, and we paid occasional perfunctory court to one or other of the reigning beauties from Somerville or Lady Margaret Hall, but men known to have sisters were apt to be treated with reserve in Trinity Term lest they should require their friends to take these sisters to Commemoration Balls.

In many respects life at Oxford seems to have altered little over the four decades since I went down, but in one respect the change has been so complete as to be scarcely imaginable in my time, namely the relationship between men undergraduates and women, whether members of the University or not. In the 'twenties there were amorous relations between undergraduates and women outside the University, but these were, I believe, unusual, and they were discreetly consummated. In the early 'sixties there was a case of a woman undergraduate who was discovered with a man in her bed, in her College; action was taken against her by the authorities. Their action provoked an angry and articulate response among many undergraduates. At a country house where I happened to be staying

the matter became the subject of discussion over dinner. Someone
said, 'There were people who condemned the action of the authorities as an infringement of human rights. Have you ever heard anything so ridiculous?' A sixteen-year-old girl (who had just left a
strict convent and won a place at Oxford) rapped the table and exclaimed in an angry voice, '*I* think that what the authorities did *was*
an infringement of human rights.' My own contemporaries, members of a generation looked back upon as wild, would have regarded
the incident and its sequels as passing well beyond the bounds of
fantasy.

The small society I am trying briefly to sketch was largely self-
sufficient: it comprised intellectual brilliance, the social graces, and
figures of great elegance and charm, as well as a few loveable individuals denied any of these attributes. In the autobiography of a poet
who was at Oxford a few years later, undergraduate society is
described as snobbish and exclusive. I formed a contrary impression.
A high proportion of the people I am writing about were of the kind
now described as 'privileged': they were largely Etonians and Wyke-
hamists, they included members of historic families, but so far from
being exclusive they were disposed to welcome those from outside
who were able to contribute intellect, wit, good looks or any other
quality conducive to the enhancement of life. 'Cads', the sort of men
who wore hair oil and possessed racing cars in which they took
women of the town, were 'out', those who were aggressively athletic
also; 'poor scholars', exclusively intent upon academic honours,
would have grudged the time, for instance, for cups of morning
coffee with Mr. Hall, the tailor in the High, still more for long dinners
at the Gridiron Club, or for endless conversations before windows
opened on to college gardens full of the murmur of summer. Sometimes there were, so to say, field days, or field nights, rather, of more
exacting pleasures, splendid occasions celebrated with a luxury
possible now only for the rich. I recall one such occasion, 'A Farewell Dinner' (according to the menu) 'held for no particular reason
in Magdalen' on 7th December 1921. An elaborate dinner was
served, and guests were offered the choice of 'Bridge, Bacarat (*sic*),
Scandalous talk, and Music,' for each of which a room had been set
aside.

It was immediately after this dinner that an incident occurred
which exemplified the homosexual climate I have alluded to. One

speaker, eulogizing our host, said that he had provided his guests with every amenity they could have dreamed of, but that 'he had only neglected to provide a naked houri crouched beside each chair'. For this observation a second speaker took him sternly to task: 'I think there are present only two who would have the slightest use for such an object.' I have beside me as I write a menu signed by a number, probably a majority, of the guests (or else my memory of the occasion would have been less complete), of whom only a small minority were homosexuals (and some of these doubtless so only in a sentimental sense), yet this rebuke provoked no dissenting murmur.

I recall another similar celebration, on the grandest scale, of the twenty-first birthday of David Cecil, at which much of the talent of a whole Oxford generation seemed to have been assembled, at which were present Anthony Eden, Robert Boothby, John Strachey, Edward Sackville-West, David Balniel, Maurice Bowra and numerous others.

The political climate of this group was one of enlightened Tory-ism, although some of us styled ourselves 'Whigs', which, still refractory to the Liberalism of my family, I found congenial. Towards the end of 1921 I began to contribute articles to a serious Conservative periodical, *The Oxford Fortnightly Review*, of which, at the beginning of the following year I became, with David Cecil, a literary editor. Its political editors were John Strachey and Robert Boothby, and its musical editor Edward Sackville-West. Shortly afterwards I was elected to the principal Tory Club, the Canning.

My religious fervour subsided a little: the happy eventfulness of the present made my soul's salvation appear, for the moment, a matter of less urgency than it had on my solitary walks over the arid summit of the Cotswold Hills. I occasionally frequented Campion Hall—not Lutyens' ample building off St. Aldates, but the modest house in St. Giles beside the Lamb and Flag public house—where I had first called with a letter to Father Martindale from Eric Gill. The Catholic society of Oxford was very different from the large and predominantly indigenous society it has since become: in those days it was easily roused to the kind of truculent defensiveness most eloquently voiced by Hilaire Belloc, who was in fact the hero and exemplar of many of the Oxford Catholics. It was moreover a society which, although by no means dominated by, was at least strongly coloured by, the presence of a number of Continental *grand seigneurs*, several of whom I knew and liked but whose presence overshadowed somewhat that of both the intellectual fervour of the converts and the tenacious faith of the Old English Catholics.

I used to become restive at the undue importance that seemed to be attached to the possibility of the restoration of this king or that archduke, to the alleged piety of the peasants in this or that area of Europe, and at the inclination towards unreflective sympathy with the policies and attitudes of foreign ultramontanes and the idealization of the Age of Faith (when was it?).

Among my friends was a strange man, disapproved of by the rest. I was warned that it would be best for me to avoid him, but I was so far from heeding this advice that for a term or, perhaps for two, I shared rooms with him at 50 The High. His name was Tom Darlow; he was the son of a prominent Congregationalist and he had recoiled violently, even savagely, against his puritanical upbringing. What made him an exceptional being was the coexistence in him of much generosity and a warm and enduring affection for his friends with something approaching moral anarchy. Most immoral conduct is simply selfish impulse translated into action, but with Tom Darlow this was not the case, for, with him, the dubious shifts to obtain money, for instance, to which he sometimes resorted (and which became fully known only after he had left Oxford) were prompted, I believe, far more by the desire to help or rather to please his friends than for the gratification of some taste of his own. Perhaps his need to please his friends arose from the need to compensate for some obscure sense of failure. Whatever its cause, it was a besetting weakness, and it involved several of his friends as well as himself in awkward predicaments. If the recollection of certain of his actions sometimes provoked doubts, these were apt to be set at rest by the presence of Tom Darlow himself, immense in height and breadth with a hint of the lay preacher in his dark, well-made clothes, intelligent, genial and courteous. A chronic sufferer from insomnia, he was extremely well-read, especially in the works of William Morris and the Victorian novelists. One summer evening we met after dinner by arrangement but with no particular end in view. 'You're reading *The Return of the Native*, I think you told me,' he remarked. 'We're going to see Eustacia Vye.'

We got off the 'bus at Iffley and strolled along the river bank, saying little, my imagination faintly stirred by the name of Eustacia Vye, and wondering idly what my friend had in mind. Some joke, probably, but I forebore to ask him. 'There she is,' he said, and in the distance, coming slowly towards us, was a girl. I could see that she was tall and dark haired, but her most noticeable feature was her rhythmic unhurried walk. As she approached I experienced a momentary disappointment, for her face, though touched with beauty, was not pretty as it seemed to be at a distance, but her figure was of an extraordinary grace and it was soon apparent that she was incapable of an awkward movement. 'Hullo Tom,' she said, and turned and walked beside us. While they talked together I listened, but neither before nor since have I met anyone about whom, on first acquaintance, I could make out less. I gathered that she knew almost nobody, did not read the newspapers but was familiar with the names of trees and flowers and with a number of the English classics. I could not even make a guess at her background: she had none of the distinguishing marks of class. Who was she, this girl, so serious, so dignified, who seemed to be solitary as the scholar-gypsy and to belong nowhere, except perhaps beside this reach of the Thames? Presently we came to a high stone wall pierced by a door through which she admitted us, and led us to a summer house beside the river. Here we sat, talking until far into the night, the murmur of the lazily-flowing water in our ears. It was characteristic of Tom that he should have had the generosity to present me to this rare being and yet, as though to assert some proprietory right, to have talked much himself, encouraged her to talk a little, and relegated me to the part of silent listener. As the hours passed, I felt myself more and more drawn to Tom's Eustacia, whoever she might be, and more and more beset by a loneliness due to my virtual exclusion from their enchanting companionship. The time came for us to leave. In the darkness I was aware that he was holding her in a long farewell embrace. 'Come on, Johnny, we must be off,' he said, and walked briskly towards the gate. An instant later I felt myself in a bear-hug of extraordinary power and, incredulously, I heard the words, whispered very quietly into my ear, 'Come tomorrow night, if you want to, by yourself.'

On the walk back to Iffley I kept secret the whispered words that had transformed my mood from loneliness to exaltation. I have never been a gambler, a man who invites the undeserved bounty of fortune, but I have always understood the delight in such unmerited bounty. Before we had boarded the returning 'bus I had learned about all that I ever learned of Eustacia's circumstances: she was the daughter, according to Tom's account, of a landowner at whose house I was later a frequent visitor, and a village girl, and she had been adopted by the generally absent owners of the house near Iffley. But if this was all that I ever knew about her circumstances, it was not all that I knew about her herself. For I returned the next night and many other nights, and we walked the countryside or lay in the summerhouse while the murmuring waters of the Thames flowed by. She was the first girl to be devoted to me, and this was an exhilarating revelation of things before suspected, hoped for but unknown. Inexperienced as I was, I had little difficulty in refraining from taking the fullest advantage of the devotion of this wild, guileless being, in whom I never discovered any trace of malice, avarice, jealousy or ambition. Nor must I take any credit for what I did not do, for even at this time of my life women were too fascinating to approach too intimately, as they were too alluring to keep away from. Where did this idyll lead? These pages are autobiography, not romance, and so it must be admitted at once that it led nowhere. Life seemed to me a vast expanse, crowded with possibilities of adventurous happiness, and it beckoned me away from this quiet companionship which, if I had had the wit to recognise it, could itself have yielded extraordinary happiness. But I had not, and my visits became less frequent and then ceased. A year or so later Tom mentioned that she had disappeared from Iffley, and I never heard of her again.

It was about the time when my visits to Iffley were dwindling that I met another girl who was to become one of my closest friends. I shall not forget the occasion of our meeting. It was at a lunch party at John Strachey's. I had scarcely entered the crowded room when there occurred a violent explosion, followed by the tinkle of shattered glass. For an instant I had the impression that there was blood upon some of the guests, but what had happened was that John had placed some bottles of claret beside the fire forgetting to remove their corks, and for one of them the internal pressure became too great. The guest of honour was Elizabeth Ponsonby, a stylishly slender girl of about twenty-two, with an oval pale face especially modelled, it seemed to me, to express an aristocratic disdain, crowned by a helmet of honey-coloured hair. Already she was something of a legend, born of parents both of ancient families—her father had been a page to Queen Victoria—who had become Socialists. Elizabeth herself, reputedly born in St James's Palace, was the personification of sophisticated independence. I was pleased to have seen and heard her, but it did not occur to me to regard her as anything except an elegant monument. After lunch I sat down at the end of a sofa in the corner of the room. Elizabeth placed herself beside me and said that she heard much about me from John. For some reason I made, after a time, as though to get up, at which with a brisk gesture she straightened her legs so as to pen me into my corner. At the end of an afternoon that should have been given to Bishop Burnet's *History of his Own Times* or Rousseau's *Du Contrat Social* I had entered into one of my most intimate friendships. The recollection of this friendship impels me to reaffirm the truth, more frequently affirmed than believed, that it is possible for much intimate friendship to flourish between a woman and a man which is entirely free not only from sensual acts but from sensual tensions of any kind. Elizabeth Ponsonby was a girl of whose attractions many different kinds of men were aware, often violently aware; she was ardent, reckless and without permanent attachment. As for me, I was particularly susceptible to the allure of women, yet even when I followed her a couple of years later into a society in which human relations were kaleidescopic, in which late hours and heavy drinking were the rule, our relationship would have done us no discredit had we been priest and nun.

About the same time I had another encounter which brought me an interesting acquaintance, and gave me intermittent insights into yet another, although contiguous, society. I was dining alone one night at the Golden Cross, a comforting fire at my back, an open book beside me on the table, far from the stresses and delights of university life. I was just aware of the only other diner, a woman in black, seated with her back towards me. Hearing the sound of something fall heavily, I looked round to find that my solitary neighbour had collapsed face downwards over her table. I went over to her and enquired whether I could be of help. After a few moments she was sufficiently recovered to sit upright, and I found myself looking at an arresting and remotely familiar face, with broad cheekbones, dark, bold, humorous eyes set very wide apart, a blunt, impertinent nose, an almost teak-hued complexion. Just then her eyes were red-rimmed with crying. 'I'm sorry I disturbed you, but my husband has been killed, murdered I mean and. . . .' She was so evidently ill and distressed that I suggested that she ought to go straight to bed and, since she seemed incapable of returning to wherever she might have come from, that she should stay in one of the rooms upstairs. 'But I've no money. I only just managed to pay for my dinner,' she objected. Asking the manager of the hotel to look after her I walked back to College, wondering who this strange being talking of murder might be, and why it was that her face should stir an echo in my memory. Next morning my curiosity was at once satisfied and further excited. There was a tap on my door and in she walked, transformed by a good night's sleep. Her face showed no trace of tears; her movements were marked by energy and decision. 'I'm sorry,' she said, 'for the bother I gave you last night. You were awfully kind. I'm afraid I can't stop thinking of the way my husband was killed, and I'm in Oxford to collect some of the things he left at his college.'

'You haven't told me your name,' I said.

'I'm Betty May,' she explained, and I understood how it was that I knew the face of this legendary bohemian: it was from having seen her bust by Epstein. 'Now I'll tell you,' she continued, 'how Aleister Crowley killed my husband.' My memory of her narrative has faded, and the—greatly exaggerated, to say the least—story must have been told often enough, but I listened entranced to her account of her marriage to Raoul Loveday, a man some years her junior, of their invitation by the sinister hierophant Aleister Crowley to his house at Cefalu, and in effect of his sacrificial killing of her husband. As I sat listening I looked at the face of this woman who personified in the eyes of my generation the bohemian, whose own morality was thus defined by the man whom she accused of her husband's murder: 'Do what thou wilt shall be the whole of the Law.'

I did not see Betty May again until I had left Oxford, and not often then. I could more readily suspect her transgressing any moral law than of harbouring an evil thought. The last time I saw her I was coming out of a theatre, and there she was in the crowd, so drunk that she could barely stand up, and supported by a companion on either side. As soon as she saw me she dragged these companions towards me repeating, 'I must speak to John—it's important.' She whispered a name in my ear, adding 'You *must* back him tomorrow.' Not being a betting man I disregarded her advice, but I remembered the name next day: it was the name of the outsider who had won the Derby.

In the course of my three years at Oxford I made two expeditions abroad. The first to Dublin, during the Long Vacation of 1921, in the company of my father.

Although I did not know it, I was a witness of the climax of Ireland's struggle to free herself from British rule.

We arrived early in the morning and wandered about the almost deserted streets, still strewn with the wreckage of war. Glimpses of sky could be seen through the windows of gutted and roofless buildings, their bullet-pitted walls bearing illiterate scrawled slogans attacking the Forces of the Crown.

Later on the people came out into the streets; the British troops, thanks to the truce, moved unarmed among the crowds and they appeared to provoke no sign of hostility. At certain street corners there congregated slouching young gunmen-out-of-work. On the invitation of Desmond Fitzgerald, one of the Sinn Fein Ministers, we visited the seat of the rebel government at the Mansion House, from which the rebel flag was flying. The big seedy-grandiose building was a vortex of furious activity. A crowd of workmen were preparing a big circular hall for the first meeting of the Dail. There was an eerie coexistence of two systems of government, the one busily taking over, the other 'withering away'. Indeed it was strange that there should still be a Viceroy in Viceregal Lodge, but when he arrived at the Horse Show he was virtually ignored by the crowd whose cheers were reserved for a political prisoner just released.

There was one conspicuous respect in which the Dublin of 1921 contrasted with the capital of the Republic of Eire. Politics were discussed with passion. We attended parties where political controversy raged and speculation often passed the borders of fantasy. These parties were filled with characters out of Dostoievski, but who argued about the destiny not of Russia but of Ireland. Nothing could have been less characteristic of the commonsense, slightly complacent, Irish Republic that watches with disinterest, and as it were from afar, the great struggles that afflict the greater part of mankind.

One day we were driven by Dermod O'Brien, the President of the Royal Hibernian Academy, and his wife, to Glendalough, in the Wicklow Mountains, where there stands a group of seven churches of great antiquity. In the villages through which we passed the police barracks were either blackened ruins or else transformed into forts by sandbags and barbed wire. The road had been trenched and filled in, retrenched and refilled in respectively by the Republican Army and the British Forces. On our way back the car lurched into a shallow Sinn Fein trench, and we were pitched gently out on to a soft, grassy bank—I had never experienced so comfortable an accident, and it increased the friendly feelings which my contacts with the rebels had implanted. The car suffered a broken back axle and we left it lying on its side.

We managed to escape from time to time the pervasive atmosphere of politics. We called on James Stephens, temporarily Director of the National Gallery of Ireland. The author of *The Crock of Gold*, a tiny leprechaun-like creature, whose talk was even bolder in its imaginative sweep than his poetry or his prose, was the most improbable bureaucrat I had ever encountered. We called, too, on George Russell, or AE, who was busy putting fairies into a landscape which in intention at least was as realistic as a Courbet.

On account of the influential part played in it by poets and other writers, I had heard the Irish national movement made light of in England. My own experience in Dublin was of hearing good sense and generous sentiments expressed by the writers, and painters too, as by no-one else. Especially by one who spoke through the mouths of actors, for we heard *John Bull's Other Island* played at the Abbey Theatre, to the accompaniment, incidentally, of occasional rifle shots in the street outside.

I returned to Oxford despondent after this enjoyable expedition. It seemed to me a matter for despondency that the outstanding political talents of the English and the Irish were proving inadequate to devise a common system of government welcome to both, and that as a consequence a people who, however different from the English, were members nevertheless of the same family, was in the process of breaking away. I know little of politics now and I knew less then, but having experienced at first hand the positive goodwill towards England among the Irish rebels I met, at the very moment when there was cause for greater bitterness than at any other, I believe that an offer to share our destinies as equal partners, an offer coming manifestly from the heart as well as the head, might even then have not been without effect. The irreconcilable Irishmen I have met have almost all been Irish-Americans.

The following winter, with John Strachey and Edward Sackville-West, I spent some weeks in Vienna, a city still suffering from hunger and the shock of being deprived of the function for which it was built with such magnificence, of serving as the capital of an empire. It was in Vienna that I first heard of one of the writers whom I admire most. The three of us had taken a young French journalist, Yvette Fouque—with whom we became lifelong friends from the moment of our first meeting—to a music-hall where one could dine or have supper in the auditorium while the performance was in progress. We had just seen a team of parrots who had been taught to ride bicycles—I have never seen such looks of concentration as those parrots gave to the steering of their mounts—by a husband and wife who themselves bore a close resemblance to parrots. The spectacle, from some irrational cause, moved us to speak of Henry James. 'I find that I read him with less interest,' Yvette said, 'since I began to read Proust. Henry James' novels now seem to me to be such conscious aesthetic constructions; Proust's are too, of course, but they are so close to life that one doesn't notice the artifice; as one reads one seems simply to be living. . . .' 'But who,' one of us asked, 'is Proust?' Yvette's eyes opened wide, and she set brilliantly to work to repair our ignorance, and as the parrots pedalled on for their encore we watched them with an abstracted gaze, for we were hearing, for the first time, of the progressive analysis of the Guermantes, of M. de Charlus, of Mme. Verdurin and Saint-Loup and of the revolution that this to us unknown writer was likely to bring about in the psychological novel.

On account of Eddie's passion for music John and I spent more time at the Opera than we would had he not been with us. His hypersensibilities, always a source of respectful amusement to his friends, were raised by music to their highest pitch. One night, at the conclusion of a Wagner opera which to me had seemed interminable, I made a movement of relief which caused my chair to creak. Eddie winced as though pierced by a hatpin. 'Really Johnny, it's too bad,' he said in his flat, cold voice, 'that awful noise has spoilt the whole effect: now I've got to listen to it all again tomorrow night.'

We made expeditions along the Danube—not a blue but a khaki river—and on one of these someone offered us, licitly or not I do not know, the Castle of Dürnstein, where King Richard I was imprisoned, for about £40, so depreciated was the currency of Austria.

We dined at Sacher's; we frequented cafés and music-halls, but Eddie's devotion to classical music drew us more often into the Opera House and the concert hall. His influence in this direction was reinforced on the evening of our arrival. As we entered the big dining-room of the Erzherzog Karl Hotel there were only two diners, who were sitting together and speaking in English with the freedom of people unlikely to be overheard. As we passed by their table on our way to our own I heard one of them mention my name—in some quite trivial context—and I did not resist the temptation to materialize before them on the instant. One of them was spare and sardonic; the other rotund and genial. Both looked as astonished as I hoped, and introduced themselves: Edward Dent, shortly to become Professor of Music at Cambridge, and Arthur Bliss the composer. At their invitation we attended a performance of an orchestral work by Bliss. The occasion was awaited with interest, for the Viennese were apt to complain that they never heard the work of English composers. Such complaints were less frequently heard after the performance in question, for the harsh and continuous roll of drums at its climax was accompanied by a crescendo of hoots and boos by the audience, which were intended to assert the classical purity of its taste.

While we were in Vienna the death occurred of the former Emperor, and the streets were impressively draped with long black hangings, some of them stretching from upper windows almost to the ground. We all three of us were oppressed by the sense that this magnificent city was slowly dying, that before long its baroque splendours would be deserted. We were, happily, mistaken: there was certainly much misery; there were painful readjustments to be made, but the city was not dying. A Second World War was needed to demonstrate the full resilience of human society, especially urban society. Berlin, Coventry, Warsaw, the Ruhr, these suffered disasters incomparably more severe, yet they not only survived but after a few years they flourished.

For all the experience I gained and the pleasure I derived from my visits to Dublin, to Vienna, and my occasional sorties to Iffley and elsewhere, Oxford itself and my friends there remained the focus of my most ardent interests. The sense of surprise at the sheer and almost continuous enjoyment I derived from a world which the morose and lonely schoolboy of only a couple of years ago could scarcely have imagined was continuously renewed.

I read avidly—Shakespeare, the Elizabethan and Restoration dramatists, James, Hardy, Thackeray, Joyce, Wyndham Lewis, Yeats—indeed a large part of my reading would have been more appropriate to the School of English than to that of History. I also read, of course, a good deal of history, but in too unsystematic a fashion to enhance my prospects for my Final Schools; indeed with an insolent lethargy that cost me dearly I neglected even to finish reading one of my 'set books', namely Bishop Burnet's *History of his Own Times*. My patent dissipation of my energies in journalism, social life, indiscriminate reading and caricature (likenesses of several of my friends, David Ceecil and Edward Sackville-West among them, were reproduced in *The Isis* and elsewhere) caused my tutor to warn me that the first-class honours which had once been considered within my reach I was now unlikely to obtain.

Patient readers who have arrived at this point in my narrative may perhaps be surprised that one whose life has been lived among the visual arts, who might be presumed to be something of a visual man, should have touched so lightly hitherto upon painting and on sculpture not at all. Indeed I was surprised myself that, considering my heredity, the relative facility with which I could draw, the friendships I had already formed with artists, and above all my fascinated response to the external world, my interest in the visual arts should not have been more lively. I was mortified on more than one occasion, after a visit to the Ashmolean Museum to look at paintings and drawings, by the recollection that it had been made not on my initiative but on that of some friend less innately visual than I and whose opportunities of cultivating his understanding of the arts were far inferior. This want of interest disturbed me the more because I could not discern its cause. There were even times when I felt a hypocrite, for I allowed myself to be drawn into several art activities: I helped to organize an exhibition at the Oxford Art Club of drawings by Max Beerbohm; I played some part in the activities of the Uffizi—a club so exclusive that it withered away because eventually nobody was considered worthy of election. It was at the Uffizi that I heard Anthony Eden deliver his lecture on Cézanne. This lecture caused something of a sensation, for it was regarded as audaciously incongruous, rather as a lecture by a general on Jackson Pollock would be today. Anthony Eden, although only in his middle twenties, was already an august and highly traditional figure, and

Cézanne, outside a narrow circle, was still a controversial painter. Anthony Eden was not only august, he was positively regal: he had a fine presence; he was as serious and gifted as he was handsome. Had the Oxford of those days had occasion to elect a president, he would surely have been the overwhelming choice. I never knew him well, but there was a link between us: Whistler had quarrelled with my father, on account of his refusal to break with Eden's father, Sir William, when Whistler quarrelled with him.

My want of enthusiasm for the visual arts troubled me the more because I knew that somewhere in the recesses of my mind enthusiasm did smoulder but, for some mysterious reason, was unable to secure, so to say, the oxygen needful to enable it to burst into flame. I used to recall exceptional moments of exhilaration in the presence of works of art. At home at Oakridge a few years before, in the same cellar, among the same discarded books where I discovered New-man's *Apologia*, I came upon a small booklet, bound in a sort of rice paper. As I turned its pages of reproductions of paintings by a hand unknown to me, my heart beat faster. On the title-page I read an unfamiliar name: El Greco. But how was it that I experienced so few such moments?

During the next few years the cause became gradually apparent to me, and it was chiefly on account of it that I decided for a time to make my home in America. It was, quite simply, the character and experience of my father. He was a man of preternatural dynamism who had been intimate with many of the masters active in his time, and a multitude of lesser artists; he had seen so high a proportion of their significant works in so many countries; he had formed an opinion on each and every one of them, and he constantly voiced these opinions. So much experience, such passionate and continuous didacticism, combined to make it difficult for me to enjoy the visual arts, for it left me with so little scope for personal exploration. I was at once brought up short in head-on collision with some fully formed opinion about it which my father ardently desired to impart, even to impose. I felt myself in a maze that Kafka might have described from which there was no exit to any personal experience and so to any personal conclusion. The finding of the little book of reproductions of paintings by El Greco was a memorable occasion because I had never seen them, never heard of them, never heard my father pronounce the name of their creator.

This situation was complicated by the fact that I was deeply devoted to my father and that I believed his judgments to be generous and wise. Had I not had an impulse, strong yet frustrated, to form conclusions of my own, it would have been of no consequence. But there had been a time, when as a boy I even wanted to be a painter myself, and he had successfully discouraged me. Towards the end of my time at Oxford I became more than ever aware of an uneasy stirring of my interest in the visual arts, an interest which, however, no sooner stirred than it was smothered. The realities of the situation, so clear later on, were entirely hidden from me then.

The impulse was fostered by contacts with artists outside the circle of my parents' friends. From the summer of my second year I had the privilege of frequenting the Manor, at Garsington, a house about five miles distant from Oxford, the already fabled home of Lady Ottoline Morrell and her husband Philip. Fear has stamped my first visit upon my memory. One hot Sunday afternoon in the summer of 1922 John Strachey, Edward Sackville-West, David Cecil and I had been invited to their house. On arrival we hesitated at an open french window that gave upon a lawn, at the far side of which a tea-party was in progress. We hesitated because the lawn was not so wide that we could not discern among the tea-drinkers the figures of Lytton Strachey, Aldous Huxley and Duncan Grant, as well as that, so awe-inspiring at a first encounter, of our hostess, and this modest patch of grass seemed to us an alarmingly wide space to cross exposed to the gaze of so many august eyes. So it is that I still retain so clearly a picture of the group: Lytton Strachey limply inert in a low chair, head drooped forward and red beard pressed against chest, finger-tips touching the grass; Aldous Huxley talking, with his face raised upwards staring at the sun; Duncan Grant, pale-faced, with fine, untidy black hair, light eyes ready to be coaxed out of their melancholy, and Lady Ottoline, wearing a dress of lilac silk more appropriate to some splendid Victorian occasion, and an immense straw hat. Our hesitation lasted only an instant, and presently we were seated in the circle around the tea-table. I found myself beside Duncan Grant, but one had to be alert to catch his scarcely more than whispered words, which towards the close of his sentences were almost soundless. His friendliness did not, however, disguise even from my inexperience his membership of a society

with a means of communication peculiar to itself. After listening to
him and to Lytton Strachey I vaguely apprehended that in this
Oxfordshire village were assembled certain luminaries of a then to
me almost unknown Cambridge world. All Lady Ottoline's guests,
however, remarkable as they mostly were, assumed in her presence
the look, almost, of conventional nonentities. Her great height, her
wasted gothic face, the Victorian ornateness of her clothes, her quiet,
lowing voice, her 'advanced' opinions and her general freedom from
inhibition, made her one of the most spectacular figures of her time.
Speaking of her some years later Arthur Ponsonby said to me that he
saw her come into a café in Rome 'wearing a hollowed-out swan on
her head', and that people 'stood on their chairs the better to see her'.
Of the several characteristics which made Lady Ottoline memorable
the most arresting was the contrast between her fantastic appearance
and the sober and benevolent quality of her mind and character. In her
house (which I thereafter visited often) I heard in the course of discussions many extravagant and many unkind words spoken, but I
can recall no occasion on which she did not herself speak with wisdom and kindness. Showing me round the house on my first visit
she took down a book from a shelf, opened it at its title-page and
pointed with a long, bony finger at the author's name: T. S. Eliot.
I told her that it was a name unknown to me. 'I'm not surprised,'
she answered, 'but it's a name that will soon be known to everyone—
the name of a great poet.' I found that the pictures I saw at Garsington—by Augustus John, Gertler, Gilbert Spencer, Henry Lamb and
others of their generations—and the painters I met there, perhaps
because it was a house into which I had found my own way, made a
livelier impact upon me than those I encountered in houses where I
accompanied my parents. At all events they rekindled my fitful
interest in the visual arts. Whether the diffidence which afflicted my
three friends and me at the moment of our entry persisted with them
I cannot remember, but with me it intermittently recurred, so that
I sought refuge with the only entirely reassuring person present, a
big, bluff, commonsense man, with a remarkably acute intelligence,
who seemed something of an 'odd man out'. As we drove back to
Oxford I remarked that although I had immensely enjoyed Garsington I had found it something of a nervous strain, at which my
three friends laughed and told me that I had an original way of
showing it, by foregathering with the rudest and most arrogant

person present, J. B. S. Haldane. As we drove through Cowley we
encountered a procession led by the Cowley Fathers. John, who was
not particularly hostile to the Catholic Church, was fiercely opposed
to any Catholic pretensions on the part of the Church of England,
which he regarded as a department of state created by Acts of Parliament. Inflamed by the sight of processional crosses, banners bearing
the name of Mary and such-like manifestations of Anglo-Catho-
licism, he ordered our driver to slow down while he stood up in the
car and kept shouting 'no popery! no popery!' to the evident astonishment of the Cowley Fathers, whose irreproachable conduct as a rule
disarmed the prejudice of opponents. (Was it not a Jesuit who said:
'We have made the rules, but the Cowley Fathers keep them'?) So
ended a memorable day.

*

Suddenly—it seemed but a few months ago that I had been a freshman—the Trinity Term of 1923 had come and almost gone before
it was borne in upon me that in a few weeks I would have left Oxford.
I looked eagerly forward to the beginning of what seemed to me then
the endless journey of adult life, little foreseeing how fleeting this
was also, how little time it allowed for the fulfilment of one's aims, or
what a makeshift affair it was to be. Just as one may begin to suffer
from homesickness before leaving home, so I began to feel during
the last weeks of term the pains of my impending departure. There
crowded in upon me miscellaneous memories of things about to be
carried far away on the stream of time. The unmistakable fusty smell
of undergraduate rooms; the smoky smell of the mist that gathered
in the streets on autumn afternoons. Lying on my back in a canoe as
it floated slowly on the current through the narrow tunnel (closed
sometime in the 'thirties, I believe, after sundry drownings)
between St. Ebbes' and Christ Church Meadow, and listening in the
darkness to the thumping sound that I eventually recognized as the
beating of my own heart. A walk with David Cecil on which a long
silence was broken by his exclaiming with passionate vehemence,
'I can so understand killing people for religion's sake, can't you?'
Helping a very drunk friend into Magdalen one night who, catching
sight of the immensely dignified figures of the President, Sir Herbert
Warren, and Lady Warren, pointed at them screaming, 'Why there's
the Pre. with a whore!' My first visit to J. C. Masterman (afterwards

Provost of Worcester and Vice-Chancellor, but then a Student of
Christ Church and temporarily my tutor) when he asked me for the
principal causes of the French Revolution. I gave the elementary
textbook answers. Justifiably annoyed by my glibness he answered,
'Isn't it odd that you should be able to account so easily for what
continues to elude the greatest authorities?' Near collision at a street
corner with two figures with scarves flying in the wind, one fair,
shortish, with fanatical eyes set wide; the other tall, dark, with an
expression of pride oddly blended with courtliness: Evelyn Waugh
and Harold Acton. Looking at Uccello's 'Forest Fire at Night' with
David Balniel. Visits to obscure cinemas where good films were
showing with Anthony Asquith as guide. The sight of the Oxford
Brewery burning, also at night, and its high tower falling in a roar of
flame. A party disembarking from punts into a moonlit college
garden, one man after another climbing over a wrought-iron gate
except the last, who tried the lock, opened it and walked nonchalantly
through. This last man was Gladwyn Jebb. The recurrent fits of
agitation, near madness almost, of Gerhardi, due to suspicion that
his scout day by day was stealing his marmalade spoonful by spoonful.

*

Academically I wasted much time at Oxford, and for more than a
year before I went down was manifestly destined to disappoint the
hopes of my tutor that I would take first class honours. But there's a
sense in which, looking back, it seems to me that I never used time to
greater purpose. Most of my friends, coming from the major public
schools, took somewhat for granted the dreaming spires and the
daisied lawns, the free life, offering the widest choice of friends and
of books; they were certain of easy access to one of the ancient
universities and they were in every way prepared for the experience
which Oxford fostered: for most of them it was no more than the
precisely anticipated sequel to their lives at school. A few, particularly Etonians, even enjoyed it less. (I remember one of them,
Cyril Connolly, a member of a generation immediately following
my own, describing his disappointment with Oxford.)

But for me most of what, at school, I had known or imagined
(apart from my father's happy recollections of a Trinity Term a
quarter of a century before) was drawn from what I had read, and of

the experience of it I was all but deprived by my own ineptitude and poor teaching at school. Therefore I experienced Oxford with extraordinary zest, sustained until the last instant of my last term; zest for the beauty of the place, the privilege of multifarious friendships and of continuous converse with some of the finest minds of my generation. I learnt what it was like to be constantly happy, though not what a rare experience this was. I came to Oxford diffident, inclined to moroseness, somewhat lost and aimless. I left it zestful, genial, with some notion, so to speak, of the lie of the land, with intellectual perceptions deepened and sharpened by interchange with minds superior to my own, and the determination to be a writer. Oxford gave me much of what I needed when my need was greatest. As an inhabitant of an unkind world I would like to record that I cannot recall, during those three years, being the victim of a single unkind act.

CHAPTER FOUR

LONDON: EARLY FAILURE

WHEN I found I had taken only third-class honours I was not surprised: indeed I was fortunate not to have done worse, for I have already mentioned my inexcusable failure to read one of my set books to the end. I did well, I was told, in some of my papers, and the examiners therefore perhaps dealt leniently with one outright failure, on which, had they been so minded, they could have failed me altogether. Never in recent years, I suppose, had undergraduates attached so little importance to obtaining degrees as those of the immediate post-war generations. A number of contemporaries went down without taking degrees, among them, I recollect, Evelyn Waugh, John Betjeman and Alan Pryce-Jones, while Richard Hughes took fourth-class honours in— of all subjects—English Literature. The mediocrity of my own degree is not to be excused by the prevailing indifference to academic attainment: on the contrary, having already experienced failure I ought to have taken the warning to heart. Instead I had allowed this indifference and my sheer fascination with the life of Oxford and with its incomparable beauty—I used to go at weekends on sightseeing tours to other colleges—to lull me into forgetfulness.

There I was, then, in the outside world, without academic distinction, without specialist aptitudes or training, without money, and, what was more disadvantageous still, without definite aims. Certainly the intention to be a writer was steadily taking shape as a principal objective, but I entertained some justifiable doubts whether my writing would enable me to maintain myself on even the most modest scale, and was determined to find other work such as would leave some time and energy to spare for my chosen vocation. The story of the four years after I went down from Oxford is the story of successive failures to find such work. I was a leader-writer on *The Daily Express*, where I found that I was unable to write fast and indeed that I could scarcely write at all about subjects which did not arouse my interest, and had I not been taken ill and gone abroad to recover, I cannot believe that so inept an apprentice would have been tolerated for long. I worked with a literary agent, where I felt my faculties deteriorate from the effects of the vast mass of rubbish that it was my duty to read. I failed an interview for a junior post in the Victoria and Albert Museum.

My parents allowed me the use of the top floor of their house in Airlie Gardens, which consisted of four small servants' bedrooms, and these I transformed into a pleasant flat. The windows on the south side looked out onto the big garden which the residents of Airlie Gardens shared, and far beyond over Kensington, Chelsea and Battersea right to the Surrey hills. This splendid prospect would raise my spirits and restore my sense of proportion in the face of failure. There were dark moments. I remember walking along Notting Hill High Street with Evelyn Waugh (who had not yet published anything and who had some miserable position in a school in the neighbourhood), discussing the bleakness of our prospects. I mentioned that I had only just rejected, after the most serious consideration, the offer of a junior mastership in a fashionable school in California at a salary of only £250 a year, out of which I would have had to pay for the upkeep of a horse. 'Give me the address, and I'll put in for it, if you've really decided to turn it down,' he said. I was about to agree, when a recollection of a recent event decided me to refuse. I told him that a few nights ago his brother Alec had shown me the typescript of a highly entertaining story that he had written and that Alec had expressed confidence in his abilities as a writer. 'So I'm not going to give you that address.' Perhaps my solicitude was misplaced; perhaps the earlier opportunity of visiting Forest Lawns that this mastership would have offered might have hastened the appearance of *The Loved One*.

One afternoon I opened my door in response to a tap and admitted a tall, thin young man, with fine-spun, straight gold hair, who told me that he was a poet, and he handed me a letter of recommendation from Richard Hughes. As though to substantiate his claim to be a poet, he presented me with a slim volume entitled *Masques and Poems*. The poet's name was Peter Quennell, and he was an undergraduate at Balliol. On my inviting him to inscribe his gift, he not only did so but embellished a preliminary page with a pen drawing of the wide and complex view from my window. We spent the rest of the afternoon talking as though we were already the friends that we never quite became. Peter Quennell was the only poet I have known who looked poetic; he was moreover responsive and sophisticated. From time to time he wrote, in a beautiful hand, lively and affectionate letters from Balliol, from which it became apparent that his academic career, at least, was not prospering. They are undated, but were written, I would suppose, in 1924.

'I am ending up,' runs one of them in part, 'with all kinds of embroilments—poor Balliol is getting so annoyed with me—and has said how much it would like to take my scholarship away and send me down. So I have had to not go to bed—and read Plato—very hard.

'I am almost—no, I am quite—out of love with . . . for the time. It's infinitely so much better and happier—to be not a poodle and a private detective and a provider of meals—all in one . . . But . . . is vaguely, I think, rather relieved not to have me any longer—being absurd and unhappy always just behind her.

'Oxford has been so amusing and very delightful—but an immensely impossible place to write poetry in . . . If God doesn't fuss about it and stop me, I shall go to Paris and discover something about French paintings.

'O my dear John—what a preposterous and most foolish and egotistical letter.'

Gradually he ceased being a poet, an impractical and romantic-looking person, and he became a social historian, a leading authority on Byron, a writer with a rare sense of style and acute perception, and a practical and highly successful man.

Although I did indeed experience many dark moments, my life during these four years was not an unhappy one. Occasional articles —I contributed to *The Times Literary Supplement*, *The Architects' Journal*, *The Sunday Times*, *The Spectator*, *Artwork* and *Apollo*—and tutorials brought in enough to enable me to survive and at moments even to survive in comfort. Credit was easy to obtain. When, for instance, I offered to pay my expensive tailor, he enquired whether I was dissatisfied. Depression at my failures in finding work of a more or less permanent kind was more than offset by the sense that I was beginning to learn how to write and by the gradual clarification of my aims as a writer and, as always, by the society of my friends.

There was during the nineteen twenties one circumstance in particular that mitigated my estrangement from the visual arts. This was the opportunity that my father's Principalship of the Royal College of Art afforded me of coming to know artists of my own generation. When I called there with my father after his appointment but before he assumed his duties, the place had the look—and even the smell—not of an art school but of an inferior elementary school: the members of the staff whom I happened to see resembled clerks; the retiring Principal wore a morning coat, and the students seemed to have sunk into apathy. Certain members of the staff occupied the spacious studios intended for the students, who were exiled to the smaller rooms intended for the staff. My father's dynamism, which could be oppressive at times in a confined place such as a home, had a most fruitful theatre of action in the College. In no time at all artists were appointed in place of pedagogues to teachings posts (then a startling innovation resented by the art teachers' organization), and a generation rich in talent was gathering in the classrooms: Henry Moore, John Piper, Ceri Richards, Edward Burra, Barnett Freedman, Edward le Bas, Charles Mahoney, Albert Houthuesen, Barbara Hepworth, Edward Bawden and Eric Ravilious, to name but a few of the most talented members of it. The sheer volume of unfolding talent, the interplay between individual talents, the sense of new beginnings, the benevolent, electric presence of my father, and —as at Oxford—the sense of awakening from the nightmare of the war, combined to make the Royal College of Art an exhilarating place. The virtual coincidence of the university and college terms set a limit to my visits while I was an undergraduate, but once I settled in London my relations with a number of the students became close and friendly. Henry Moore, however, I came to know, I fancy, soon after he came to London in 1921. We first met at one of the Sunday evening gatherings when my parents kept open house. He talked in his slow, pleasant Yorkshire voice about the sculpture of ancient Mexico with such penetration that after he had left I asked who he was. 'He is the most gifted sculptor at the college,' said my father. 'He is going to be a *great* sculptor,' my younger sister added. Henry Moore, who was then twenty-four, could more than hold his own at students' parties, for instance, in a manner that might surprise those who came to know him later on—he had been a bayonet instructor not long before—but few people I have known so long ago have changed so little. He showed then the same unassertive assurance, tempered by a readiness to admit to error, the same profound good sense, kindliness and sense of justice, and above all the same nearly imperturbable serenity as he does today. His appearance, too, has remained much the same: the face has been furrowed, but the short, strong figure, animated by an energy as strictly disciplined as it is abundant, has scarcely broadened or relaxed.

If Moore was the student most widely admired as an artist, the dominant personality was Barnett Freedman. The unimpressiveness of his appearance was such as to enhance by sheer contrast the impressiveness of his presence. He was short and pot-bellied; his complexion was greyed by the heart-disease from which he suffered and eventually died. The powerful, richly cockney voice, uttering, in season but preferably out, opinions sometimes whimsically perverse, sometimes original but mostly challenging, issuing from so unlikely a source, had a strongly mesmeric effect on those who heard him. Soon after his arrival his nonconformist wisdom, his satire, his irony, his candour and his racy stories about the East End—where his father pushed a fruit-barrow—had become celebrated throughout the College. I had not known him long when he invited me to dinner and to his room to see his work. He took me to Bertorelli's, a restaurant in Charlotte Street long known to students of the Slade and lately come into favour with certain students of the College. We had a splendid dinner, but on visiting his tiny studio-bedroom in Euston Road I realized with affectionate dismay that he had probably spent everything he had, possibly even more, on my entertainment. Barbara Hepworth was ambitious, cool and hard-working, one eye ever attentive to what Moore was doing. Albert Houthuesen was an Anglo-Dutchman who lived and worked in the presence of the great Dutch masters like a religious man in the presence of God. Several of his contemporaries are now illustrious, many more are successful, but Albert Houthuesen alone is still unplaced, for the mass of work, accumulated with almost a lifetime's untiring industry, was scarcely seen save by a few intimates until his first exhibition in 1961. Although it is out of harmony with prevailing taste, its combination of intensity of emotion and painterly skill is likely to enable it to survive. But I must not give way to the temptation of writing at length about this remarkable generation of students: it merits extended treatment, but by someone more closely involved with it than I. My debt to the painters and sculptors whom I came to know at the College is very great. They gave me an insight into the ideas that

THE AUTHOR *aet.* 19, BY WILLIAM ROTHENSTEIN

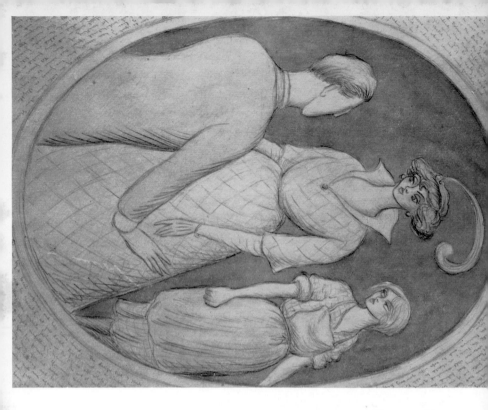

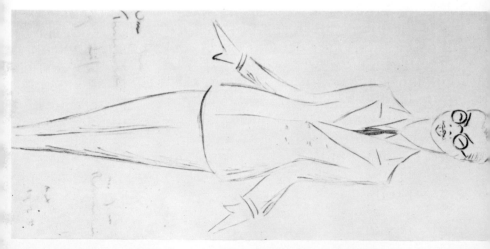

(left)
ZULEIKA DOBSON
BY MAX BEERBOHM

(right)
ON THE THRESHOLD
OF LIFE
BY MAX BEERBOHM

were of the most urgent concern to the artists of my own generation, and they gave me the germ of the idea—which determined the subject of most of my writing later on—that I would be happier in bearing witness to the activities of my own times than in researching into things past. In some degree, however, my friends and acquaintances at the College suffered in my eyes from the fact that, like almost all other artists, they formed part of my father's prior experience. I had only to name one of them for my father to give his opinion of him, thus hindering me from forming my own, by transforming the subject into something placed, classified and, in a sense, done with.

In any case, for all my curiosity and affection, the College was but one of several interests. It meant even more to me in retrospect than it did at the time when it was often eclipsed by the multiple excitements of setting out upon my life's journey as an independent person.

These excitements were heightened by a growing awareness that in London life was as real and as earnest as Browning pronounced it and that in comparison the life of Oxford was enchanted make-believe, in which it seemed no more necessary to pay for one's errors than one's debts. Tragedy—there were of course tragedies at Oxford—seemed the result of some chance inadvertence on the part of providence rather than of the action of the slow-grinding mills of God. It could not escape my notice, for instance, that amorous relations between men, which at Oxford had seemed in general harmless and sometimes idyllic, in the world outside often had sinister accompaniments. One incident touched me more nearly than considerations outside my personal experience. My attention was caught late one afternoon by a familiar figure walking in front of me in crowded Piccadilly. When I called her name she did not seem to hear. Pleased by this chance encounter I quickened my pace and caught up with her. 'What's wrong?' I asked, when she turned towards me a face harrowed with distress. 'It was all so lovely at Oxford, but things are different now, and you're never to try to see me,' she said, and walked quickly away. I recalled the summer afternoons I had spent on the river in the company of this perfect little being, with eyes like morning glories, a skin in which you could not have discovered a single flaw even with a microscope's help, tight golden curls, white dress always freshly laundered; her happy, mindless face upturned to chatter while I lazily manoeuvred the punt.

I had often noticed her walking about the streets of Oxford, head held high, looking neither to left nor to right, ever followed by the attentive glances of men, but knowing that she was a 'town girl' I did not expect ever to meet her. One day when I was kept in my room by a chill, she was brought to see me by some friend. 'I hear you think I'm like Dresden china,' she said, pleased by the trite observation I had doubtless made, and from that moment and without premeditation or explanation she attached herself to me. Now, two years or so later, she was, almost inconceivably, earning her living, and maybe someone else's, by walking the streets.

This encounter was a shock, but it was not a shock that sobered.

I was leading a life so confused that even now, looking back after the passage of nearly forty years, I can discern in it no pattern, no development, only an avid blundering after experience and pleasure.

I explained in an earlier chapter how it came about that my innate love of the visual arts (and it was in some degree the case with literature as well) was diverted by my father's wide knowledge and positive opinions, resulting in the deadening impression that every smallest foot-path was charted, that I had little chance of a personal discovery or experience. But once established in London I began to form friendships with writers as well as painters. Among younger writers those whom I first came to know were Edith, Osbert and Sacheverell Sitwell, who were not only immensely entertaining but shared, although in a far more militant form, my own recoil from paternal influence. Their father, Sir George Sitwell, figured in their conversation as the possessor of fewer redeeming qualities than he is allowed in Osbert's memoirs. I remember Osbert relating an incident, not mentioned, I think, in his memoirs, which was evidently a landmark in their relationship. He was arranging flowers when his father entered the room and watched him with an increasingly sardonic expression. 'I've made plans, Osbert,' he eventually said, 'for you to develop the *other* side of your character: you're going to Sandhurst.'

A few years earlier, during the war, I had been so moved by a poem, signed 'Miles' in *The Nation* that I had written to its anonymous author, from whom I shortly received a friendly letter written from the Western Front. The letter was signed 'Osbert Sitwell', and when I encountered the author, with his brother and sister, in 1923 or thereabouts he at once recalled my letter. I was greatly touched by this, and the Sitwells on their part treated me, without prelimin-

aries, as a friend. This was an indication of one of the engaging
traits of the three Sitwells: they behaved as though all the people
they knew were either their friends or their enemies—there was no
grey intermediate class, none worth a thought, at all events—and the
people whom they did not know were likewise either potential
enemies or potential friends. If one were a friend, one became part
of a vast conspiracy of light against darkness personified by school-
masters, militarists, telephone operators who gave wrong numbers,
Royal Academicians, people we used at Oxford to call 'hearties', but
above all people hostile to the Sitwells. Their attitude in this warfare
was not one of aggression but of what I believe strategists term
'dynamic defence'. One evening Lady Colefax telephoned to invite
them to some function but for some reason or other they considered
the invitation discourteous. 'No, I'm afraid we *can't*, Sybil, but won't
you dine with us—*last* Thursday at eight?' I heard Osbert say. But
like others with a satirical turn of mind and the power to discomfort
their enemies with the barbed retort, the Sitwells were extraordinarily sensitive to any criticism, any joke even, directed against
themselves. A song about them—could it have been *Three Chelsea
Buns* in a revue by Noel Coward? Something of the sort at all
events—caused them distress painful to witness; there was even talk
of a challenge to a duel.

Their principal theatre of action was 2 Carlyle Square, the house
in Chelsea where Osbert and Sacheverell lived; Edith was frequently
there, although she had a flat in Moscow Road, Bayswater. This
house, full though it was of the paintings and drawings of advanced
contemporaries, Modigliani, Picasso, Gaudier-Brzeska, Sickert and
a score of others, also contained family portraits and a mass of other
inherited possessions of every kind. This extraordinary profusion
gave the effect of a Victorian rather than a contemporary interior.
It was a house where the unexpected happened so often as to become
the expected. At an evening gathering there entered a pale man with
a nimbus of fair hair, and catching sight of me he came briskly up
and said, 'Just before I left New York I consulted a fortune-teller,
who described somebody who, later on, was to have a decisive effect
on my life: the person whom he described could be nobody but you,
so I thought we'd better meet.' This man was the celebrated con-
ductor, Leopold Stokowski, whom I have never seen on any other
occasion.

They were an impressive trio. Edith had a face like an Elizabethan portrait, hieratic and waxen, but lit often by the distant smile to be seen on the faces of archaic sculptures. In those days the editor of *Wheels* and the author of *Façade* was the personification of sophisticated anarchy, yet she said to me with the utmost earnestness, 'You know, I don't like to hear people question the divine inspiration of the Bible.' Osbert, blondly Hanoverian, solidly built and very much the family's head, possessed the sharpest and widest-ranging mind. Sacheverell was lanky and avid of things to read and to look at: even in those early days he told me that there were few serious books in French, German and Italian as well as English about painting and architecture that he had not read. This he told me not boastfully, but mournfully, as another might say, 'I don't know what to do: I've read every readable book in the ship's library.' All three were tall, and all spoke in drawling voices, choosing their words deliberately as though they had something amusing or instructive to impart. They usually had. They all talked well, but unlike some other good talkers they were always eager to hear what their friends had been doing, and hearing, and always ready to enter fully into any situation, tragic or comic, in which their friends were involved. I have never known members of the same generation of a family so closely united.

Most of the brief notes we exchanged concerned arrangements for meeting, but such notes, written by them, sometimes contained something more. Osbert, writing to change the date of a lunch, added:

'I went to the London Group Dinner last night. Very good speeches from Sickert and Virginia Woolf.

'Sickert said that Clive Bell had stated that Cézanne was the Columbus of a new world of painting—but that all he (Sickert) knew about Columbus was that he had succeeded in making an egg stand upright—which was more than Cézanne had ever done!'

About the same time as I came to know the Sitwells I also came to know two beautiful Canadian girls, Frances and Georgia Doble; with Frances I was half in love; Georgia and I became lifelong friends. We met constantly but, apart from our respective parents' homes, mostly in frivolous places, nightclubs and the like. One day they said to me, 'You know writers and people like that. Couldn't you arrange for us to meet some?' Accordingly I asked the Sitwells whether I might bring the Doble sisters to see them. 'If you must,' Osbert said. The day after their visit, happening to meet Osbert in the street, I thanked him for their kindness to my friends. 'But we *liked* them,' Osbert said, 'Sachie particularly one of them.' So began a protracted courtship that did not always run smoothly. One night in August 1934, staying at Weston Hall, Sachie's house in Northamptonshire, I was woken up successively by Osbert, Willie Walton, and finally Sachie himself, in order to advise upon some difficulty that had loomed up suddenly. It was evidently solved, for Georgia and Sachie were married the following year. It was the Doble sisters who obtained for me through their friend and fellow Canadian, Lord Beaverbrook, the post on *The Daily Express* in which I acquitted myself so poorly.

Looking back over these years I cannot see how I sustained life with the occasional articles I wrote, almost all of them for highly respectable and therefore meagrely paying publications; my occasional teaching was of a similarly unremunerative kind. But sustain life I did: I belonged to the Savile Club, then next door to the St. James's in Piccadilly, and I frequented restaurants and nightclubs. I even travelled abroad. After the illness that probably spared me dismissal from my leader-writing post in Fleet Street, I went in September 1924 to Rapallo, by way of Turin, to stay with Max Beerbohm; about this visit, however, I recall little beyond the leisurely and civilized way of life observed at the Villino Chiaro, which directly overlooked the coast road to Genoa. We had breakfast brought to our rooms and we met on the terrace; at eleven a bottle of the white wine of the district was served. We talked until lunch and again after our siesta. How melancholy that I should remember so exactly the combined taste of the dry white wine and the sweet small macaroons served with it, and almost nothing of Max's flow of conversation, so admirable a combination of wit, satire, reminiscence and the precise assessment of human character and situation. General ideas and the larger movements of history meant little to him—so little that he was able to declare, and with emphasis, that he did not believe that Russia had any significant part to play. Max's interest lay in people he had known, or else in a repertory of historic 'personalities', which included Goethe, George IV, Byron, Disraeli and the Pre-Raphaelites, about whom he could tell one as much as if he had known them himself. Disraeli, Byron and Rossetti he declared to be the most fascinating personalities of the nineteenth century. He would open an old *Who's Who* and allow the sight of the names of those whom he knew to act as a stimulant to his memories. His old hatred of Wells flared out: 'H.G.'s behaviour', he said, 'is, I suspect, not so much a consequence of his philosophy of Free Love as of sheer local over-development.' In addition I recall two of his general observations: that no idea was worth dying for, and that love—in the sense of love between man and woman—could offer the most intense happiness that it was given to human beings to experience. The only observations on literature that I have not forgotten were those that he made in response to my enquiry about his opinions on Proust and Joyce. While he did not question the talent of either, he said that he was convinced that the power of selection was one of the prerequisites of mastery and that it was one in which both were conspicuously lacking. He was avid of news of London, and the arrival of *The Times* offered occasions for asking me many questions. Although I remember so little of what he said, I can see him as clearly as if I were looking at him still: urbanely rounded features, wide long-lashed eyes, 'boater' worn at a rakish angle; languid figure in white linen suit of old-fashioned cut, walking slowly back and forth across the terrace in the dazzling light. Max appeared to know few people in Rapallo or indeed in Italy except for old friends from England.

It so happened that living within easy walking distance was an old friend of his and ours: Gordon Craig, to whose villa I shortly received an invitation. Green shutters opened somewhere above and Gordon Craig called 'come up,' and presently I was seated in his book-lined study. As often, he spoke of the theatre. 'No purpose whatever,' he said, 'would be served by a National Theatre or any administrative reform: two or three theatres should be run by gifted men—that would be the only hope.' As he talked, with such vision, such sparkle and so little regard for the laws that govern human nature, he put me in mind of something he had written—on what occasion I could not remember—about a scene he had designed: 'Quite an impossible scene; that is to say impossible to realize on a stage. But I wanted to know for once what it felt like to be mounting up impossible ladders and beckoning people to come up after me.'

Next day I received an invitation to call again. 'I've asked you to come,' he said, 'to answer the question you put to me yesterday. You asked me what I would suggest as the first reform necessary to improve the English theatre,' and he spoke with his accustomed eloquence on his favourite theme. With an eye to defraying the cost of my journey, I wrote an account of our conversation, of which I subsequently sent him a draft. I came upon the following letter he wrote me by way of commentary—I hope my 'interview' is buried for ever between the covers of some obscure theatrical journal:

My dear John Rothenstein,

Your uncle Max[1] has sent along the 'interview' which, to me, is full of good points.

Will you object to hear them—allow me. First of all the thing none of us have you have—a way of writing clearly—separating your lines and your words so that human beings are saved from worry. Don't think this is a little thing—it strikes me as first class —I suppose it has not occcured to you but I see how cramped are these lines and words—can I mend matters?—I am wondering.

Then the interview itself—a glimpse is a glimpse and you've again done what almost everyone forgets to do—given a glimpse instead of a tedious long explanation. Again—you've barely mentioned yourself or your opinions. That's well nigh a miracle nowadays when an interview is generally packed full of portraits of the INTERVIEWER and his notion of what the victim should say.

Altogether, Mr John, allow me these *complimenti*: you are like your father and won't like them but tolerate them and surely they'll do you no harm.

The rude part comes now—

Perhaps one isn't a man of genius, you know: and when one realizes that its awfully uncomfortable for one's eye to rest upon the dreadful words—As for 'prophet'—you are unkind—For while the old 'uns, not stopping to study what I was up to, rushed in like angels and dismissed me from the world with the word 'Prophet' the younger fellows have for some years now set themselves right against that feathery verdict—and find that half of my work is quite useful—they are about to find the whole of it useful, so I hear.

By the way about 'Rule Britannia'. Not IN the theatre—I meant out of it and whenever played—Speed up that tune and all England might unconsciously speed up too: their pulse would come to beat a bit faster—their ideas and the execution of them would

[1] Max Beerbohm, an honorary uncle only.

come pat one on top of the other—and this would affect our theatre—and all else. I meant that the bands in the parks—in the streets—take the pretty fine tune at a quicker temp—not three times the pace, exactly—though I expect I said that. But quicker—incisively—with the same attack that we hear used by the military and naval bands here—were the jolly tune in the least sad—at all soothing and tender—anything but rousing, I would not dream that improvement were possible. Its the same with the song 'The British Grenadiers', they always drag that too—just a bit—enough to queer it. Their notion is to give Dignity and weight to all music —to all books (I refer to the bindings) to all theatrical performances—'The Merchant of Venice' is as solemn as 'Hamlet' in the hands of an English theatrical company—I almost believe 'The Geisha' had a like Dignity and as much weight—

And to speed up a play—to lighten a book cover or shorten a sermon (even one upon Rule Britannia!) would have a 90th part of the value which I believe would result from speeding up our half dozen national songs.

All this I ought to have stopped to say to you when you were good enough to come over to the villa—but I was in my riveted half hour over that damned Patience, a game at which I prefer not to be obliged to cheat—and it held me—so you must please excuse my seeming rudeness.

So now—if you care to delete the words '*at any performance*', and add 5 or 6 lines more, I don't think it would be bad.

Give my affectionate remembrances to your father and mother please—and will you say I was going to write and tell them how you brought a lot of good things with you to our house—and the best of all, youth which made us feel younger.

My family send you every good wish

As I do,

Gordon Craig

Oct. 29th—Torino—and now going on to Geneva probably—as it's rather cold here.

I left Rapallo—where I had been since 27th September—on 19th October, with the utmost regret, taking with me a caricature of Lord Lonsdale which Max gave me as a parting present.

By way of Genoa and Milan, experiencing the extraordinary

exhilaration that the Northerner generally feels on his first visit to Italy, and Dresden (where I stayed with my father's old friend, the artist Ludwig von Hofmann), I went to Silesia to stay with Gerhart Hauptmann at Agnetendorf, the house presented to him by the German State. Also there were Frau Hauptmann and Benvenuto, their son, Mrs. Edward Shanks, whom he was later to marry, and the secretary Fraülein Elisabeth Jungmann, who more than thirty years later was to become the wife of Max Beerbohm, whom at this time she had never met. I had never stayed with a national hero before and the experience was an interesting one. Hauptmann had become illustrious as a radical, but during the period of self-doubt and disintegration that followed their defeat in the First World War Germans tended to rally to men who had become landmarks in the days of their country's greatness, and they were many, too, who attempted to use his celebrity for political or personal ends. It was evident even to me who knew little of Germany and no German at all that this illustrious old radical was being courted by Junker neighbours, by sections of the army—General von Seckt called later on when we moved to Berlin—and that, having a broad streak of vanity, Hauptmann enjoyed it, yet mindful of the values he had stood for he was also reserved. No wonder that many of his fellow-countrymen regarded him as a father-figure, for he was in fact an ideal father-figure: strong, handsome, just and benevolent, and a splendid host. The household's way of life during the day was comfortable, but it ended with a dinner such as is served in other houses only on Christmas Day, to which we sat down at eight and did not rise until between one and two in the morning. There was a largeness, an almost regal quality about Hauptmann—he looked and behaved as a great man should look and behave. Benvenuto, Mrs. Shanks and I drove and walked over the pine-covered Riesengebirge, encountering sometimes companies of young men on the march, in military formation, who more often than not would hail us in a friendly fashion. When Benvenuto talked with them they seemed free from any trace of aggressive intention, positively well disposed to the world in general, except for occasional expressions of hostility to the distant French. On one occasion he and I fired one of their illegal automatic weapons. It did not remotely occur to any of us that these para-military formations were the near ancestors of Hitler's storm troops. The Hauptmanns presently took me to Berlin, where we

stayed at the Adlon. It was astonishing to me to witness the deference
accorded to Hauptmann by people of every class—a deference almost
impossible to imagine being accorded in England to an intellectual.
At home Shaw was regarded as a highly quotable *enfant terrible*;
Wells as a subversive vulgarian; Kipling as another kind of vulgarian
who spoke too loudly about the White Man's Burden; Chesterton
as a fanatic who disarmed by his paradoxes and his twenty stone;
Belloc as another fanatic whose combativeness made him impossible
to ignore—all, in a word, were 'outsiders', whom it never occurred
to anyone to treat with the respect due to generals and politicians
(however disastrous their records) and of course to footballers and
cricketers. Before returning home I visited the big house in the
Pariser Platz of the celebrated painter Max Liebermann, then aged
about seventy-seven but still energetic in word and gesture, melan-
cholic in looks, scathing in comment but, I felt, fundamentally
generous and humane, and the possessor of a fine collection of works
by the Impressionists and by his German contemporaries. Next time
I visited his splendid house some twenty-two years later it was a
charred and roofless shell.

Back in London I resumed my frivolous life. The friends of whom
I saw most were John Strachey, Joseph Brewer, the Sitwells, the
Doble sisters, Alec Waugh and Elizabeth Ponsonby, who telephoned
to me almost every morning with the latest news of what was going
on among our friends. Among those on my return whom I saw with
increasing frequency was Alec Waugh. As a friend he has many
virtues: first an inner serenity which he is able to impart in moments
of a friend's distress; he is endlessly curious about the springs of
human action, especially as they operate with regard to sex and
money, topics about which he talks well because what he says is
based upon lifelong and dispassionate observation. I often went down
to his flat in nearby Earls Terrace in the evenings and listened to
his candid, sensible words—uttered in a voice as tiny as his handwriting—not always easy to catch against the rumble of High Street
Kensington's traffic. Just as I recall the taste of white wine and
macaroons at Max's, so at Alec's do I recall the smell of a luxurious
Russian Leather soap he used which pleasantly suffused his flat,
rather than his actual conversation. One evening he invited me to a
small party and to remain for dinner afterwards. At the party my
attention became focused upon an unusual situation: a young

woman of spectacular beauty sitting neglected almost to the point of boycott. Time and again I saw Alec introduce fellow guests who drifted almost immediately away, men no less promptly than women, leaving her alone. When I was introduced I awaited intently the disclosure of some repulsive characteristic, but I could discover none, but, on the contrary, she was amusing and sympathetic. Better still she showed, by keeping our conversation running continuously, that she was anxious that I should not leave her. I was enjoying—it would surely have been a very false modesty to see things otherwise—a conspicuous success with a spectacular beauty. When all the guests had gone and Alec and I were alone, I made haste to ask her name (which I had not heard when pronounced in his tiny voice against the party's din). 'Do you mean,' said Alec with a broad grin, 'that you don't know who she is? She is Mrs . . .' I will not repeat her name here but then it was on everyone's lips; it was the name of a woman whose lover her husband had killed with six revolver shots—and been acquitted. So much for my success.

Another writer of whom I saw something about this time was Sinclair Lewis, to whom I was introduced by Joseph Brewer. To Sinclair Lewis I am twice indebted. His talk about provincial America, which was largely amplification of *Main Street* and *Babbit*, quickened in me the particular and romantic interest I had felt for some years in the United States, which originated perhaps with my American friends at Oxford, notably Joseph Brewer himself. The odd thing was that this interest, far from being deadened by the grotesqueness of which Lewis's books first made me aware, was actually enhanced by it. Someone said to me that I never fully enjoyed a joke until it had been carried too far, which I had to admit was perfectly true. There was an extremism about American absurdities which I found immensely appealing: they seemed to me to be a species of fantastic rococo ornament that this great society could afford. One evening when Sinclair Lewis and I met for a drink together—an evening I am not likely to forget owing to the way in which I incurred my second debt—began with Joseph Brewer showing us a printed invitation he had received from his old college in America inviting 'Alumni' to attend 'A Grand Pow-Wow, to encourage Dartmouth thinking by Dartmouth Men along Dartmouth Lines'—and ended by my falling out of the taxi at Hyde Park Corner—the door was evidently incompletely closed—and Sinclair Lewis jumping out and dragging me with the utmost promptitude from in front of an oncoming 'bus. My sentiments for the United States, fostered by these friendships, were to exert a critical influence upon the course of my life—but not just yet.

I lived beneath my parents' roof and in touch with my family, especially my father whom I talked with almost every day, often earlyish in the morning before he left for the Royal College of Art. Around the middle 'twenties he began to suffer from a seriously over-strained heart and would stay in bed, reading and writing, until the moment of his departure. While he guarded, like most of us, an inner sanctum of privacy, outside it he was one of the most candid human beings I have known, and although capable of keeping a confidence, his natural impulse was to speak his whole mind. Conversation between us was salted by a fundamental difference of outlook. He had a strong, indeed an almost passionate belief in an essential unity, even an essential likeness, among mankind, which led to the further conviction that difference between people could be resolved by honest discussion, and that sensible men of all parties were in agreement: in short he believed with Montesquieu that 'all wise men have the same religion . . .' It led him, too, to see history as a continuous recurrence of situations essentially similar. To me, on the contrary, what seem most significant in human beings are the differences between them; history—except in the most superficial sense—never repeats itself, and wide generalizations are in general either truisms or falsehoods. These lively early-morning talks are among my happy memories of these years, although I often left my father with apprehension that a man so candid and so guileless, so easily disarmed by the expression of generous ideals, should be so exposed by his high position in the world of art. (My apprehension would have been still greater had I known the art world as I came to know it later.) He himself was not unconscious of his situation: 'an artist,' he used to say, 'is only safe when he's at his easel.' What impressed me beyond anything else about my father was his disinterestedness; the entire absence from his mind of any thought for his own advancement, of the remotest sense of rivalry with other artists. On the contrary, when people used to call with the intention of purchasing one of his pictures, they often left empty-handed after having been persuaded to promise to buy an Augustus John, a Stanley Spencer, a Paul Nash, or something by a talented but indigent student. My other principal points of contact with my family were my parents' Sunday Evenings. Many who frequented them regarded these evenings as unique occasions—unique in several respects but in none more conspicuously than for their extraordinary intermingling of the brilliant with the tedious. I can best perhaps convey their peculiar character by describing briefly a single one of them, although it will certainly be a composite impression of several. There would be a miscellaneous contingent of downright bores, people who, intrigued perhaps by a lecture or a pamphlet of my father's about some such topic as the wider use of craftsmen, and having not much else to occupy them would take advantage, quite legitimately, of my parents' comprehensive welcome. To these would be added, although remaining for the most part separate from the first group, students from the Royal College of Art. (Indeed it was to enable them to meet older artists, collectors and others who might be of service to them that these evenings were originally planned.) Henry Moore, Barnett Freedman, Barbara Hepworth, Albert Houthuesen, Percy Horton, Edward le Bas, Cyril Mahoney, Edward Burra, and Harold and Eric Jones were among those who appeared most often. Another distinct group would consist of Indians. Ever since my father's visit to India in 1910 his house had always been a place where Indian visitors to London almost invariably called, the most illustrious among them Rabindranath Tagore. Bearded, wearing a turban and a long soutane of undyed silk, he would be seated serenely like a Buddha with worshippers at his feet. In the presence of worshippers, as he was too often, his eyes would assume a faraway look and his voice a dreamy intonation, which together evoked an ideal personification of the Wisdom of the East. Nothing could have been more different from this than the aspect of his character that he showed to his intimates, which was down-to-earth, amusing, wise, modest and affectionate. My father loved and admired Tagore, but he often became impatient of the attitudes of the public personality. I have even heard, and on more than one occasion, some high-flown pronouncement with mystical overtones cut short by my father's abrupt, 'Nonsense, Tagore,' and a brief factual justification of his rebuke. There was one person, however, whom Tagore's public personality completely mesmerized: this was C. F. Andrews, at one time a missionary in India but latterly more Hindu in spirit than the Hindus themselves. One night, dressed in a flowing robe of indeterminate shape and colour, he came into the room, and with his arms extended straight above his head, ran round it crying out 'The Babu is making lines, the Babu is making lines . . .' When he could be induced to sit down and explain himself, it appeared that what he intended to convey was that Tagore had taken up drawing. Finally there would be other illustrious persons who belonged to no particular group. One of these—a frequent visitor—was Ralph Hodgson, seated in an armchair, his long narrow skull tilted back, pipe clenched between jaws, bulldog at his feet and some children gathered about him; talking mostly about poetry, but also about animals, and with fury of the cruelties they suffered at the hands of men. He would emphasize his points with minatory gestures of a gnarled forefinger: he seemed to be made of some substance much tougher than flesh. Most men have an element of the feminine in their make-up, as most women of the masculine, but Ralph Hodgson's masculinity was unalloyed; shaking his forefinger at my brother (who had shown him some of his drawings) he once exclaimed 'Poor boy; you were born in a kitchen so there's nothing for you but to cook.'

James Stephens was a frequent visitor—of whom an anonymous friend well wrote: 'Sheamus fills a room; he passes for a city . . . he has the vision and the report of a prophet, spellbinding, aweing . . .' The others I have mentioned spoke quietly, to their immediate neighbours. The melodious Irish voice of James Stephens rang round the room, bringing to life the ghosts of Irish legend, or else elevating into legend some everyday event; or again, calling on men to leave all work to women and to devote themselves to drinking and to talk. In contrast to Stephens was T. E. Lawrence, who usually called unheralded and left when he found the family was not alone, but now and then he would steal quietly and, in spite of his celebrity, unnoticed into a Sunday Evening, and after an hour or so he would be found to be there no longer. Another guest, like an apparition from one of his own stories, an elusive combination of the tangible and the mysterious, was Walter de la Mare, small, dark, pale and serene, and welcome anywhere he cared to go. He exercised an invariable attraction: at least I never met anyone who knew him whom he did not captivate; I doubt whether he ever had an enemy. The spell of de la Mare was peculiar in that it was apparently effortless. Silent, he was a delightful presence, but even his conversation had few of the qualities that spellbind or even beguile: there were no arresting phrases; he dwelt seldom on religion, politics, absent friends, money, or the passions, nor was there any evident magic in his tone of voice. The power of endowing the most ordinary things and events with beauty and an aura of strangeness difficult to define and of expressing the quiet affection of the speaker for most of creation were, I suppose, what made his listeners wish that he would talk on for ever. This was the impression he made on me and those whom I knew, but of what he said I cannot remember a word. De la Mare also radiated sheer goodness, and the memory of it prompts me to wonder whether this quality of goodness has become less marked among persons of comparable eminence in literature and the visual arts today. During my early years I can recall so relatively many men who were so largely motivated by an ardent goodwill towards their fellow men; in some cases towards mankind in general, in others towards a wide circle of friends and acquaintances. Of such a high proportion among those I have mentioned in these pages, more especially the writers, Hudson, Conrad, Bennett, Max, Stephens, Tagore, de la Mare, Lawrence, Hodgson, to name only a few, all seemed to me men of immense goodwill. Today self-seeking, but above all ill-will, active or latent, frank or masked, seems to me to be far more prevalent than it was. Is this due to my suffering, unconsciously, from the disease that caused Ruskin in his later years to believe that not only human society but nature herself was deteriorating? Or to the devotion of my father (himself a man of radiant goodness) to good men that led to those he frequented being exceptional in this regard? Or is it that the harder, vulgarer, more competitive society in which we live today has brought out uglier traits? Or again, are such traits to be found more frequently in the world of the visual arts than in that of literature— though more conspicuously among critics (as seems to me to be the case) than painters and sculptors themselves? I do not know, and I am too much implicated in the present to judge it; I only know that I am acutely conscious of a change of moral climate, and of a sense that the men of luminous goodwill today—and happily there are many—are pessimistic, defensive and content themselves to act in accordance with their convictions and their finest impulses, but less ready than their predecessors directly to challenge, in particular, sly malice or even flagrant malevolence.

Such then was the kind of assembly to be found at my parents' house on Sunday nights, even though my memories of several are telescoped into one, for not even on the most exceptional of them would so many notable persons be present.

I was in the meanwhile also coming to know several people who in one way or another contributed in some special way to the enlargement of my ideas. One of these, to whom I look back with particular affection and gratitude, was Arnold Bennett. It is evident from these pages that I knew, had always known, writers, but it so happened that I met Bennett at the very time when my own desire to be a writer was taking direction and form. Moreover, in contrast to a number of others who happened to express their ideas by writing, Bennett regarded himself as a 'writer' in the strictly professional sense in which another man would regard himself, say, as a solicitor or an accountant. He used to discuss with me the problems of writing in a practical and downright fashion: his interest reached beyond the making of lucid, lively, flexible and abundant prose to such implements of his calling as pens, paper and the like. He was justifiably proud of his own methodical procedures: once he showed me a beautiful MS of *The Old Wives' Tale*—so elegantly written and so little corrected that I wondered afterwards whether it might have been a fair copy. Output was a topic to which he often reverted: could I be mistaken in supposing that he told me of his writing ten thousand words at a stretch? The problem of how best a writer could market his work, the advantages and disadvantages, for instance, of employing an agent, was one on which he was always prepared to discourse. It was his belief that good writing was a marketable commodity and that the marketing of it was an integral— and not the least enjoyable—part of the writer's profession. He impressed it upon me that taking account of the market need not involve any sacrifice of independence. 'It's a mistake to write an article and then consider where to send it. Before you begin your article, decide where you'd like to publish it; get a copy of the publication in question and study it carefully; note the *length* of the contributions—so many contributions get turned down simply because they're the wrong *length*; and note the kind of public that it caters for. Then, having mastered the obvious facts, get down to work and write exactly as you wish.' The readiness of Bennett to discuss with me the technicalities of his profession, his assumption that I would be a writer, and his apparent conviction that my writ-

MAX BEERBOHM

By John Rothenstein

aricature of the famous caricaturist, who is
living in retirement in Italy. Mr. Max
rbohm is a brother of the late Sir Herbert
Beerbohm Tree

During a performance of 'The Rheingold' Mr. Sackville
West's neighbour whistles the tune.

By John Maurice Rothenstein.

THREE CARICATURES BY THE AUTHOR

(*below*) THE AUTHOR IN HIS ROOMS

AT WORCESTER COLLEGE

THOMAS ROWAT

ATHOLE HAY

ings offered some degree of promise, gave me pleasure and confidence, as well as cause for surprise, for I had no illusions about the meagreness and ineptitude of everything I had written, which included a particularly unworthy (and fortunately unsigned) little monograph on Eric Gill in Benn's series, 'Contemporary British Artists'. I was deeply touched that he should perceive in any of it a gleam of something worthy of cultivation. One day, however, seeing me off after a visit to his house, he looked, characteristically, inside my hat. 'Lock!' he said with a touch of whimsical reproof, 'my dear John, you've no business to get your hats at Lock's until your earnings are up—let me see—by at least 150 per cent.'

Apart from all this, the society of Bennett was a delight and I looked forward to my visits to his house—a delight chiefly, perhaps, because he himself was so delighted with the world that he had conquered. He never lost the feeling of being a 'card' from the Five Towns who had come up to London and made good, and his enjoyment of the things brought him by success, wealth, good food and wine, smart resorts, freedom to travel at will, access to any society that took his fancy, never lost its freshness, nor did his sense of wonder at what the poor boy from the Potteries himself had become. It was perhaps an unconscious understanding of all this that caused him not only to refrain from any attempts to become a conventional 'gentleman', but to preserve and indeed to exploit his idiosyncrasies: his high coif of hair that rose from his head like a cockatoo's crest; his stammer that he adroitly exaggerated in order to bring an element of suspense into his conversation and as a discouragement to interruption, but above all his frank relish of the glittering prizes of success. These he was able to relish without reservation and with a clear conscience because he knew that however highly he valued these things he did not put them first, and indeed he clearly saw the comic aspect of these tastes on the part of a serious writer. Of smart resorts those that he most enjoyed were big hotels.

When tired or dispirited he found that the best restorative, he told me, was not a visit abroad with all its attendant complications, but a few days in a big London hotel—the Savoy for preference. His large, red brick Edwardian house, 75 Cadogan Square, with its heavy French furniture, had a touch of flamboyance, but he had some good paintings by such of his contemporaries as Bonnard and Sickert. (Bennett was also interested in younger artists such as

Nevinson and Wadsworth for their representation in a contemporary idiom of aspects of urban and industrial life.) There was more than a touch of flamboyance about his clothes; 'I saw Arnold Bennett at the theatre last night,' a friend said to me, 'wearing a pair of women's lace drawers in place of a dress shirt.' He did indeed wear lace instead of linen shirts with evening dress.

Another whose friendship meant much to me, more particularly during these years, was Eric Gill, whom I can just remember coming to my parents' house before he became a sculptor, when he was a carver of inscriptions. At that time he was a slight, alert, red-bearded young man, dressed, somewhat according to the William Morris tradition, as a gentlemanly workman; later on, after his reception into the Catholic Church, his manner of dressing underwent a radical alteration: he wore a loose black overall with a belt, a biretta without a tassel and black or coloured stockings cross-gartered. His way of dressing was one example of the way in which every detail of his life was regulated by his principles. In another man such clothes would have appeared fantastic, but on account of Gill's dignity and good humour and their being manifestly working clothes they provoked little comment. There was nothing, I believe, of the poseur in Gill: everything he did was an expression of some clearly formulated conviction—but his friendly eye and forthright, informal way of talking dispelled any impression of pedantry. It was his being a Catholic that first drew me to him. Earlier in these pages I wrote of the processes that led me to become a Catholic myself. These processes—reading and desultory meditation—were at first almost wholly solitary; my parents had a number of Catholic friends but to none of them did I, except to Gill (and on one occasion to Frederic Manning), say anything of what was in my mind, and being at a school in which the pervading sentiment was agnostic I myself had none at all. Gill was for several reasons an exception. First perhaps because he was a man who tried to live his life in precise accordance with his beliefs, and he regarded none of his activities as lying outside the orbit of his religion. Most of us shamefacedly accept, as an inevitable part of the nature of things, the inconsistency of many of our actions with our professed convictions. It was impossible, therefore, to avoid occasions of religious discussion, and for me such occasions were welcome. There was a reason, apart from my ardent interest in this subject, that made his attitude towards it especially sympathetic to me. Some pages back I alluded to my father's dis-position to see what was common between men. He was not less disposed to see what was common to institutions, and to conclude that institutions, like men, beneath surface differences, were very much the same. It was a habit of mind founded in the widest tolerance and human sympathy, and which could lead to illuminating con-versation. To one thing it could not lead, namely any firm conclu-sions where religion was concerned. Gill's human sympathies were far less wide than my father's, but he had a more logical mind. During the time when he was becoming a Catholic he maintained close touch with my father, discussing his changing convictions with the utmost candour. Gill was deeply appreciative of my father's sympathetic comprehension, by which he was eventually misled. So complete did his comprehension appear that Gill not unnaturally came to wonder why the considerations that decided the issue for him did not lead my father to similar conclusions. When he under-stood that their minds were not so close as he had supposed, that for instance certain things that Gill had accepted literally were under-stood by my father in a symbolic sense, that certain things which he had accepted as unique were to my father things which pertained to the spirit underlying all religions, their relationship sustained a shock. They remained close friends for a time, but eventually Gill's friendship cooled and they rarely met. I continued on very friendly terms with Gill, unaware of their rift until both were dead. In spite of his Nonconformist origins there was a dry, legalistic element in Gill's mind of which I was not unaware, but dryness and logic were at that particular moment vastly more valuable to me than the noble but somewhat generalized sentiments I grew up with. These senti-ments were like handsome cheques that were often difficult to cash. So it was that Gill became a particularly valued friend.

Gill's woodcuts of religious subjects, hieratic, with a touch of archaism, but ardent in feeling and beautifully engraved, especially those which illustrated the small occasional magazine, *The Game*, that he printed and published, became for me while I was still at school moving symbols of the Catholicism that so much occupied my thoughts. I must have written him a letter in which I expressed my admiration for these woodcuts and, no doubt with extreme reserve, have alluded to the Catholic orientation of my mind. I received the following letter in reply.

JM+JD   Ditchling Common
                                         Sussex
                                         November 20th 1919

Dear John,

I was very much pleased to get your letter of the 16th. I am very glad you like the woodcuts and even more glad to hear that you are interested in the Church.

I wish we could meet and have a talk about it. I should think you are quite right not to be in a hurry, but at the same time do not delay to get into touch with someone competent to advise you on the Catholic side. If you are going to Oxford, as I understand, I do not think you could do better than to go and see Father Martindale, S.J. He is a man of extraordinary culture and sympathy, his address is Campion Hall, Oxford. But it has just occurred to me that Stroud is not very far from *Woodchester*, where there is a Dominican Priory. The Prior there is a friend of mine, Father Hugh Pope. I am sure you would like him very much, and it seems a pity, as you are so close, not to see what he says. Would you like me to write to him?

I have asked Mr. Pepler to send you the prints you ask for.

No, I do not think the 'Game' is anti-monarchical. Nobody can be particularly keen about the monarchy as at present emasculated. But the *idea* of the Kingship and the *reality* it has been and might be again are things to which the 'Game' is not opposed.

Yours very sincerely,
Eric Gill.

The following autumn I asked whether he would make me a bookplate, and he replied, on 2nd October, 'I should be pleased to do a bookplate for you and a simple one with white lines on black could be done (exclusive of prints which would be a few shillings a hundred) for about two guineas . . . I am very glad,' he added, 'that you want to see Father Martindale . . . I enclose a letter to him herewith.' During my years at Oxford it so happened that I saw less of Gill, but not long after I went down we resumed our meetings and our desultory correspondence.

Many pages back I told, and in some detail, of the processes of mind which led me to embrace the Catholic faith, but the day of my reception into the Church was long deferred. About my decision I consulted no one, but in view of its crucial character I felt bound to inform my father of it. My father listened with sympathy to what I had to say, but he urged me most earnestly to postpone giving effect to my decision. As we walked together along the road over the bleak stretch of country which lay between Far Oakridge and Bisley —the monotonous thought-fostering road on which I had made many decisions— he spoke of England as being a Protestant country, and while he talked I caught a glimpse of the great community of Englishmen whom we both revered, Protestant or following a way of thought derivative from Protestantism, Milton, Newton, Wren, Blake, Dr. Johnson, Reynolds, Gainsborough, Pitt, Nelson, Words-worth . . . To Catholicism he had no theological objection— dogma meant almost nothing to him; indeed he had once himself been drawn to the threshold of a Benedictine monastery, and he had little love for the Established Church. I recalled his lack of interest when my sisters had gone not long before to Gloucester Cathedral to be confirmed. Although his reasoning did not touch me, I had the utmost affection and respect for my father and I appreciated the fact that I was dependent upon him. So I waited, going if not regularly at least often to Mass, but suffering at being a Catholic only by desire. But I must not exaggerate my suffering: had formal reception into the Church been my sole aim, it could have been realized earlier, but there were many times when my voracious desire for experience of many kinds made me, if not forget-ful of it, less urgent about its fulfilment. Within a couple of years of leaving Oxford I had paid off most of my debts and I had begun to enjoy a precarious economic independence. I gave myself, until the last, to the reading of much non- and some anti-Catholic philosophy and theology, sometimes discussing what I read with Gill. I lent him a book by James Harvey Robinson that had taken my fancy and I received the following letter—a letter that conveys something of the quality of his conversation :

Capel-y-Ffin,
Abergavenny.
29.3.25

My dear John,
    I hasten to write and tell you that I have got and read your gospel according to James Harvey Robinson! I began it at Reading (a good place to start one wd. suppose) and finished it (all but the

last 20 pp.) at Llanrihangel Crucorney Mon. (a good place to stop!) Well, I'm really blessed. Of course I think it's an admirable book in many ways; with its general thesis (under the circumstances in which the mod. world finds itself) I am in enthusiastic agreement. Of course—in fact what else is any decent person saying but that we've got to be as near absolutely honest and disinterested and sceptical as its possible to be? But really I am, as I said before, simply blowed! I can't imagine why the said J.H.R. doesn't play his own game—just a little bit—for practice. For ignorance, inadequacy & carelessness the book takes a lot of beating—vide pp. 167 & 168 which of course I naturally take note of. But I have made copious marginal notes & I wd. like most awfully to go through the book page by page with you and show you just what I mean when I say it is ignorant, inadequate & careless in very many instances. There's little occasion for me to praise the book to you—you already recognise its good qualities—its admirable division of thinking into reverie, decision, rationalizing and . . . the other thing, which he calls 'creative thought'—its admirable general scheme—animal, child, savage and traditional civilized mind—its historical scheme—prehistoric, classical, mediaeval, scientific. Properly worked out & viewed without prejudice there wd. have been little to complain of. Of course he wd. or might reply that the book is only journalism—written to reach the 'man in the street' & that it is not meant to be scientifically critical in style or diction. But, personally, I think there is too much of such popular slapdash & that his own cause, which is also my cause & that of any honest person (tho. I myself don't claim to be more than 'indifferent honest') wd. be better served by a more carefully written & more 'scientific' book. I'm not a learned person—yet there are many places in wh. even I can detect that J.H.R. simply doesn't *know* what he's talking about. Inadequacy—well look at the footnote on p. 125 & the paragraph on metaphysics to which it refers. What, we may ask, are 'perfectly *commonplace* conclusions'? This is simply begging the question. He does it constantly too. As for Carelessness—note the word 'Providence' on p. 61 where it can have no meaning worth mentioning—the word 'salvation' on p. 105 & the words '*No one*' on line 7 from bottom on p. 163. No one . . . well, well. This is simply damned careless or damned ignorant—& so in

many places. On the other hand the paragraphs beginning on the
bottom line of p. 200 (re modern business) are excellent and very
valuable—so are many other things in the book & I only regret
that it will only reach the 'outsiders' (except in rare cases like
mine!) and will do nothing to increase their humility but will
merely have the effect of making them think what damn fine
fellows they are compared with old stick-in-the-mud Augustine
& Thomas Aquinas. It wd. be fine if you could visit us here. Then
we could have a good talk and argument about it. Is there any
chance at all? You'd like this country. Why not come & correct
the proofs of the *biography* here?
we'd be delighted to see you.

Yours sincerely,
Eric Gill T.S.D.

. . . .

On re-reading the above I perccive that I've omitted to mention
one thing that struck me v. much in reading the book—viz: that
the 'gospel' according to J.H.R. is from an R.C. point of view
such a 'back number'. It may be news—startlingly fresh &
revolutionary to H.G.W.[1] and many other people, but really,
really, with my hand on my heart (& my tongue miles removed
from my cheek) the general thesis is as stale as anything. That's
where J.H.R. is so amazingly ignorant, living as he appears to do
in Tooting or Golders Green.

EG

By the spring of 1926 I felt free to carry out the intention formed
so many years before: I placed myself under instruction by Monsignor Moyes, a theologian and Canon of Westminster, and in June
he received me into the Church in the crypt of Westminster Cathedral.
I had wanted for my godfather someone the character of whose
faith had a particular significance for me. I always abhorred 'fideism',
the habit of assuming that nothing can be settled by the intelligence,
and that custom, tradition, convention, the prevailing opinion
among those in authority are the only safe guides. Because of a series
of historical accidents, among others the influential part played in
the Church in the English-speaking countries by the Irish—to whom
she owes so much in so many respects—'fideism' is fairly widespread

[1] Wells.

among Catholics in Great Britain as elsewhere. Since the central act of a Christian is the choice between good and evil, anything such as the habitual recourse to conventions which detract from the responsibility for those acts deprives his choice of meaning. (For the same reason a democratic system—for all its absurdities—seems to me preferable for a Christian society to any other simply because it offers wider scope for the choice between good and evil than an authoritarian system in which many vital moral issues are removed from the responsibility of the ordinary man.) Before my reception into the Church I accordingly took the precaution of discussing my religious problems with the most sceptical Catholic I knew, Frederic Manning, author of *Scenes and Portraits*, a forgotten book of dialogues which his acute sense of history, his psychological perception and the dry lean perfection of his style combine to give, for a few others besides myself, the stature of a classic.

Manning's scepticism, far from being a discouragement, assured me that there was a place within the Church for a natural sceptic such as myself. 'I wouldn't leave the Church,' Manning said to me, 'but I'm often inclined to doubt whether, were I outside, I would become a Catholic.' Shortly after my reception I wrote to him to ask whether he would serve as my sponsor at my confirmation, and I received the following letter in reply:

> Chalfont Park Hotel,
> Gerrards Cross,
> Bucks.
> 14.x.1926

My dear John,

Of course if you think my nature sufficiently godly, and sufficiently paternal, I have not the slightest objection. But I confess that, at this precise moment, I am being vastly amused by the Holy Father's disapproval, expressed through the Cardinal Secretary of State, of M. Charles Maurras and his influence on *L'Action Française*. For 25 years or more, poor Maurras has been tolerated by the Vatican, I suppose as a decoy, and now that his work has been done and his adherents duly registered among the elect, his methods are disavowed, his orthodoxy questioned and his equivocation exposed.

Admire with me the Eternal Justice which punishes eventually the disciple of Hébert because he uttered no word of regret at the condemnation of his master; and adore the inscrutable wisdom of God, or of the Holy See, which suffers evil for a time that good may come, and discards an instrument that has been the salvation of many, after a quarter of a century's use, as pernicious and abominable.

If I were you I would take the name of Anselm, but don't ask me why.

Yours always,
Frederic Manning.

I mentioned my reception neither to any member of my family nor to anyone else, but shortly afterwards I heard from Gill:

Capel-y-Ffin,
Abergavenny.
18.6.26

My dear John,

I heard from a friend yesterday of what he calls 'John Rothenstein's step' and 'more than ordinary cause for rejoicing'. I can only assume that he means that you have been 'received'. Let me know yourself that this is so. Your little article in Blackfriars seemed to me explicable on no other ground—but I do want the authentic news. What good news it will be—oh yes, and praise be to God. I am still hoping that you will be able to come and see us here. Do come while the weather is warm and the days long.

My love to you (and please remember me kindly to all your family).

Yrs.   Eric Gill   T.S.D.

On my confirming what his friend had told him he wrote:

Capel-y-Ffin,
Abergavenny.
5.7.26.

My dear John,

I was v. glad to get your letter of the 29th from Port-Vendres and to know that the good news was true news. I look forward now to your visit to C-y-Ff and hope it will be soon. Then we can discuss the matter! Meanwhile I write merely to acknowledge yours and to say that I quite understand your position as I am more or less in a similar boat or, shall I say, occupying a v. similar cabin, a department in the steerage or stokehole or lock up of 'Peter's barque'.

                                to be in the lock up anyway . . . the thing is to go blindly to the   anyway and   anyhow and any-where . . . and I think you'll find that scepticism and 'this-worldliness' and rationalism ('free thought' is of course a name without meaning) are only given their proper chance inside the said barque. As an insider you can be a sceptic to some purpose—outside—well, who cares? But will await your coming here.[1]

            Yours   Eric G.   T.S.D.

During September I asked him whether he would stand sponsor for me at my confirmation, and sent him a copy of a novel *Tony*, by Stephen Hudson, of whose collected works I had recently published an appreciation. He made the following reply:

                                    Capel-y-Ffin,
                                    Abergavenny.
                                    Oct. 16 '26

Dear John,
   I've been away a fortnight only returning last night finding your letter. I wired this morn and hope you got it in time. Of course I am only too pleased to be your godfather at your con-firmation and will do my best to live up to the responsibility. Blessings on you. I hope you are well. You say nothing of the family. How is your father and how is Rachel?
My love to them and to you.
            Eric G.   T.S.D.

P.S. I'm returning *Tony* herewith and I am also sending the Pamphlet. V. many thanks for the former. I think its a v. brave effort to do the particular thing it sets out to do. I admire it v. much. The end is horribly well done. I don't agree with you that his dying at the end spoils the thing. I think it just makes it right—because the particular quality of disillusion which runs through

---

[1] The missing words are due to the letter's having been torn by hasty opening.

the whole narrative is made credible when you discover that it's, as it were, a dead man's confession. Lor! what a gang they are— what a life—and yet and yet how poignantly tinged with the milk of h. kindness . . .

On 11th September I went to stay with the Gills at their house at Capel-y-Ffin in the Black Mountains of South Wales. It rained continuously, the house was damp—the paper in my bedroom leaned crazily away from all four walls—there was no hot water, no newspapers, spartan food—and I enjoyed every instant of my visit: Gill's sharp-edged genial talk warmed the bleak house. A few minutes after my arrival there came into the sitting-room a small man who, though I now know that he was thirty-one, looked not more than twenty-four. 'Well goodbye, Eric,' he said, 'I'm going now.' In my mind's eye I can still see the two of them shaking hands. Eric Gill, keen-glancing, energetic in word and gesture, wearing his black biretta, rough black cassock gathered at the waist by a leather belt; David Jones with pale face surmounted by an ingenuous fringe, dark and thick, his figure languid and his voice muted. He looked much younger than his years, although his skin had the delicate, tired texture commoner in old age than middle life. The dark eyes, large and mild, had in their depths a little touch of fanaticism quite absent, for all his intermittent aggressiveness, from Gill's. His clothes were anonymous. The contrast between the two men was not more apparent than their friendly understanding. David Jones and I were introduced, shook hands (his grip was soft and shyly friendly), and a few moments later he left the house. 'Who was that?', I asked, 'One of your apprentices?' (Gill usually had several in his workshops.) 'That was David Jones. He's been learning carpentry, but he's not much good at it. But he's a jolly good artist: a lot will be heard of him before long. Look at this,' he said, pointing to a big water colour lying on a table representing two horses on a hillside, 'he's just finished it.' Imperceptive of its qualities, I gave it, nevertheless, so long and hard a look as to imprint it on my memory. 'It's done from this window,' Gill explained. I walked up to it and peered out, but I could see nothing except mist lashed by driving rain. The outline of a big hill, when adumbrated by Gill, was just visible. It was many years before I saw David Jones or the drawing again, and the drawing, 'Hill Pastures—Capel-y-ffin', must have impressed me more than it seemed to at the time, because I remembered it so clearly.

The illuminating quality of Gill's conversation was chiefly due to his propensity for carrying all his arguments to their logical conclusions—a procedure that sometimes landed him in paradoxical situations but which provoked his listeners to reach their own conclusions upon important issues that supineness would otherwise have tempted them to leave unresolved. For Eric Gill religion was not a survival, a mere pious legend, but something belonging to the here and the now, something that should regulate not only human relations but the relations between capital and labour, the banking system, dress and innumerable other matters generally regarded as having only remote and theoretical connection with the teachings of the Church. For Gill failure to perceive the logical consequences of one's beliefs and to act appropriately was among the most grievous of shortcomings. 'Look at your father,' he exclaimed suddenly as we walked through the rain near Capel-y-ffin, 'he's got infinitely more interest in religion, much deeper understanding of it than, say, the average parson. When I was becoming a Catholic he showed me the solutions to certain difficulties that troubled me, but why can't he see the full implications of what he believes?'

I made poor use of an opportunity of expressing my high regard and my affection for Gill in the shape of an invitation to contribute a short monograph on his work to a series on British artists published by Benn, already referred to. My monograph is a faulty thing, and when the proofs arrived absence abroad deprived me of the possibility of effecting improvements. Gill—who had invited me to Capel-y-ffin so that we might correct the proof together—was understandably annoyed. 'I was v. disappointed with the "Benn" book . . .', he wrote on 5th June 1927, but concluded charitably 'I've an idea that you cannot have seen the proofs yourself . . . and you are probably as annoyed as, or more so, than I with the result.'

The third person to whom I owed much at this formative period of my life I met in 1920. I recall the occasion clearly. My father was entertaining some friends in the huge studio at the top of the house that we briefly occupied in Sheffield Terrace. Taking the only vacant chair I found myself neighbour to a pale-faced man with black hair, dark militant eyes, wearing a black suit and round his neck a black scarf. Hearing I was at Oxford he encouraged me to describe the intellectual life there, and in the course of doing my best to satisfy him I must have paid high tribute to the intelligence of some of my friends. 'I daresay they're a lot of fools,' he said sharply. I enquired coldly who he might be. 'Wyndham Lewis,' he answered. 'Then you're the author of *Tarr*,' I exclaimed, mollified now that I found he was a man with a right to judge—though not people whom he did not know—for I had just read *Tarr* and thought —and think it still—one of the best novels of its time. In spite of his occasional truculence I felt very much at ease with Lewis and we became friends and met at intervals until the end of his life.

The writing of certain authors is in essence a literary form of their conversation corrected and polished. I cannot read a paragraph written by Max, for instance, without hearing the words pronounced in his urbane and hesitant Edwardian tones, and I have heard my father and others familiar with Henry James remark on the similarity of his written and his spoken word. It is easy to hear in the writings of Wells the squeaky voice, now genial and now combative, of their author. With Lewis it was otherwise. He talked well: any subject likely to extend his intellect or to add to his stock of information was grist to his mill: the visual arts and literature, politics of the world and of the little dangerous world of art, philosophy, religion for preference—the same subjects, in fact, as engaged him as a writer, but unlike Stephens, Berenson, Max and Max's friend Reggie Turner, Lewis was not a great talker. There was moreover one respect in which his talk was unlike his writing. As a writer he was aggressive; he could hardly treat of any character without showing sooner or later the incomparably deadly claws of his satire; as a talker he was largely defensive, expressing his suspicions that this person or that had plotted or was plotting to do him an injury. Years later, in fact the last time I saw him in private, shortly before his death, he told me that Roger Fry and his 'Bloomsbury' circle had ruined his life and that had he known how much he would have suffered, in his own words, 'by a sneer of hatred, or by a sly Bloomsbury *sniff*' he would never have attacked Roger Fry. (Lewis was referring to his description of Fry as 'the Pecksniffshark, a timid but voracious journalistic monster, unscrupulous, smooth-tongued and, owing chiefly to its weakness, mischievous' in the famous 'round robin' in which in 1914 he announced his resignation and that of his friends from Fry's venture, The Omega Workshop.) When unconcerned with enemies, real or suspected, the conversation of Lewis was genial and relaxed.

The defensive attitude of Lewis the private individual did not express itself only in his conversation: there was something about his whole way of life that put one in mind of a defensive military operation. His dwellings were sequestered and fortress-like: at Adam and Eve Mews, off Kensington High Street, where he lived when I first knew him, his rear was protected by a high wall; his room in Percy Street was difficult to find, camouflaged as it were, while 29A Kensington Gardens Studios, where he mostly lived during his last years, was approached by a narrow many-cornered corridor leading eventually to an inner fastness, which might have been constructed with a professional eye to concealment and defence. To the sequestered and fortress-like character of the places where he lived was added an extraordinary secretiveness, as an elaborate security measure. Not for years after his marriage, for instance, did he admit to the existence of his wife. It was probably during 1938 or 1939 that I had dinner with him at Kensington Gardens Studios. Dinner was elaborate and the studio impeccably tidy. I was reminded of an occasion, some years before, when Lewis had entertained me at his studio in Percy Street. Then we had sat on packing-cases in front of a red-hot iron stove, from whose angry rays we must have suffered painfully had we not been shielded by a yard-high range of cinders encircling the fearful source of heat. Only a feminine hand, I reflected, and a feminine hand of more than usual authority, could have so transformed the environment of so formidable a man.

Lewis's defensiveness and his habit of shrouding his movements with extraordinary secrecy were, I think, partly pathological, but they were also the consequence of his deliberate intention to achieve the utmost freedom from social ties in the interests of impartiality as a critic of art, thought and life. It was not that he was an impartial person: on the contrary he often showed himself a ferocious partisan, as he was of course well aware, but rather that he wished to abstain from personal entanglements. About 1922 the mystery in which he shrouded himself grew denser still. In the introduction to his short-lived periodical *The Enemy* he wrote of his move outside the prevailing revolutionary movement—and his words perfectly apply to his disengagement from intellectual society in general: 'My observations

will contain no social impurities whatever, there will be nobody with
whom I shall be dining tomorrow night (of those who come within
the scope of my criticism) whose susceptibilities, or whose wife's, I
have to consider. If the public is not aware of the advantages it
derives from such consequences as these, it is time that it awoke to its
true interest.' This last sentence indicates a fact of cardinal importance about Lewis: his sense of being, as an artist and thinker, a
public and not a private person. In this capacity he was certainly
more fully himself, in fact. With many writers the expression of their
spontaneous thought, their asides, so to speak, are more illuminating
than their considered statements. My father, who knew Oscar Wilde
well, told me that his conversation was infinitely more amusing, far
more of a work of art, than even the best of his writings. With Lewis
this was not so: his conversation was always good, but even at its
best it fell a long way far short of his writings. I do not believe I
ever heard him express an idea that is not to be found in his books.
And he was less outspoken: on occasion I have heard him deny, with
a note of apprehension in his voice, being in the slightest degree
critical of someone whom, thinly disguised, he had truculently
indicted in some recent publication as an imbecile or a hypocrite.
Being myself one of those who did not come within the scope of his
criticism, I used to see him fairly often during his undercover years:
at tea-shops in Tottenham Court Road and Notting Hill Gate,
where, in broad-brimmed black hat, black choker and overcoat,
talking about Joyce, Benda, T. E. Hulme, T. S. Eliot or Hegel, his
saturnine figure was in strange contrast to his commonplace environment; or else in his studio.

   I am under a threefold debt to Lewis. He encouraged me, when
I was of an age to accept too readily the heroes of the time: Proust,
Picasso, Joyce, Diaghileff or whoever they might be, to scrutinize
them with a critical eye; and likewise the dominant tendencies in
literature and the visual arts. He clarified my vague comprehension
that abstract art—however natural and beautiful a means of expression for certain temperaments—was wholly inadequate as a means of
expressing the full content of the vision of others. It was not until
later that Lewis wrote, 'the geometrics which had interested me so
exclusively before I now felt were bleak and empty. *They wanted
filling*. They were still as much present to my mind as ever, but sub-
merged in the coloured vegetation, the flesh and blood, that is life

. . .' but this was often the burden of his talk. Finally he encouraged my innate propensity to favour the concrete, the exactly defined, the rational as against what was cloudy, fanciful, subjective. I owe to Lewis much clarification of my own innate predispositions towards literature and the visual arts and an enhanced confidence in their validity.

Three years after I came to know Lewis I met Stanley Spencer, who did not, like Lewis, contribute to the formation of my ideas about the arts, but who did enormously enhance my enjoyment of painting. Where I met him I cannot remember, but a few days later I received a postcard which bears the postmark 17th September 1923 and which runs thus:

3 Vale Hotel Studios

Dear Rothenstein,
    Could you come tomorrow (Tues) afternoon between 2 & 3. I will be in in any case so it does not matter if you dont turn up. On Wed afternoon I shall be in all the afternoon also, if you cant come tomorrow come then. On Thursday I may be going away. I should like very much to see you if you could come.
Yours very sincerely,
Stanley Spencer

I found the studio on top of the Vale Hotel, a big public house overlooking the pond in the Vale of Health in Hampstead. The room was barely large enough to accommodate the immense canvas, measuring some eighteen feet long by nine feet high, which leaned against the longest wall. This was 'The Resurrection, Cookham', or rather, was to be, for it was scarcely begun. Up against the canvas stood a small table—which, with two kitchen chairs, an iron stove and a small tin bath, was virtually the room's only furniture—and upon it a large teapot, half a dozen unwashed plates and some white marmalade jars, some containing paint brushes and others marmalade.

Stanley Spencer was a tiny figure with a long fringe of dark hair hanging low over a face of extraordinary earnestness and animation. The least observant would have been aware of being in the presence of a person of unusual energy and originality. After the minimum of preliminaries he began to speak with the utmost candour of what most deeply concerned him.

Sometimes the process of getting to know a person is the process, so minutely described by Proust, of stripping layer after layer of deceptive appearance and laying bare at last the unexpected and irreducible core of personality. Contrary to the creations of Proust, Stanley Spencer revealed this innermost core at once.

During the years following that first visit I had day-long and night-long talks with Stanley Spencer about aspects of his painting, but he never said anything so illuminating of the innermost springs of his creativity as what were almost his first words. At that time he had held no exhibition, and, so far as I am aware, little or nothing had been written about him, but I had the good fortune to know two of his finest paintings, 'Zacharias and Elizabeth', of 1912–13, which I had seen in Sir Muirhead Bone's house near Oxford, and his 'Self-Portrait', of 1913, in the chambers of Sir Edward Marsh in Gray's Inn. When I expressed my admiration for these he said: 'Those pictures have something that I have lost. When I left the Slade and went back to Cookham I entered a kind of earthly paradise. Everything seemed fresh and to belong to the morning. My ideas were beginning to unfold in fine order when along comes the war and smashes everything. When I came home the divine sequence had gone. I just opened a shutter in my side and out rushed my pictures anyhow. Nothing was ever the same again.' I spoke of the beauty of the glimpse of the river in the top left-hand corner of the big canvas against the wall—one of a few meticulously finished islets in a wide sea of white priming; 'sometimes,' he said, 'I get a plain glimpse of that earthly paradise, but it's only a fragmentary glimpse.' These words of his were in no sense a personal confidence; they were repeated in one form or another at that time, I suppose, to anybody with whom he engaged in serious conversation; they give a luminous insight into the spiritual predicament that never ceased to harrow and to drive him. When he met people he was prepared to treat them as friends, and he so treated me from my first visit, on which indeed he gave me the splendid pen drawing of himself which he made in preparation for the Tate 'Self-Portrait'.

In the spring of 1926, when 'The Resurrection' was almost complete, I paid a visit to the same studio that remains particularly clear in retrospect. Shareen, the Spencers' first child, had been born in November 1925. Mrs Spencer was bathing Shareen, and I was momentarily distracted from her husband's conversation by my impression that the water was too hot. Shareen yelled, but appeared to suffer no harm. I remember, too, that a boiling kettle which stood upon the iron stove filled the room with steam, which condensed upon the spacious surface of the canvas. A quarter of a century later, when certain of the greens showed a tendency to liquefy, I invited the artist to come to the Tate to examine this painting. He was as puzzled as I about the cause of this liquefaction until we recalled the baleful perpetually steaming kettle, which, he became persuaded, was the cause of the instability of certain areas of the paint.

The great canvas, which I had first seen blank except for a few minutely finished islets and—at longish intervals—seen fill gradually with figures resurrecting among gravestones and tombs, and become suffused with simple yet highly personal poetry, moved me so much that I wrote, in 1926, an article on Stanley Spencer. This was accepted by *Apollo* but remained unpublished until the following year when the gift of 'The Resurrection' to the Tate Gallery by Sir Joseph, afterwards Lord, Duveen made the picture a focus of widespread controversy. It was violently attacked and warmly praised. Stanley Spencer became a public figure—and my immature pages of eulogy became 'news' and promptly appeared.

A friendship had begun to grow up between us when, in the spring of that year, he went to live at Burghclere, near Newbury, to carry out wall paintings in the war memorial chapel specially built to house them by Lionel Pearson.

During the next decade I saw him only occasionally, but I did not cease to cherish the memory of the tiny figure of Stanley Spencer, whose prodigious flow of ideas issued in unceasing talk dwelling largely and with incredible minuteness and evocative power upon the circumstances of his childhood and their particular significance, and the memory, too, of the great 'Resurrection' leaning against the wall of his studio with the preliminary studies for what were to be the still more magnificent wall paintings in the Burghclere chapel.

It was a meeting with another painter, Walter Greaves, about the time of Stanley Spencer's departure for Burghclere, that gave me an objective that I have pursued—alas all too fitfully—ever since, the keeping of some sort of records of living artists. A vast amount of research is devoted to ascertaining facts about dead artists that might be obtained without difficulty while they are alive. Indeed it has come to be regarded as somehow more 'scholarly' to study the dead than the living. The meeting resulted from a commission from Osbert Burdett, acting on behalf of Faber's the publishers, to write a book about some of the painters of the eighteen-nineties. I was in two minds about this commission: I was becoming more and more interested in the art of my contemporaries and felt some reluctance for writing about a period which I had so often heard discussed at home that it had lost much of its freshness. In the event, on account of my particular admiration for certain of the artists who would fall within the scope of the projected book and of my pleasure at being commissioned to write a book at all, I accepted. When it was complete, Messrs. Faber lost the MS and when after much exasperating labour I produced a second MS, they asked for extensive modifications which I was not disposed to make, and the book was published instead by Messrs. Routledge in 1928 under the title of *The Artists of the Eighteen-Nineties*. Walter Greaves was one of the artists of the period whom I particularly admired, and in response to a request to call upon him I had the following letter:

Charterhouse
March 25th 1927

Dear Mr Rothenstein,
    I shall be pleased to have a visit from you, I think about 3 oc. as that is the time we come out from Dinner, and you might drop me a line when you are coming, as I should not like to be out, I suppose I can call myself a bit of old 'Chelsea' the Old Bridge Houses and Cremorne Gardens have all vanished, I often think of those happy days, there, please remember me to your Parents, and hope they are keeping well.
                                    Yours sincerely,
                                    Walter Greaves.

I went down to his little room in the Charterhouse to find one of the most delightful old men I have ever met: enthusiastic, serene, utterly without guile or ill-will. I had heard that in earlier days he darkened his hair and his drooping moustache with bootblacking, but both were now snow white.

Greaves had held an exhibition at the Goupil Gallery in 1911, when Joseph Pennell had viciously attacked him, asserting that much of his work had been 'foisted on the public as Whistler's' and that certain etchings, ostensibly by Greaves, were in fact by Whistler. From a second exhibition, held eleven years later at the same gallery, his 'Hammersmith Bridge on Boat-Race Day' was bought for the Tate. This wonderful painting—by far the finest English 'Sunday painting' of the century—has always attracted a wide circle of admirers, yet it has somehow assumed the character of an anonymous masterpiece, like a folk song or a mediaeval building, than of the work of a particular man. Its fame had accordingly shed little lustre on Greaves himself. Greaves himself was virtually forgotten; scarcely anything—apart from the controversial exchanges that had followed Pennell's attack—had been published about him. Since the time of which I am writing Greaves has all but vanished from view; the group of his paintings in the Tate and a fine example at Manchester are almost the sole reminders of his existence. I accordingly think that it is worthwhile to quote in part the account he gave me of himself, his relations with Whistler and the Chelsea of his day, for my *Artists of the Eighteen-Nineties*, for it must be among the few firsthand sources of information about this remarkable man, and my book has been long out of print.

'I was born (he said) during the late 'forties in Lindsey Houses, now Cheyne Walk, Chelsea. My father was Charles William Greaves, a boat-builder and boatman. My brother Harry and I drew and painted as soon as we could walk. We started by painting crests on boats and armorial bearings, and then, encouraged by my father, we went on to river scenes. My father didn't either draw or paint himself, but he was friendly with several artists. The one whom he knew best was Turner, who lived only a little way away from us, in Cremorne Road, I think. Although he knew Turner well, he never knew the man he was, that is, not until afterwards. My father said that Turner was fond of sketching in Battersea, and used to send his landlady, Mrs Booth, across the river before him with his luncheon. When he did that he would always accompany her as far as Lindsey Houses to ask my father what the weather was going to be like, and if he received an unfavourable reply he would say to her, "Don't go far, Greaves says it's going to be wet." My father rowed Turner several times on the water, who always, he said, was dressed the same way, in a dirty faded brown overcoat and top hat.

'Then there was another artist who lived near us, only about four doors away. He was John Martin, you know, the one who painted

'The Day of Judgment'. Whenever there was a storm and my father had to stay up all night to look after the boats, Martin used to say to him, "If there are good clouds and a good moon, ring my bell." And when there were, he would ring the bell, and in a little while Martin would come out onto the balcony of his house and start working.

'Except for those two, and afterwards Whistler, Rossetti, your grandfather John Knewstub, my brother Harry and myself, I never heard of other artists living in Chelsea in the old days. In those days it was all so different and so gay. It all seemed so lively, with people going to Cremorne dressed in bright-coloured clothes, with the fireworks and the regattas. There were two clubs, the Ranelagh and the Wellington, and their yachts used to start at old Battersea Bridge and race to Wandsworth three times up and down for a silver cup. Then there was the Female Blondin, as the girl was called, who walked five times across a rope stretched across the river. All sorts of things have changed now. I remember the old fire engine that was kept in a stable in Church Street. The man who looked after it slept above, and when there was a fire they used to wake him and he would put his head out of the window and yell, "What's up?" And when they told him there was a fire he threw down the key and went to sleep again. Then they unlocked the door beneath and brought out the engine, which ten men worked, five on each side. And how the carters used to fight in the part of the cobbled street just near our house, where it narrowed! Sometimes the barges would sink, and I saw whole families who lived in them struggling in the water, and watermen fishing them out with boathooks.

'Then one day we were painting on the river bank near our place, when Whistler, whom we knew by sight as a neighbour in Lindsey Houses, came up to us and watched us at work. He said suddenly, "Come over to my place", and we went there and he showed us his work and his Japanese things. I lost my head over Whistler when I first met him and saw his painting. Before that my brother and I had painted grey, and filled our pictures with numerous details. But Whistler taught us the use of blue and made us leave out detail. At first I could only try to copy him, but later I felt a longing for my own style, and something more my own did come back.

'We often used to stay up all night on the river with him, rowing him about. When he came to a view which interested him he would suddenly stop talking and sketch it with white chalk on brown paper, just showing the position of the lights and the river banks and bridges. Just as suddenly he'd start laughing and talking again. The next day I'd go round to his studio and he'd have it all on the canvas. He got me into the way of working like that.

'For many years we saw him nearly every day. We attended to all the work of his studio, mixing his colours, stretching his canvases, preparing the grey distemper ground he used to work on, and painting the mackerel-back pattern on the frames. We must have done all this for close on twenty years. Besides this we helped to paint the inside of his place in Lindsey Houses. When he gave dances we used to play the piano, but he only liked one tune, and he couldn't dance —not really. Of course, we never got so much as a shilling for all that we did, but we never minded that.

'I very well remember Whistler's mother coming to stay there. When he went away I used to go and stay at his house in order to look after her. She was a religious woman, a bit too religious, I thought sometimes, but she was a perfect lady and very fond of me, too. I often used to see Carlyle—everyone about there did—but I never got to know him even when I painted his portrait. He seemed a gruff man, and hardly answered when you spoke to him.

'As I said before, I went mad over Whistler. I can see him now, with his scowl and his top-hat over his eyes. He used to dress peculiarly—long yellow frock-coat. A regular Southerner he was: West Point, wasn't he? He always used to say so. People ran him down, I know, but he was a very nice fellow, and very hospitable, too; but he wanted knowing. He considered himself the greatest artist of all—that was Whistler. Then one day he got married, and vanished. I know Pennell said that Whistler worked on my etching of 'Lime Wharf'—why, Whistler never even saw it. He said he could detect Whistler's work in my 'Battersea Bridge', but Whistler never saw that, either. I never could make out Pennell's reasons for going on as he did. I had never done him any harm, and he came along to me when he was writing Whistler's *Life* to ask for what I knew. But don't let's talk about Pennell.

'I still draw. In fact, I couldn't pass the time without it. I think I could draw all old Chelsea by heart. I don't suppose I'd get it extraordinarily exact, but I can *see* the place all right as I do it.

'I never seemed to have any ideas about painting—the river just *made* me do it. You see, you have to have them if you paint in a studio; but if you are outside all day, as I was, by the river, all you've got to do is to watch the red-sailed barges passing. And then there was the bridge—I suppose Battersea Bridge got a bit on the brains of all of us.'

The image of him—a small grey figure in the sunlight—standing in his door in the Charterhouse waving goodbye when I saw him for the last time, is something that remains clearly in my mind's eye. The consequence of my coming to know Greaves was to make me feel it both a privilege and a duty to preserve against oblivion some memorials, however slight, of artists whom I have known—especially those whom fashionable opinion passes by.

The impulse was fostered by the commission to write *The Artists of the Eighteen-Nineties*, since the writing of it involved my seeing such of my subjects as were still alive, in particular (besides Greaves) Steer, Charles Ricketts and Charles Shannon. The book, published in 1928, was vitiated by many and serious faults: the historical introduction was too long and appropriate to a study of far wider scope; a number of obvious subjects, William Nicholson and James Pryde, for instance, were omitted for no valid reason; opportunities of recording illuminating facts, now irrecoverable, were missed; it was without a bibliography—in fact it was a very amateurish affair. My nerve, however, must have been steady in those far-off days, for looking at a copy of it as I write these lines I am reminded that I dedicated it to Jacques-Emile Blanche—and to Berenson!

Ricketts and Shannon I had known as occasional visitors at my parents' house, but the occasions of seeing them with a particular end in view enhanced the pleasure I had in their company. They shared Townsend House, in Albert Road, off Regent's Park—they had lived together since they were students at the Lambeth School of Art in the 'eighties—which was filled with the objects of beauty that in earlier days they had starved to acquire: I have never seen finer drawings in a private collection.

Each complemented the other: Shannon was tall, palely and idyllically handsome, but without the lifelong stimulus of Ricketts he would have been, I suspect, a dullish man; Ricketts was small and animated, enquiring, witty, learned and positive in opinion. The poet Sturge Moore, one of their oldest friends, telling me about his early memories of them, thus described Ricketts: 'The most original person I had ever met; he looked in those days, with his thin

colourless face and long light hair, more like a dandelion puff than
anything else. He was blithe, alert, active, and an extremely fast
walker.' The description fitted Ricketts well enough in the 'twenties
but his hair was no longer pale but reddish. In spite of the wide
range of their friendships and their social graces, there was something
cloistered about them both: it was evident that their wide knowledge
of the world was derived from art rather than from experience. Both
men were urbane when I knew them, but their cloistered character
may have been more aggressively manifest before they had been
mellowed by success and a lifetime's dedication to the most reward-
ing connoisseurship. This indeed was maintained by Ricketts himself. To a young fellow guest at tea one day, who made some enquiry
about their early life, Ricketts asked, 'Hadn't you always heard that
we were pedantic and disagreeable?' The young man answered without conviction that he had heard no such thing. 'Yes,' said Ricketts
genially, softly striking the table with flattened palm, 'I *insist* that we
were pedantic and disagreeable.' Oscar Wilde, who had learnt from
Whistler to attach importance to the printing and binding of books
and who first suggested to Ricketts that he should design them, was
a regular visitor to the house, formerly Whistler's, in The Vale,
Chelsea, where Ricketts and Shannon had previously lived. 'The
Vale,' said Wilde, 'is one of the few houses in London where one
is never bored,' but he also considered it 'too self-contained', by
which he meant over-precious and exclusive. One day, Ricketts told
me, Wilde brought a friend to see them who was an admirer of his
writings but destitute of any feeling for the visual arts. As soon as he
he had left Ricketts asked angrily, 'Why did you bring this man
here?' 'An obscure worshipper who bowed in the outer court, so I,
the god, beckoned him in,' Wilde answered. 'But Wilde,' replied his
host, 'you said that gods should never leave their temples.' 'You, my
dear Ricketts,' said Wilde, 'belong to an older type of deity, who
mistake worshippers for food and when they see one they tear him
to pieces.' A not very remarkable fragment of dialogue, but, as
Ricketts repeated it, Wilde himself might have been speaking.

Ricketts and Shannon, the fruits of their audacious and impeccable
connoisseurship glowing upon the walls of Townsend House,
showed little interest, and that unsympathetic, in the contemporary
movements that were transforming the visual arts. Imagination was
the quality that they valued above all others, and they believed that

there was little place for imagination either in impressionist or in post-impressionist art. Even as students, they told me, they had become convinced that impressionism, with its fostering of acceptance, passive and uncritical, of glimpses of nature, was particularly inimical to the transforming imagination, and that Puvis de Chavannes, whom they revered above all living painters, dissuaded them from studying in Paris, where the imagination was ever becoming of less account. The only painter belonging to the modern tradition of whom I heard Ricketts speak with enthusiasm was Delacroix, an enthusiasm clearly reflected in a number of his own paintings. They were almost as critical of their contemporaries' means as they were of their ends: in particular they believed the direct method of oil painting all but invariably practised was limited in its range of colour effects and liable to deterioration. They accordingly used the glazing method of the old masters. I regret not having spent more time in the company of these two. Ricketts was probably the most sensitive and scholarly connoisseur in England, and the walls of Townsend House offered an education in European drawing.

Another of the great connoisseurs, Bernard Berenson, I came to know about the same time. In 1927 I spent about two weeks at I Tatti. I had not, nor have I since, stayed in a house where the art of living was brought so near to perfection, symbolised by the carnation placed diagonally across the breakfast tray that was brought to one's room. Life at I Tatti was luxurious, but the luxury was tempered by the atmosphere of quiet purposefulness that, emanating from Berenson himself, pervaded the whole house. There were none of the cloying, eventually debilitating effects that luxurious houses are apt to have for those unaccustomed to them. At I Tatti a guest who wished to work could do so without interruption and in perfect quiet for the whole morning, after lunch and before dinner. The serene and studious atmosphere of the house and the invisibility of Berenson himself during working hours provided the ideal circumstances for his emergence at mealtimes: during the whole of my visit each one was an occasion to be remembered. But alas, as so often, my memory is unequal to those occasions. But although I am able to recall no more than the merest snatches of his conversation, its range and incisiveness made on me—as on so many others—an impression that has lost nothing of its distinctness.

Berenson would walk briskly into the drawing-room as though

reluctant to keep waiting guests who he knew expectantly awaited his presence among them, and as though he himself looked forward to conversation as a welcome change from writing or research. He was small and pale—as he grew older his pallor became so extreme that he assumed an almost translucent look—and dressed with meticulous care in clothes of a somewhat Edwardian character. The thickness of his neck was in odd contrast to the delicacy of his features and the stylish cut of his short white beard. His hands were of a delicacy fitting to a critic who first made lovers of painting consciously aware of its 'tactile values'—a favourite expression. They were raised to his face in expressive gestures of mock boredom or despair and sometimes one of them would take with a caressing gesture the hand of some woman guest who stirred his sympathy. In spite of the almost incredibly wide range of his interests, he possessed a salient characteristic which gave a sort of unity to the immense diversity of the objects of his conversation. His disposition was empiric. He delighted in facts: 'I could happily spend an afternoon reading a statistical report on, say, Nicaragua, its population, commerce, crime, literacy and so forth.' Conversely he expressed impatience of psychology and even of philosophy because they did not rest upon bases of sufficient ascertainable fact. Religion, on the other hand, although his attitude towards it was ambiguous, he valued for its immense influence over the imagination and for the beauty of its liturgies and of the works of art that it inspired: in any case it was one of the paramount *facts*. Of so arbitrary and artificial a subject as heraldry he was contemptuous. Pedantry, especially when it sprang from a disproportionately exhaustive study of the second rate or the tenuous, was apt to provoke him. He was a humanist, and his interest was quickly aroused by anything that added to his knowledge of mankind, particularly of the means whereby their lives—to use a favourite expression—might be enhanced. Gossip gave him evident pleasure, partly because it satisfied his insatiable curiosity about his fellow men, partly because it helped to keep him in touch with his many friends in London, New York, Paris, Boston and other cities which he knew intimately but rarely visited. His own comments on his fellow human beings and their work were as candid as they were original. He illuminated whatever subject he touched. To walk with him round his garden (which I did every afternoon) was a delight, so acutely perceptive was he of the beauties of trees and plants. There were two subjects, however, that he not only never spoke of in my hearing but did not even distantly allude to: the buying and selling of pictures, out of which he had made a fortune, and his early life in Lithuania and the slums of Boston.

Once or twice I had the exhilarating experience of looking at paintings under his tutelage: he showed me for the first time the Massaccios in the Carmine: he said little but he made me *see* them. Every evening he would question me minutely about the churches and galleries I had visited. This drawing me out, this helping me to set my impressions and information in their proper context, was an act of rare benevolence, for nothing that I could have said about the arts of Italy could have added one jot to his unapproached knowledge. One afternoon when I returned from Florence I found him examining a fragment of a stone carving. 'Who do you suppose it's by?' he asked me. Seeing my hesitation, he said, 'Begin by establishing the obvious facts and approach the question of attribution gradually. Now when do you think this carving was made, and where?' 'In the sixteenth century and in Italy,' I said. 'And where in Italy?' 'In Florence,' and so by gentle easy stages he led me, from the general to the particular, to a point when I expressed the tentative opinion that it was the work of Michelangelo. 'I believe you're right, you know,' he said, and with a warm congratulatory smile, as though the attribution were entirely my own.

I have little reason to suppose that Berenson thought especially highly of my capacity, but he invariably encouraged my efforts. In 1930 I was invited to address the Royal Institution, and I sent him the printed account of my lecture.

'My dear John (he wrote, 16 June, 1930, from the Palazzo della Fonte, Fiuggi)

I am much pleased with the abstract of a lecture contrasting Flemish & Italian painting & thank you for sending it.

The subject is most fruitful & I wish you would penetrate & comprehend it & present it to us in a book—in a real book, not a Cleverbelly nor a Floppetry. Such a way of approaching art might at last be appreciated even in Anglo-Saxonia, & would certainly be acclaimed elsewhere. Try.

Where are you & what?
Sincerely yrs.
B. Berenson

If his prevailing mood was of benevolence tempered by an acute critical faculty, he was quick to administer a rebuke when he judged it necessary. In the cool of the evening we used sometimes to go driving through the Tuscan countryside, so magical yet so familiar from the rocky landscapes of Florentine paintings. On one such drive we passed by a peasant family seated on the verge of the highway eating their supper, who were covered by the dense cloud of white dust raised by the car. I was sitting beside Berenson, who detected my slight gesture of compunction. 'You must'nt allow yourself to attribute sensibilities to the Tuscan peasants that don't belong to them: they delight in dust and noise and they wish Florence were more like Wigan.'

Occasionally I visited one or other of the expatriate collector-scholars. The villa of Charles Loeser I remember chiefly for the impression made upon me by his group of fine Cézannes. Against the Florentine background, the resonant blues, reds, lilacs and golds, the assurance justified by the profusion of genius and vast competence, the painful unending struggle of Cézanne to realise his extremely complex vision, and the pride that prevented him from setting down a single brushstroke beyond what he felt, were to be seen in moving isolation. It seemed to me that I was seeing Cézanne for the first time. 'I intend to leave my Cézannes,' Loeser said, 'to the White House, on condition they're hung, and if they're refused, to the Vatican.' They now hang in the National Gallery of Art in Washington.

I used occasionally to go to the Viale Milton to see Reginald Turner, one of the ugliest men and most entertaining talkers I have ever encountered. After lunch one afternoon he took me to a café in the Via Tuonaboni where there awaited us a man of remarkable appearance: wide forehead, reddish hair and beard and brown, slightly protuberant eyes like those of an untamed animal. It was D. H. Lawrence. I had expected him to be a touchy and aggressive man, as indeed he sometimes was. Throughout this long, hot afternoon he was serene and gentle. The only touch of asperity he showed was his exclamation at the mention of the characters in the writings of Wyndham Lewis: 'How they every one of them stink in his nostrils.'

It was while I was staying at I Tatti that an idea that had been in and out of my mind for several years became a resolution. I have already alluded to the sense of frustration caused me by my father's seemingly all-embracing experience of modern art and by his strong opinions. That most of these opinions were well-founded I did not doubt. Doubt indeed I hardly could, in the face of the generous promptitude with which his wisdom and his perception led him to acclaim the work of artists of many kinds in their earliest days: Augustus John, Epstein, Paul Nash, Stanley Spencer, Henry Moore and how many others. His perception was not confined to painting: Oscar Wilde had asked him why he did not write literary criticism and told him that the letter he had written about *The Ballad of Reading Gaol* had given him 'more pleasure, more pride than anything has done since the poem appeared'. Conrad, Hudson and a score of other writers had expressed themselves in like terms. Had the opinions of my father been egregiously stamped with the prejudices of his generation they would not have troubled me: they would have been easy to dismiss. But since I was convinced that many of them were true, I wanted to reach them independently, and not simply by inheritance. In fact I felt altogether too deeply involved in the art world in which my father held so important a place. The resolution I have referred to was to escape from my frustration—a frustration which became more acute with my ever-growing passion for the arts—by quitting the environment that caused it, and emigrating to America. To Berenson I confided my resolution (but not the circumstances behind it), and he encouraged me to carry it out. America, he was convinced, offered far greater opportunities than Europe for those concerned with the arts; he urged me to try for a post at Harvard—the only *institution*, I fancy, that held any romance for Berenson, who, while conceding their uses, was apt to be unsympathetic to academies of learning as well as the honours they conferred. A little later he sent me a letter in which he warmly recommended me to his friend Professor Paul J. Sachs, of the Department of Fine Arts at Harvard. A passage in his covering letter (written from Settignano in February 1927) expresses his regard for his alma mater: 'I should be delighted if you could find a perch at Harvard. I sincerely believe that just now it is as pleasant a place, humanly speaking, as one can easily find.' He added a word of warning to one who had never held a post of any kind: 'You must, however, be prepared for disappointments. Americans judge by impressions, and with rare exceptions judge badly. I have one piece of advice to give you. When you find a job, stick to it as long as you can. If you "can't be on your job", should they think over there, you'd better come back at once. America is no longer a Golconda, but luck still reigns there as nowhere else.' Not long after my return home I was the guest at lunch at the London School of Economics of one of the professors—a man of brilliant intellect and a prominent Labour politician. He questioned me closely about my impending departure for America, and when I mentioned the letter he exclaimed, 'B.B. and Paul are among my oldest friends. Send me the letter and I'll add a hearty endorsement to B.B.'s recommendation of you and send it on.' Although I wondered what weight the endorsement by a professor of economics, who was moreover ignorant of my own small professional qualifications, could add to Berenson's word, I did not feel able without discourtesy to resist this pressing invitation. I sent him the letter: it was never received by Professor Sachs, nor ever heard of again.

Not long after my visit to I Tatti I accepted an invitation to stay with Jacques-Emile Blanche, an old friend of my father's. I landed at Dieppe briefed with elaborate directions for the taxi-driver for finding the way to the Blanche's house at nearby Offranville. The taxi-driver looked puzzled, and asked the name of the owner of the house. When I uttered it he grinned approval and exclaiming, 'Ah, le grand peintre!' drove off certain of his route. How unlike an English taxi-driver, I thought, who would have known a man of Blanche's eminence not on account of his being 'a great painter' but as a public personality or simply as the owner of a more substantial house than most of his neighbours.

Blanche was an extraordinary combination of unreconciled characteristics: he was frankly self-interested yet exceptionally generous, acutely intelligent yet capable of the wildest absurdities. One day he said something about the Dreyfus case, and I, supposing that I had misheard, asked, 'But surely the innocence of Dreyfus is beyond question?' 'My *dear* John,' Blanche exclaimed, '*Nobody* in France believes today in the innocence of Dreyfus, but nobody!' To a young neighbour who expressed regret at the early death of some common acquaintance he said, 'What does it matter, somebody dying young? It's when an *old* person dies, with the accumulated wisdom and experience of a lifetime—someone such as myself—that there's serious cause for regret.'

There was virtually nobody in the artistic or intellectual life of

Paris active during his long life whom he had not known and whom he was not willing to speak of in the frankest terms, sometimes imparting to them vices and malpractices that I had never even heard whispered of them before or since. Like Berenson he was little interested in philosophy or abstract ideas but his interest in literature, painting, politics and his fellow-men was passionate. Also in England, and I was able to repay, however inadequately, his flow of pungent gossip about Proust, Valéry, Gide, the impressionists and their successors with news of his English friends and, what was not less welcome to him, news of what the younger generation of English painters and writers were doing and of the evolving pattern of English social life. One of his most endearing traits was his desire that his friends should share his experiences, and he drove me about the country to see places and people to whom he was particularly drawn. Once, driving through Lisieux, I asked him if he had ever seen Saint Thérèse. 'I don't remember,' he said, 'but everybody knows her family, in fact there are some of them'—and he indicated two or three very ordinary-looking people—'standing over there.' We had passed by before I could focus clearly upon them, but there was something moving in the sight of the immediate family of a saint— even though it was one who had probably inspired more tawdry art than anyone who ever lived.

I had not appreciated how exceptional were Blanche's powers of concentration or his facility as a painter until I sat to him for my portrait—intended by him as a present for my parents. In two hours he had completed a head and shoulders, talking the while as though he had nothing to divert his attention. Then he insisted upon a frank criticism and when I pointed to what seemed to me a weakness in the modelling, he said cheerfully, 'You're quite right, I'll do it again.' Next morning he repainted it entirely, setting right the weakness I had pointed out. I liked the portrait, and its being the work of a pupil of Manet gave it a special aura.

One consequence of our talks was to stimulate the always latent curiosity in Blanche about English painting, and since he was one of those fortunate beings for whom the transition from thought to action is easy, he decided to write an article on certain members of the younger generation, and I agreed to help him to procure reproductions. A letter dated just two weeks after my departure shows his continuing interest:

Off.   24 Aug 27

Dear John,

I wonder, have you asked S. Spencer's permission for reproduction? I wish you did.

P. Nash sent me six or seven photos of light, awfully French looking, Cézannesque water colour drawings. The editor of *L'Art Vivant* thought them (between ourselves) of small interest. What I want is a p.c. of one of the War pictures. Both Nashes did excellent war pictures. Considering what my article means to convey (purely *British* modern art) I fear the present style of P.N.'s work won't exactly meet with my personal views. What am I to do?

In great hurry
Yrs
JE.Bl.

We miss you very much.

But my London life, with intermittent expeditions abroad, was nearing its end with gathering speed. The idea of going to America took an ever firmer hold upon my mind, and events combined to bring about its realization. My parents no longer felt themselves able to allow me the free use of the flat in Airlie Gardens where I had lived since leaving Oxford. I received an invitation to meet him from a certain Mr. Carol M. Sax. Could he be Berenson's friend in some sort of disguise? After all, there were Americans who spelt night nite. Sax was not Berenson's friend, but he offered me an assistant professorship in art history at the University of Kentucky. Even though the salary was only $1,500 a year—about £300 at the prevailing rate of exchange—I was relieved, for I had already been granted my immigration number, which obliged me to arrive before a fixed and not far distant date. Having heard nothing from Professor Sachs I had faced the prospect of landing without work or money in a strange continent. (Knowing my predicament Audrey Mildmay— later the wife of John Christie—had suggested that I should join the company that was about to tour the United States with *The Beggar's Opera*—and was not even deterred by my telling her that I was the least musical man imaginable.) In order to avoid the by all accounts unpleasant if not degrading ordeal of examination on Ellis Island, off New York, I booked a passage to Montreal, where I could of course land without formality. Crossing the border between Canada and the United States, I gathered, was a matter of no difficulty at all.

CHAPTER FIVE

EMIGRATION TO AMERICA
AND RETURN

IT is said that a drowning man relives his life at the moment
before death. As I walked the deck of the *Ascania* memories of
my own life, in particular the chapter of it just closed, the four
years since I left the University, crowded upon me with a trance-like
vividness. I realized that, however my American journey might turn
out, I was wise to go. My intimate involvements with it had obscured
my view of a whole world that I must either see clear and with
detachment or else fail in the course I had set myself.

There were supporting reasons for my departure also: I was
becoming too much attached to a way of life that was leading nowhere in particular. I had not the facility to make a living by writing:
my monograph on Eric Gill, my massive catalogue of my father's
portrait drawings 1889–1925, published in 1926, to which Max
Beerbohm generously contributed an introduction, for instance, had
probably made less than £100 between them. From this distance of
time I cannot see how I survived. But somehow I did more than
survive: I frequented the Savile Club, but although I enjoyed its
genial atmosphere, especially the sight of Sir Edmund Gosse, Lytton
Strachey and other illustrious literary figures sitting at their special
table, I was not a clubman but was more at home at nighthaunts, to
one or another of which I went most nights with parties of friends. I
went, of course, to all the art exhibitions and I explored London far
and wide. I had gained, during those four years, a wide variety of
experience but the time had arrived for me to lead a more purposeful
life. But as the liner ploughed its way out into mid-Atlantic how
bitterly I missed my family, my friends and great grey London, so
noble in spite of its multifarious disfigurements. What I then experienced was a kind of death, but at twenty-six this kind of death is
usually of short duration. It is an eerie feeling to be an emigrant with
a home neither behind one nor ahead: to be without possessions

other than the contents of a couple of suitcases (the few trunks of books and pieces of furniture packed away in an attic back in Airlie Gardens seemed no longer effectively mine) was a bracing experience, for almost as satisfying as accumulating objects in which one delights is the sense of liberation that comes from parting from them.

I sent a cable to two Canadian sisters with whom I had been on friendly terms in London. 'Come and stay,' they cabled in reply, 'but why make us spend a dollar and a half on a cable?' No doubt, I thought, the parents of these two girls have saved up for years to enable them to be presented at Court, to enjoy the London Season, and I envisaged the small suburban house in which, unless I were more careful, I would hardly be a welcome guest.

Presently we entered the wide St. Lawrence. It seemed incongruous that Quebec, the first town of the New World I saw, should be so old. I had not yet set foot upon another continent, so that landing on the prosaic quay at Montreal was an exhilarating event. The taxi brought me to an imposing building. 'Mr. Dawes' apartment?' I enquired of the manservant who answered the bell. 'This', he replied with a certain hauteur, 'is Mr. Dawes' residence.' So the dollar and a half the Misses Dawes had expended upon their cable did not matter, I thought with relief. But neither the attractions of these sisters, Betty and Connie, nor the warm hospitality of their household, nor the proffered opportunity of exploring the Province of Quebec weakened my conviction that the sooner I began my new life the better; so I left for New York next day.

Among the letters of introduction I had brought was one to the great banker Otto Kahn, who entertained me to a luxurious lunch in a private room in the offices of Kuhn Loeb. This intelligent and powerful man was benevolence itself, but I was vaguely disquieted by the way, tactfully varying the form of the question, he asked what he could do for me. It did not seem to occur to him that I had called on him as a friend of whoever had given me the letter to him, just as I would have called on anyone else, and without ulterior purpose. The more I reflected upon the kindly, gently insistent enquiries of Mr. Kahn the more clearly did an intuition form in my mind that America was not a country in which, as in Europe, young writers, artists, friends of friends, however obscure, could foregather with important people, sometimes even on intimate terms, but that I was now in a country in which people moved in the society of their equals as measured by the income they enjoyed and only approached the important, above all the very rich, for some specific purpose. It was an intuition which, as I later discovered, somewhat oversimplified the facts, but it was not entirely ill-founded. At all events it so coloured my view of the American social structure that I put aside the numerous letters of introduction I had brought, and never during my years in the New World did I make use of another. This action made the break with the art world of England, which was, after all, the principal reason for my emigration, the more complete. No more influential friends of friends for me: henceforward I would foregather only with those whom I came to know on my own account.

At Lexington —where the University of Kentucky is—I was met by Professor Sax and taken to the Lafayette, a big hotel on Main Street which was to be my temporary home.

That evening I was invited to dinner at the comfortable, Edwardian red-brick house of the President of the University, Dr. Frank McVey, a tall dignified man with a genial manner tempered by the expression of his eyes that suggested a melancholy that he was unable to dissimulate. The Head of the Department of Fine Arts offered the sharpest contrast to the President: Professor Sax was short and pale, his watery eyes were of an unusual lightness, his indeterminately coloured hair was as though bleached by the sun, or rather by arc-lamps, for he was an impassioned man of the theatre, of the Little Theatre in particular. His knowledge of the fine arts was sketchy, and the vagueness of his manner when they were the subject of discussion seemed to me to have a touch of the defensive, but in what pertained to drama he had an easy and practical grasp. And he was evidently, like the President, a benevolent man of liberal mind. In England, in university circles at least, a degree of liberality of outlook is taken for granted. Here in Kentucky, as I understood before dinner was over, it was a somewhat exceptional quality, calling for some courage to sustain it. The University of Kentucky stood, evidently, for the liberal values, but it was on this account under intermittent and sometimes vicious attack from certain of the local sectarian colleges and their supporters in the State Legislature, more especially for its teaching of science, which was considered an affront to the fundamentalist doctrines propagated at these seats of learning.

Although I closely observed these two men, on account of the interest which they evoked both as characters and as men upon whom my immediate future would be largely dependent, my attention was more imperatively drawn to another member of the party. This was a young girl, a student at the University, named Elizabeth Smith. Her appearance alone—she was tall and slender, with a glossy helmet of dark hair—would have in any circumstances engaged my close attention, but her expression, which conveyed humour and high-spirited courage, and, what is rarer still, a generosity of spirit, a virtual absence of self-interest, made our meeting, though brief and formal, memorable for me.

Throughout my journey from England I was uneasily aware of an impending ordeal, namely my first lecture. So far as I can recall I had never spoken in public, and I had no notion how to prepare a lecture. Did one write the whole thing out, and read it? Or learn it by heart? Or speak extempore? The first course seemed to me to be liable to foster dullness—the other two were beyond my powers. While crossing the Atlantic I tried to envisage my ordeal and worked out a method of speaking from notes, which included quotations written out in full. Because it was far off I worked only languidly at the preparation of my first lecture: an ordeal sufficiently remote holds little fear; the young and healthy do not fear death. At last it was upon me, early on a brilliantly sunny morning. I went into the huge empty cafeteria and seated myself in a far corner with a cup of coffee for a last look at my notes. Presently a man came in, and of the hundreds of empty chairs he settled into that next to mine and began to talk. I did not conceal my exasperation, and it did not occur to me until weeks later that he had joined me out of sheer friendly concern for my solitude. My first lecture, which did not turn out as badly as I had feared, had one singular consequence: several students resigned from my course on the grounds that they could not understand me, and others joined because they liked to listen to the kind of English I spoke. One of my students, a hillbilly from the mountains who fell into neither of these categories, hearing that I had been in the United States for no more than a week, declared approvingly, 'You sure have learnt American fast.'

The early mornings are the times mostly clearly imprinted on my memory. The dazzling blue of the sky; in the big dining-room at the Lafayette the waiters, of every hue from ebony to peach, gathered gossiping round my table—I breakfasted late and almost alone after my early morning lecture—friendly disposed towards an Englishman. Of this friendliness on the part of negroes I was made aware even before I set foot in the South: I engaged a black porter in Pennsylvania Station, New York, and as soon as he heard me speak he exclaimed, with a grin, 'I'm British too.' One such lovely morning I said to Elizabeth Smith, looking up into the blue, 'We ought to go for a walk.' 'Oh,' she answered, 'the weather is likely to be sunny for quite a while, and we don't walk much—but we might ride.' And ride we often did, out along the Winchester Pike and past Ashland, the house that had been the home of Henry Clay, Kentucky's best-loved statesman, returning to the Art Department just in time for my first lecture. This place, a temporary single-storey structure, long since demolished, comprised a little theatre where the lectures as well as dramatic performances were given, an art library and some studios where painting and drawing were taught. Mr. Sax presided in his amateurish, unmethodical but humane and easy-going fashion over his Department, which he had made into a place that fostered lively appreciation of the arts. He was, moreover, rich and a bachelor, who himself financed some at least of the theatrical performances and art exhibitions at the Department. Painting was well taught by Edward Fisk, brother-in-law of Eugene O'Neill, a talented painter, who first drew my attention to the strange work of Charles Demuth, an American, whose art and style had the disturbing overtones of James's *Turn of the Screw*, of which he was the appropriate illustrator. Some acquaintance with Demuth led me back to Thomas Eakins, a puritan Pennsylvanian Courbet, and Albert Pinkham Ryder, a painter-equivalent of Herman Melville, brought up among the whalers of New England, for both of whom I felt an ardent admiration. So ardent that I prepared a short series of lectures about their work. In those days Americans, outside a few sophisticated centres, had not become proud of their native school, and my students, after listening to one or two of these, petitioned me to desist and to return to the painters of Europe. 'After all', the petition concluded, 'we signed on for your course to learn about artists, not Americans.' I grieved at these fine painters being unknown abroad and rejected at home, and prepared brief appreciations of their work. That on Ryder fell by the wayside but my *Note on Thomas Eakins*, published three years later in *Artwork*[1], was the

---

[1] Autumn 1930.

first tribute to this painter, so I was told long afterwards by his biographer, to be published outside the United States.

Elizabeth Smith I found was a student of mine. From the beginning she showed me much kindness and introduced me to her family. Through these introductions and owing to the friendliness of the people towards visitors from England and to the encouragement the University gave to members of the faculty to accept lecturing engagements—as a means of fostering goodwill—in other parts of the State, I came to know Lexington and the surrounding Bluegrass region more quickly and less superficially than might otherwise have been the case. The Smiths were at that time, with the exception of Elizabeth's brother Gilbert, living in a red-brick house of Georgian character, built in 1840 for Mrs. Smith's great-grandfather. It was situated at 225 South Limestone, a long street crossing the town from North to South. During the Civil War its cobbles echoed to the tramp of both the Union and Confederate armies, who successively occupied what was in effect a frontier city.

At least a dozen branches of Elizabeth's family had lived in America since Colonial days. There were Kings and Kennards and Spencers from the Eastern Shore of Maryland (the latter were related to the Washingtons and one of them had shared the Original Grant at Mount Vernon with his Washington cousins; another had been Governor of Barbados).

The other side of the family was Puritan in its origin and Elizabeth's father was descended from the first Governor (and also historian) of Plymouth Colony.

In the early 1830s the Kennards, with their grown-up children, crossed the Alleghenies to settle in Lexington. Their first place of residence was close to Christ Church and not far from Cheapside, where their son-in-law, Whittington King, founded the insurance brokerage firm which continued as the family business for more than a hundred years.

Subsequently the Kennards and their children chose a site for a family home on the south side of the Elkhorn river, which ran only a few hundred yards south of and parallel to Main Street. The site was on a hill above the river and therefore more healthy than the older part of the town, which was often ravaged by cholera epidemics. It was in more or less open country where only a few large houses had as yet been erected, and the view over the river and the little town below made it a particularly beautiful situation. At the same time it was quite close to the centre of urban life.

The house was a double house built in the shape of a U with wooden balconies facing each other across the gardens at the back and an iron balcony in front. At the end of the garden were the slave quarters, and there were stables for both houses.

The choice of site, however, turned out eventually an unhappy one. When the railway came to Lexington it was routed along the bank of the Elkhorn; soon the river was covered in and the character of the district altered considerably. The old families sold up and escaped. The Kennard branch of the family migrated to St. Louis. The King family remained, however, probably because the death of Gilbert King after the Civil War, in early manhood, left insoluble problems for a young widow with three children. One of these children was Elizabeth Whittington King, who became Mrs. Charles Smith, the mother of Elizabeth Smith through whom I came to know this remarkable family.

In 1927 when I first saw their house six or seven generations had lived at 225 South Limestone and, even though the district was one either of commercial buildings or of University lodgings or residences and a less pleasant place to live in than it had been, the family was far too deeply rooted to conceive of migrating.

The house was a dominating influence in the lives of the five children who lived in it with their parents Mr. and Mrs. Charles Smith and the latter's sister Miss Margaret King. The outside was austere in a Georgian style imported from Baltimore by the original Maryland family and in its truncated form (the other half of it has been repulsively altered) was not conspicuous. But the interior had a serenity and a beauty not entirely accounted for by its Georgian spaciousness and large windows; it may to some extent have been due to the house's island-like existence in its then shabby and noisy environment. It had a peace and a grace that reflected the lives of the people who had lived there and a romantic evocative presence like an old sailing ship washed up on a cluttered unlovely shore.

Elizabeth's father, Charles Judson Smith, was a partner in the old-established family firm of insurance brokers, Whittington King, but his interest was in English poetry rather than insurance, although the prosaic character of this occupation was somewhat redeemed by its bringing him into regular contact with a number of the splendid farms where horses were bred and trained in the parklike surroundings of the city. His kindness of heart, which led him, on occasion, even to pay his clients' overdue premiums, prevented, I fancy, the firm's prospering on a scale commensurate with his abilities.

Elizabeth's family, which had long played a prominent part in Lexington life, was intimately connected in particular with the University, of which Elizabeth's mother was a graduate and her aunt Margaret the eminent Librarian who built up the very fine library that now bears her name, and with Christ Church, the Episcopal cathedral, that had grown from the little frame house, built at the end of the eighteenth century in a city dominated by the ideas of Rousseau and Paine, into a large building of considerable distinction.

It quickly became apparent to me that Lexington was a town of fascinating character, with its old squares and streets, its buildings of Colonial aspect, but of later construction, and the opulent, undulating Bluegrass country that stretched away on every side. At that time this countryside contained all or almost all the most famous racehorse studs in America. I have a vivid memory of undulating fields and white-washed fences, of the finest mares and foals grazing in them, sheltered under huge trees—Kentucky was just beyond the ice-spread and its flora is of great variety and sub-tropical in profusion. But it was not primarily the visual charm of the place which held me fascinated—there were many towns in England of far higher architectural interest with environments still more beautiful—but a circumstance from which I enjoyed an experience entirely new, namely, a sense of the nearness of an epic period of history. The unfolding of history is, of course, a continuous process, but in British history the dramatic events belonged mostly either to the distant past, or they took place in foreign lands. In Lexington, on the contrary, I was constantly reminded by buildings, but more vividly still by near relations of principal actors, of the great dual drama of the Civil War and slavery, of whose aftermath evidence was conspicuous either in the form, for instance, of Colonel Dick Redd, who wearing the grey uniform of the army of the Confederacy would ride onto the University campus and, causing his horse to rear, would utter 'the Rebel Yell', or else in that of discernible silences and evasions, symptoms of tensions between families, between members of families even, which were legacies of the conflicts of the recent past.

Lexington was founded (if the term is not too formal) in 1775 by a party of hunters, but it was not until twelve years later that it possessed a newspaper, *The Kentucke Gazette*, the first to be published west of the Alleghenies. This, besides giving foreign news, usually some four months old, contained such notices as that subscribers to the meeting-house could 'pay in cattle or whiskey', and warnings that certain caches of 'wheat, corn, and potatoes are impregnated with Arsenic or other subtil poison' for consumption by raiding Indians. But within a few decades Lexington had become a thriving and even a sophisticated city: 'the inhabitants', wrote a traveller in 1816, 'are as polished, and I regret to add as luxurious as those of Boston, New York and Baltimore', and its surrounding scenery 'almost equals that of the Elysium of the Ancients'. Its beautiful University, Transylvania, had about as many students as Harvard.

In the meanwhile a generation of children was growing up, and some of them playing together, who were destined to be actors in the great dramas to come: among others, Mary Todd, who was to become the wife of Abraham Lincoln, John C. Breckinridge, one day to be Vice-President and candidate for President against Lincoln. At Transylvania was a fair-haired boy from Mississippi, born, however, in Kentucky, who lodged over what is now a grocer's shop a few paces from the Smiths' house on South Limestone: the boy's name was Jefferson Davis, afterwards President of the Confederate States. In a log cabin at Nolin's Creek, in the western part of the State, Abraham Lincoln was born. At Ashland lived Henry Clay, sometime Secretary of State and the dominant figure in Kentucky politics. The newly invented steamboats diverted trade from Lexington, but it remained a political centre of great importance on account of the stature of a number of its public men, the unique fertility of its soil, and as the centre of power in a key border State. 'I think to lose Kentucky', wrote Lincoln in a critical hour, 'is nearly the same as to lose the whole game.'

The circumstance that made the political situation so violently combustible was the existence of the 'peculiar institution', that is to say, of slavery. Lexington was the largest slaveholding community in the State, and it was upon the conclusions Lincoln reached upon its workings on his visits to the city that his attitude towards the slavery question was primarily formed.

When I lived in Lexington the 'peculiar institution' had been abolished barely sixty years, and relics and memories of it abounded. Slave cabins, abandoned or converted to some other purpose, were fairly common both in the city and its environs, and only a few minutes' walk from the Smiths' house and in full view of the office of Whittington King was the site of the slave auction block. On Cheapside 'bucks' and 'wenches', as well as children, had been sold 'separately if desired'—irrespective, that is, of family ties; marriage between slaves had in fact no legal status—and a few yards away from this site was the three-pronged poplar established by law as 'the public whipping-post of this county'. Near the Kings' first residence, too, had stood the slave jails of negro dealers, Pullam's, on Broadway, where the inmates were confined in verminous pens, eight feet square, which Lincoln could not but see from the home of one of his wife's relatives, and Megowan's, on Short and Mulberry. One of the Smiths' servants, old 'Uncle Anthony', had been born in slavery; another was the daughter of a slave.

In spite of the misery and degradation that the 'peculiar institution' involved, it was widely believed to show, in Kentucky, its least inhuman aspect.

By the middle of the century an agitation, courageous yet moderate, for the eventual abolition of slavery was being conducted in Kentucky, yet its effect was to provoke its defenders to an ever greater militancy; 'the peculiar institution' seemed indeed actually to flourish upon opposition. Although Lincoln believed that the issue was one which could 'never be successfully compromised', his experience of Kentucky made him aware of the adverse effects of abolitionist agitation and convinced him that slavery must never be allowed to gain the slightest foothold in new territory.

The leader of the abolitionist agitation in Kentucky was the most flamboyant public figure to emerge from the flamboyant political life of the State: Cassius Marcellus Clay.

Kentuckians are to this day high-spirited and prone to violence, and violence is still treated with a tolerance which at first surprises the visitor from abroad. During the nineteenth century it enjoyed a wide toleration. The slavery question roused unprecedented passion, and the emancipationists were often in danger of assault and threatened with death.

Born in the Bluegrass, a son of the largest slave-owner in the State, Clay became a convinced emancipationist while he was still at Yale, and on his return to Kentucky his dedication to the cause, his imposing presence, his eloquence, his resonant voice, his unflagging energy and his courage—conspicuous even in a society in which courage was a common virtue—gave him a prominent place among the emancipationists. Before he joined them the emancipationists were intimidated by the aggressive slave-owning interest, which commanded a very wide measure of popular support.

From the time when he joined them, however, Clay's own militancy made them the aggressors, and he accordingly drew upon himself an egregious volume of malignity, on which he thrived. The history of his leadership is a saga of bloodshed and controversy. At a political meeting he was attacked by a crowd of thugs, and an assassin especially imported, armed with a six-barrelled pistol, called out to him, 'Run or be shot'. Clay stood his ground; he was shot. Feeling the ball under his left rib, and knowing he might be shot five more times, he closed on his opponent and 'cut away in good earnest' with his knife, cut open his skull, and, after depriving him of an ear and an eye, threw him over a wall. After a trial that was a sensation throughout the State and beyond, Clay, eloquently defended by his illustrious relative Henry Clay, was acquitted, and the emancipationists had won their first victory. But what still better illustrates the climate of violence were the defensive precautions that Cassius Clay found it necessary to take to protect the office of *The True American*, the anti-slavery paper he founded in Lexington by the corner of Main and Mill streets. He lined the outside doors with heavy sheet iron; the only approach to the office, a steep narrow stairway, was guarded by two loaded brass four-pounder cannon, mounted behind folding-doors. The office was equipped with rifles, shotguns and lances. There was an escape hatch, and a device which would enable him to blow up the office were it invaded. It was largely on Clay's advice that Lincoln proclaimed the emancipation of the slaves. Disappointed of a place in Lincoln's cabinet, he went as ambassador to Russia. Back at Whitehall, his large family house outside Lexington, a festive occasion was disturbed by a Russian ballerina with a boy of whom Clay admitted the paternity. His wife left him and Clay lived by himself in his forty-roomed house, some-times so lonely that he opened the windows to admit the bats. At the age of eighty-four he married a girl of fifteen. The sheriff's posse which arrived to remove the child-bride he treated to a Churchillian oration, and after firing at them with a cannon he charged, armed with his famous bowie-knife and a pistol given him by Lincoln. 'We went out to Whitehall', the sheriff reported to his superiors, 'but it didn't do no good. It was a mistake to go out there with only ten men.' Clay died alone, in his great house, at the height of a tempest, at the age of 93, in 1903—within my own lifetime.

These and innumerable other such events were still part of living tradition: the family of Henry Clay still lived at Ashland, and I knew members of it; I was on friendly terms with Miss Laura, daughter of Cassius Clay, with members of the Breckinridge family (Robert J. Breckinridge saved Kentucky from secession and a near relative, John C. Breckinridge, was the Vice-President who sacrificed a great career to fight with the Confederates); Mrs Margaret Preston John-son, whom I knew well, was the granddaughter of Robert Wickliffe, the most ruthless upholder of the slavery interest and Clay's princi-pal opponent—a woman of unusual liberality of outlook and en-lightenment, and an active ecumenicist long before it was fashionable to be so.

In this brief sketch of Lexington I have dwelt upon controversy and the violence that it so often provoked, but in spite of this, even perhaps because instincts elsewhere repressed had been given free rein in Kentucky, I found the majority of the people I came to know there not only high-spirited but exceptional for their kindness and their enlightened values and their loyalty towards their friends. Before many months had passed I became not only greatly attached to Lexington but, such was the warmth of my welcome, I began to feel also a sense of identity with it. My welcome was of course largely due to my intimacy with the Smith family. Of this family the dominant member was Elizabeth's mother, Elizabeth King Smith: a warm and vivid personality, deeply involved in numerous charitable and other fruitful public activities—in particular those connected with Christ Church Cathedral (of the official history of which she was the joint author). Into these multifarious activities she threw herself, not in a spirit of self-sacrifice, but in one of zest—a zest which she communicated to a wide circle of friends. In contrast to this ever youthful and gregarious character was her sister Margaret, the University's reticent and scholarly Head Librarian.

Two of Elizabeth's sisters, Frances and Cynthia, were also students at the University. In spite of being strongly partisan in both religion and politics, the interests of the Smith household gave 225 South Limestone something of the character of a college common room, and its situation between the University and the centre of the city made it a natural meeting place for the Bluegrass' livelier minds. The family at that time were Republicans in the Cassius Clay tradition: they had been liberators of their slaves and opponents of secession. But in spite of these attitudes they fully shared the indignation of their friends of every outlook at what they believed to be the greatly distorted picture of slavery as it existed among them in *Uncle Tom's Cabin*, and in particular in the households of those in which Harriet Beecher Stowe stayed as a guest when she visited Lexington. The book was accordingly forbidden reading for Elizabeth's mother and aunt.

The extreme reluctance of Kentuckians, particularly marked among the older generation, to mention slavery, much less to discuss it—I understood that it was rarely referred to even among intimates —suggested to me that it had caused a kind of collective trauma (for it affected alike those whose families had been involved and whose families had not), a deep sense of guilt. The reason was not, I thought, as complex as it at first seemed to me. Had the institution flourished in a primitive and brutal society it could have had no such effect, but the society of mid-nineteenth-century Kentucky was a highly civilized one, and, although more violent, it was neither more nor less brutal than that of any other part of the English-speaking world, and the institution was accordingly utterly incongruous with the prevailing moral sense. The very ferocity of the slave-owning power was indicative, I think, of a conscience that was at bottom uneasy.

Another popular classic in which Lexington was drawn upon is *Gone with the Wind*. The engaging 'Madam' kept a 'house' in the red-light district, north-east of the old post office. When she died one of our most intimate friends, Joseph Clark Graves, a scholarly man of taste, a bibliophile who established a private printing press, sent to a wide range of Lexington's most respectable citizens heavily black-bordered cards in unsealed envelopes, purporting to come from the 'house', thanking the recipents for the 'magnificent floral offerings' that they had sent for her funeral. There were many angry wives in Lexington that day, and many puzzled, disconcerted, but not invariably innocent husbands.

Kentucky was pervaded by sentiments of aggressive Protestant-ism, and many of those whom I came to know, especially among the older generation, however liberal their attitude towards negroes, socialists, and other suspect classes, were distinctly anti-Catholic and this is a rather different fashion from an equivalent Protestant society in England. For English Protestants Catholicism is primarily something that England is considered to have outgrown, a system of ecclesiastical organization and of belief which, however much it may be resented, is widely recognized as something deeply implicated in English history: the Common Law, for example, being so largely the creation of mediaeval legislators, many of them ecclesiastics; the Established Church deriving its organization and much of its liturgy directly from the Church established by a papal emissary. To travel anywhere in England is impossible for anyone with a sense of history without constant reminder of how recently, in the long vista of time, England was a Catholic country. But in most parts of the United States such is far from being the case. So much that is noblest and most characteristic has been the work of Protestants—Washington, Jefferson, Lee, Lincoln, the makers of the New England Spring, statesmen, lawyers, poets, for whom the religion of their remoter ancestors in the countries on the far side of the wide Atlantic which their families had left, often as refugees, was something so distant as to be scarcely more than fable. Even leaving remote ancestors aside, there has never been in English-speaking North America a Catholic society—not even in seventeenth century Maryland—that has been regarded with such respect as that enjoyed by the English Catholic minority. The steadfastness and courage of the recusant gentry, for instance, were admired however much their religion might be abhorred, while a remarkable number of men of genius and talent sprang from or else joined this minority—St. Thomas More, Charles II, Dryden, Crashaw, Pope, Newman, Acton, Hopkins, to name a few of the most illustrious. Moreover, in North America Catholicism has been believed by innumerable liberal-minded people to represent a threat to liberty of thought and even to demo-cratic institutions, and it has long disposed of far greater political power than it did in England under the last two Catholic sovereigns, and this power was predominantly concentrated in the hands of members of a single race. Denied full scope for their conspicuous aptitudes for politics by British rule, the Irish, possessing the added advantage of arriving as immigrants with a full, indeed an exceptional, command of the English language, became in every field the leaders of their fellow emigrants, nowhere more conspicuously than in the Catholic Church, which became, so to say, a polyglot army largely at every level under Irish command. While ardently loyal to the United States the Irish were, consciously and unconsciously, resentful of the specifically English traditions and affiliations of those who continued to be, even after they had become a minority, in many respects the leading citizens. So it came about that the Catholic Church in the United States had come to be regarded as the antithesis of much of what was most characteristically American and of what innumerable Americans in general regarded as most precious in their heritage.

American Protestantism itself showed some bizarre aspects in Kentucky. Elizabeth and I, driving into Lexington by an unfamiliar route and short of petrol, saw a neon sign which bore the words 'service station' and the familiar upright cylindrical forms, painted red and white, beneath. Closer inspection suggested that there was something unusual about the construction and texture of the pumps. Then we noticed, in small letters beneath 'Service station', the words 'for Souls': we had been lured by what was in fact an unusual façade of a tabernacle of some enterprising sect. There was a clergyman, a minister of some 'fringe' sect, or even, perhaps, 'self-employed', named, or self-nicknamed, the Reverend Tornado Jones, who, after condemning sin with a robustness unusual even among evangelists, got drunk in a neighbouring town and shot two people to death.

The fact that I was of partly Jewish descent, intimately connected with the art world (which had not assumed the prestige which later attached to it but was widely regarded as somewhat disreputable), uninterested in games or sport—all this seemed to count for nothing in my disfavour in Kentucky, but my being a Catholic was another matter. I avoided theological discussion and my observance was inconspicuous, but I was frequently conscious of my friends' uneasy awareness of my religion, more particularly those of the older generation. (In this atmosphere my friendship with Elizabeth's two younger sisters Cynthia and Peggy was particularly warming. They appeared to be congenitally free from every sort of religious bigotry, to have been born indeed with built-in principles of toleration and mutual respect. Peggy's holidays from school I always enjoyed: her wit delighted me and she on her side gave my jokes a very spirited reception.) My increasing friendship with Elizabeth and her sisters accordingly provoked in their parents a concern that all their kindness to me did not mask. This concern would doubtless have remained somewhat academic—what parents are there who have no occasion for concern about the young men who become their daughters' friends?—had not my prospects been suddenly improved as a consequence of a long telegram I received from Paul J. Sachs, of Harvard, in February 1928, telling me that he had recently heard from Berenson that I was at the University of Kentucky, that he would not himself have thought of my entering the American academic world in that particular way but he gathered in the event all had worked out very well, but that he considered it time to make a move. In reply to my acknowledgement came a further telegram that read in part: 'Please meet me Schenley Hotel Pittsburgh on Tuesday February twenty eighth at three o'clock'.

In the sombre Victorian hotel where Duse died, at once dowdy and opulent, I met Paul J. Sachs. A first glance suggested that this short, solid figure, discreetly but expensively dressed, belonged to the world of business, of banking perhaps, rather than that of scholarship. A second, especially at the benevolent, sharply perceptive brown eyes, gave intimations of the qualities that had made him the dean of teachers of art history in the entire United States and the confidant of the leading members of the profession. How, he asked me, did I happen to be at the University of Kentucky? He frowned at my account of the retention of Berenson's letter and laughed at the confusion of Sax with Sachs, then briskly recalling how little time we had together told me that I had spent long enough in Lexington and that, were I willing to consider it, he was prepared to offer me an assistant-professorship in the newly established Department of Fine Art in the University of Pittsburgh.

I returned to Lexington in low spirits: there was no doubt in my mind that Professor Sachs' offer must be accepted, for the University of Kentucky, where the teaching of Art History was concerned, was a dead-end and I could scarcely exist on my tiny salary, out of which I was still making remittances for Oxford debts. I looked forward with prospective nostalgia to the impending end of the academic year when I would see the last of Kentucky, where I had so many friends and where, in a beautiful setting, were so many vestiges of a civilization which, as in the other Southern States, exercised over me, as I believe over most English people, an irresistible attraction. But what troubled me more was the impending separation from Elizabeth. I was immensely attracted by her but what moved me even more was the realization that by the purest chance I had become friends in this distant place with one who was, quite simply, the best human being I had ever known, the freest from self-interest and the readiest to extend a helping hand to anyone in need and who thought by instinct for other people before herself— a person who in more dangerous days would have accepted martyrdom. But no one could less have resembled the professional doer of good, the enthusiastic supporter of the underdog, right or wrong, than the slender, smiling figure on horse-back, with the dark glossy hair. As the end of term approached it became clear that a choice must be made between losing the companionship of this unique being and proposing marriage. I felt unready for marriage, however; I had not journeyed four thousand miles in order 'to settle down'; the very idea of marriage (in relation to myself) was something that I could not contemplate without shock. And my income was some £300 a year. But the truth is—although I had not learnt it then—that one is never ready for the great events in one's life; they have a way of coming inopportunely, in a way that upsets one's plans—especially death, even though it relieves one of all one's earthly responsibilities. One is never prepared—one has always at too short notice to prepare oneself. Luckily for me I did prepare myself, however imperfectly, and, not without the overcoming of many—and how well justified—doubts, I was accepted. I wrote 'luckily for me' because my love of beauties, hitherto passionate but irresponsible, might so easily have led me to disaster instead of to the wisest action of my life. Elizabeth's parents accepted our engagement with goodwill shadowed by anxiety about my being a Catholic—unsuspecting that what they reckoned to be my gravest disability was the most substantial among my slender assets.

Absence of possessions over the past months had brought a

simplicity to my life which I found novel and welcome—not that I had ever possessed anything of substance—but the prospect of marriage brought a change of feeling. I remember many occasions when Elizabeth and I, without even a nickel between us to buy a cup of coffee, walked for hours up and down South Limestone and Walnut Streets oppressed by possessing nothing at all but a few clothes and those books and pieces of furniture in a far-away London attic. I had not even a room of my own, but shared one with a furniture salesman—a man whose recurrent shocked solicitude for what he believed to be the morals of European women prompted him to ask questions which interrupted my sleep.

That summer Elizabeth, accompanied by her sister Frances and me, paid a flying visit to England to enable her to meet my parents. In the autumn I plunged into the murk of Pittsburgh. Natives of this city and visitors of later years speak of it as a place transformed, but in 1928 and 1929 it was not an agreeable place, for an outsider at all events, to live in. As a producer of steel it made a memorable impression: the huge mills emerged out of the low-lying fog over the Monongehela River like battleships out of a sea mist, and by night low-hanging clouds reflected the satanic red of the flames from the blast furnaces. However memorable, this was not sufficient to sustain the visitor's spirits. Pittsburgh University seemed to me to be an inhuman place, an institution like an office which students attended for the sole purpose of securing the degrees necessary for their several careers, and which, unlike the University of Kentucky, generated no life of its own. My lectures evoked little response; I varied my approach, but with minimal success. For one thing many of the students were tired by the outside work they were forced to undertake to maintain themselves: I remember my chagrin at the discovery that a student whom I had rebuked for some stupidity had come straight from an all-night petrol station. But the exhaustion of many of them does not explain my want of success: I simply failed to discover a way of stimulating their interest, as it seemed to me I had quickly succeeded, although entirely without experience, in Lexington the year before. The newly established Department of Fine Arts was an island, somewhat isolated from the rest of the University, which was predominantly devoted to technology and business—that, at least, was how it appeared to our small staff; we were isolated, too, from the social life of the city, in spite of the efforts made on our behalf by the founder of the Department, Miss Helen Frick. Nor was our Department a place that offered much solace to an exile, or anyone else, I fancy. Professor Clapp was often tense and anxious; he was a scholar of distinction, and the cares of organization in such unresponsive surroundings must have tried him severely. Under his direction, however, the Department maintained high standards; my two other colleagues, Walter Hovey and Marvin Ross, were able and well-trained art historians. But although we all got along well enough our companionship lacked warmth.

My year in Pittsburgh was not without compensations. I made friends with Andrey Avinoff, a Russian of extraordinary intellectual versatility, who served on the staff of the Carnegie Institute, and his colleague Elliott Martin Browne, an Englishman who was building up a lively Department of Drama; the Comès family, whose house was a genial and kindly place that would have made it unusual anywhere, so that in Pittsburgh it was particularly unusual; the Mann family—the father was the Episcopalian Bishop, who said to me, 'Remember, here in Pittsburgh whatever religion we may profess, we're all of us really Presbyterians'; and lastly Father Coakley, Rector of the Church of the Sacred Heart, a liberal-minded Catholic priest, a man of exuberant spirits and a generous host, whose Sunday luncheons with his curates, occasions of lively conversation and gargantuan consumption, I am unlikely to forget. Pittsburgh seemed to me like a vast encampment encircling the steel works, peopled by Italians, Czechs, Hungarians, Irish, Germans, and ruled by a tightly-knit coterie of Scots. One of my pleasures was attending boxing matches in the steel works at night between the men who worked there: I have rarely heard silence more pregnant than the silence of the crowds of watching men, in the presence of the huge still machines, that was broken only by the impact of leather upon flesh and bone.

Among the memorable experiences that Pittsburgh afforded were my visits to the painter John Kane, who lived in a ramshackle wooden frame house near the railway tracks, made available to him, he told me, by an Order of nuns. Kane was a Scottish Catholic and upon the walls of his room hung paintings of subjects recollected from his youth in Scotland, Highland dancers and the like. 'I'm always thinking of when I was a boy and I've always wanted to go back and see what it's like now', he said. Unlike those of many emigrants in whom success has loosened the bonds with the country of their birth the sentiments of Kane for Scotland were intense. But emigration at about the age of nineteen had not brought him success: Pittsburgh, where he had worked as a coal miner, carpenter, labourer and house painter, had dealt hardly with him, and even when I knew him and he had begun to be known as an artist he had to accept occasional employment as a house painter. 'I don't mind doing it,' he said to me, 'except it's a bit of a waste of time for a man who's not got much time left. All the same it was house painting and railway coach painting that gave me the idea of painting pictures.'

The first time I went to see John Kane, probably towards the end of 1928, I was deeply impressed by an uncompleted 'Self-Portrait', the finest 'primitive' I thought, and think still, to be painted since the death of Henri Rousseau—though John Kane, lacking all training and, what was a far graver disadvantage, access to the world's masterpieces, was as a 'primitive' far more authentic than he. In the 'Self-Portrait' he is represented against a black background full-face and stripped to the waist, his features spare and taut, his body, although he was approaching his seventieth year, of startling strength. John Kane was gnarled and battered, of a philosophic and benevolent disposition—the only spark of vanity I ever detected in him expressed itself in the meticulousness with which he brushed his, I think, black-dyed hair, in particular his prominent forelock. He was amused by the degree to which I was fascinated by this 'Self-Portrait' and the way I went straight up to it on arrival to follow its progress, for he seemed to prefer his 'recollections' of Scotland and his Pittsburgh landscapes. One day he said, 'You'd better have my portrait; nobody's ever liked it so much. You take it away with you.' I answered that it would be a great privilege to possess it, but as he was beginning to be recognized he must keep it by him. With the reckless generosity sometimes found among the very poor he insisted, but I would not accept it. A few years later I saw it in the window of a dealer's gallery, and in 1939 it was presented by John D. Rockefeller, Junior, to the Museum of Modern Art, New York.

Towards the end of my first academic year I began to be concerned about my future. In spite of the kindness of friends my life in the grim twilight of Pittsburgh afforded me meagre satisfaction. Continuing to teach a subject in which I possessed no degree offered doubtful prospects, and after several changes of intention a project inspired by Elizabeth took an ever firmer hold upon me, that of returning to England after our wedding to take a degree in the History of Art, and giving Elizabeth in the meanwhile an opportunity of coming to know the country that I was determined should be our eventual home. After paying off the last of my Oxford debts I had accumulated a sum sufficient to maintain us for about a year, mainly from a bequest of £500 from my uncle Charles, my father's elder brother. My confidence in my prospects of an academic career in America were heightened by the reception on both sides of the Atlantic of my book *The Artists of the Eighteen Nineties* (the New York edition was titled *A Pot of Paint*, from Ruskin's attack on Whistler). It was treated a good deal more seriously than it deserved —it was given nearly a column in *The Times* and more in the *New York Herald Tribune* and long reviews in many of the serious and even the learned weeklies and monthlies, but in fact it largely deserved the savage unsigned review contributed by Clive Bell to *The Nation & Athenaeum*. Its redeeming features were, in spite of the lost opportunities to which I have earlier referred, the inclusion of much unpublished information, and an occasional flicker of intellectual liveliness and independence. One consequence of its publication was a letter from Arnold Bennett which, notwithstanding strictures upon my grammatical and stylistic shortcomings, suggested that he was not altogether disappointed in my first serious book.

75 Cadogan Square S.W.
21st January 1929

My dear John,
    I have much enjoyed your book, and I must write and tell you so. The Introductory Essay is in my opinion rather wonderful. The second Introductory Essay is also very good indeed. But the first one contains ideas I have never seen expressed before, and which I had certainly never thought of for myself, even in a vague way. There is a lot of genuine sociology in this part of the book, and a large part of it is original work. Or so I think. . . . The sooner you leave your present wigwam [i.e. Pittsburgh] and return to this city, the better it will be for the said city. You evidently have something to say. I congratulate you on 'The Artists of the 1890's' . . .

A review by another old friend gave particular pleasure. In *The Mask*, the esoteric and beautifully printed journal he produced in Florence, Gordon Craig wrote of it glowingly. The suspicion that I owed his praise to his goodwill towards me rather than to the merits of my book did not diminish my pleasure.

At the end of the Summer Term I left Pittsburgh, without regret, and returned to Lexington. On 11th June Elizabeth and I were married at Christ Church Cathedral by Dr. Lewis W. Burton, formerly Bishop of Lexington, a venerable whitebearded figure of transparent goodness. Also of singular unselfconsciousness. When I arrived in the vestry before the ceremony he was enquiring of the Dean, Dr. Charles Hale, 'When the congregation enters, shall we be discovered at prayer?'

I recall as clearly as though it were yesterday the rapt look on Elizabeth's face, as though she were looking at something unseen by the rest, and next the happy faces of the Negroes as we emerged from the Cathedral into the fierce sunlight. The Negroes have the capacity shared by no white race except the Italians for a total participation in joys and sorrows not their own. We took the night train for New York and left a wonderful demonstration of goodwill—for the Smith family was greatly beloved—before it had reached its zenith.

After we had left the luxury of the Plaza Hotel and the affectionate little world of Lexington receded into the past we began, on board the England-bound *Tuscania*, to take stock of the prospect before us: Elizabeth with more confidence than I who was beset by secret misgivings, due partly to being without employment, partly to a sense of being weighed down by responsibility, as though I had married, not a wife far more capable than I, but a whole family of helpless dependents. (Had I known that within a few months the small sum I had set aside for our maintenance during the year or two ahead would have all but vanished in the impending slump, my forebodings would have been more sombre still.) To have been married anywhere in Lexington except Christ Church Cathedral, to which Elizabeth's family had been devotedly attached since its early days, as well as most members of her own and her family's friends, would have inflicted an unforgivable public insult upon them all. Before the ceremony I wrote to the Catholic parish priest to acquaint him with these circumstances. My letter was returned with a rudely phrased sentence of prohibition scrawled across it against taking the course which I proposed. Back in London I obtained permission from the Westminster Cathedral authorities to marry according to the rites of the Catholic Church, for failure to do so would, of course, have involved my excommunication, a condition which Elizabeth, in spite of her anticatholic sentiments, would not have tolerated. 'Why', asked the priest to whom I applied, 'did you marry in an Episcopalian church?' I explained the circumstances, adding that I did not recognize in the Lexington priest's voice the authentic voice of the Church. 'I sympathize', said the Westminster priest as he signed the relevant form.

A few days later I experienced for the first (though not for the last) time the intrusion of the press into matters of private concern. A harsh-voiced lady journalist telephoned on behalf of *The Daily Express* to say that she had ascertained that the impending marriage ceremony was in fact a second, and unless I was prepared to make a statement explaining the reason for it, she would draw her own conclusions and print them. We were anxious that the ceremony should not be made public, lest it should hurt Elizabeth's family by suggesting that the previous ceremony was defective. Fortunately my brief service with the *Express* enabled me to frustrate her. We were married on 11th October by Father Holland in the private chapel at the Brompton Oratory, in the presence of my parents and my sisters; Richard de la Mare, the publisher son of the poet, and Thomas Emmett, were the witnesses. When I was required to produce a silver coin with which, symbolically, to endow Elizabeth with my worldly goods, I searched my pockets in vain. Neither of us, in fact, was able to produce so much as a penny, and the necessary shilling had to be borrowed from Thomas Emmett. Outside the Oratory when the brief ceremony was over we encountered W. R. Inge, the militantly anticatholic Dean of St. Paul's, who enquired how it was that virtually the whole Rothenstein family should be standing on the pavement in the Brompton Road at midday. My father, who was not only strictly truthful but unusually outspoken, mildly replied, 'Just going for a walk, Inge'. I never heard him tell a lie, before or since.

For the next two and a half years we occupied my old flat at the top of 13 Airlie Gardens, where we led a precarious existence. I enrolled as a student at University College, London, with the intention of obtaining a doctorate in the History of Art, but at once encountered an unexpected difficulty. Professor Tonks, Head of the Slade, objected to the proposed subject of my thesis, and when pressed by Tancred Borenius, the versatile and prolific Finn who was Professor of Art History, declared that he saw no reason why degrees in the History of Art should be granted at all: Borenius persisted—'don't worry', he said to me, at a difficult moment in negotiations, a wide grin on his wily cherub's face, 'Ve unhook a degree for you—only you must be patient', and thanks to his benevolent persistence my subject, 'the interaction of Classicism and Romanticism in Nineteenth Century Painting' (or something of the sort), and in the fullness of time my thesis, was accepted, defended in a viva and I became, in 1931, a Doctor of Philosophy. The dreaded viva took an unexpected turn. The two examiners, Borenius and Louis Clarke, Director of the Fitzwilliam Museum, Cambridge, were quickly at loggerheads, and I found myself the arbiter between these two men, both infinitely beyond me in learning. My thesis, in modified form, was published as a book under the title *Nineteenth Century Painting*.

Our life during these years was a strange one, chiefly on account of the dichotomy between its public and its private aspects. Outwardly we appeared, in a modest way, successful: my writings were well received; I had returned from two years spent in American universities—which was far from the routine operation it has since become—without discredit, and we lived in a house where many of the most interesting personalities in London foregathered. To ourselves our situation had a different look. Owing to the loss of the small sum just now referred to and the lack of other means of support I was compelled to break one of the conditions governing my admission to the University, which forbade the undertaking of paid work, by tutoring. I was anything but a brilliant tutor, and engagements only intermittently came my way. There was little in my academic record to justify my regarding my doctorate as a certainty. As I became absorbed in the multifarious interests of London the prospect of academic life in America seemed every day less inviting, although present poverty and an uncertain future at times weighed heavily.

These years offered opportunities of hard work which I did not neglect as I had at school and university: besides writing my thesis I finished my novel *Morning Sorrow*, begun in America, and compiled a book of reproductions of paintings and drawings entitled *British*

Artists and the War and in the Introduction I expressed a positive attitude towards the visual arts. I called in question the validity of the doctrine of Significant Form, and of the assumption of the advocates of Abstraction that form and colour were in some mysterious way superior when divorced from representation, and I maintained that the contrary was true; I challenged the validity of a statement by the immensely pugnacious and influential Clive Bell that the development of art was 'conditioned mainly by its own nature', that it was a hermetic activity deriving from a life independent of the world outside and evolving according to its own laws.

This formulation of my attitude towards the most controversial issue in the art of the time—my book was more widely read than I expected—had lasting consequences for me. My father and Roger Fry had around 1910 had a serious disagreement. This is not the place to add to what has been written about it elsewhere, but owing to the fact that a number of Roger Fry's 'Bloomsbury' friends took his part with varying degrees of militancy, from that time onwards my father stood somewhat apart from the 'progressive' forces with which his liberal mind and predominantly French formation had identified him. The opinions expressed in *British Artists and the War* caused me—until then too obscure to warrant attention—to be identified with him as unfriendly or at least indifferent towards the avant-garde movements. These were not my only publications. Being one day entirely without resources I asked my father for permission to publish the letters written to him by Oscar Wilde, and as a consequence *Sixteen Letters from Oscar Wilde* appeared, elegantly produced by Fabers, with two unpublished caricatures by Max and one by my father drawn specially for the book. I had discussed the project with Gide some time before, who warmly approved it, describing letter viii as the most important unpublished letter from Wilde he knew of. Gide wrote in acknowledgement of the copy I sent him:

Cuverville en Caux, le 4 Juin 1930

Cher Monsieur,

Est-ce bien vous que j'ai connu tout enfant, dans ce très court séjour que je fis en Gloucestershire, dont j'ai gardé si excellent souvenir? Combien me touche le reflet que je trouve de mon passage auprès de vous, dans votre preface. Ce précieux petit volume, présenté de manière si exquise, me fait le plus grand plaisir, et je vous remercie d'avoir bien voulu me l'envoyer. Je viens de relire ces lettres avec une émotion bien vive. Cela à laquelle votre note préliminaire fait allusion, est, en effet, des plus belles, et mérite d'être également connue par le public Français. Je vais la signaler à Jean Paulhan, le directeur de la N. R. F., et pense la traduire moi-même s'il accepte, ainsi que je l'y engagerai à la publier (mais peut-être jugera-t-il qu'il est préférable de la donner dans le texte original).

Veuillez me croire très sensible a ce que vous me dîtes de mes 'Faux-Monnayeurs'. Ce livre n'est sans doute point fait pour ce que l'on appelle le 'grand public'; il n'est d'autant plus précieux de savoir qu'il put occuper l'attention de quelques lecteurs d'élite, pour que je l'écrivais.

Croyez à mes sentiments bien attentifs et cordiaux.

André Gide

The writing to which I gave most thought and labour was *Morning Sorrow*. My interest was engaged by writing not less than by the visual arts, and had the circumstances of my life developed otherwise, had I been possessed of independent means of support, I would have given all my time to writing, imaginative and historical as well as critical.

Being determined to free myself from the temptation to write disguised autobiography—a besetting temptation to writers of first novels—I made three sisters, country girls, the principal characters. To anyone wishing to treat of the springs of action, the secret reasons of the heart and their consequences in terms of the most intimate relations between one human being and others, the novel must be an attractive medium. The opportunities of treating of them with anything approaching candour in a biography of a contemporary are in general restricted by the family and friends of the subject, and in that of someone belonging to the remoter past by an insufficiency of knowledge. My own novel was a mere apprentice work, but the writing of it gave me some insight into the possibilities of a medium in which motives and their results in terms of action may be treated with all the insight which the writer has at his command.

An odd circumstance was my calling one of its principal characters 'Lord Chalgrove' (on account of my reverence for John Hamp-

den who died there), for many years later we made our home near
Chalgrove and Elizabeth became so closely involved in a controversy
relating to the future of Chalgrove airfield that for a time her name
and that of Chalgrove became almost synonymous.

By this time I was able to place without much effort my writings
on the visual arts, but I was doubtful whether my novel would be so
readily accepted.

I accordingly sought the advice of Arnold Bennett but the moment
was unpropitious.

> 75 Cadogan Square S.W.
> 10 May 1930

My dear John,

In reply I will be frank. I should be delighted to read your
novel, but one cannot read and criticize a novel in less than a
day, and just now I am exceedingly busy on a little affair of my
own amounting to 240,000 words. The affair will not be concluded until the end of June. Until it is concluded the Empire,
my relatives, my child, my friends may go to the devil as far as I
am concerned. But of course you rightly want it to be handled at
once. Have any of your people read it? If so, send me a certificate
that it is a remarkable work and I will give you a special instruction to a good literary agent . . . Have I made myself clear, and am
I sure of the continuance of your affections?

> Yours
> Arnold Bennett.

One day I was invited to call at Constable's offices in Orange Street.
Elizabeth and I walked all the way back from Orange Street to Airlie
Gardens, *Morning Sorrow* accepted and its praise by Michael Sadleir
sounding in our ears and the green of the foliage in Hyde Park and
the red of the 'buses heightened to trance brightness by our happiness.

Morning Sorrow was benevolently received—its defects, improb-
ability of theme, weaknesses in construction, thinnesses of characteri-
zation, and others, were noted, but its virtues—such as they were—
evoked praise quite beyond their deserts.

One of the odd experiences that comes to an author is the assurance with which reviewers express contrary opinions upon the same
subject. 'The author of this book', according to *The Catholic Herald*,
'ought not to have written a number of the scenes that are described',

while according to *The New Statesman* mine was an 'old-fashioned story—almost one hears Bow Bells chiming'. One review gave me particular pleasure: that by Arnold Bennett in *The Evening Standard* in which he wrote that I had 'many of the qualities of a born novelist'. This from the author of *The Old Wives' Tale* meant much to a writer so painfully aware of his defects. Likewise the verdict of Max Beerbohm, 'I admire it very much. It is a subtle and searching work, and seems to me to have great beauty in a way of its own'. A letter that especially pleased me came from Florence, the widow of Thomas Hardy. This read, in part: 'I hardly like to mention your novel to you yourself as I know the best writers hate the insincere flattery that is so often poured upon them, and I really do feel shy about praising a man's work to his face. However, I am so pleased that you do know now how I liked your novel: indeed I am just re-reading it.'

This letter had a consequence that I could not have remotely foreseen. It concluded with an invitation to meet Desmond Flower, who worked at Cassell & Company (of which he succeeded his father as chairman). We became friends and his firm published, two years later, my *Introduction to English Painting*. After the Second World War he gave a fellow officer an introduction to me, which secured him a junior temporary post at the Tate. It was he who eventually succeeded me as director—but more of this in its proper place.

But I was not to be a writer of novels. In the winter of 1930, very shortly after the publication of my book, Elizabeth and I were invited to a small party by W. G. Constable, then Director of the Courtauld Institute of Art in London University, after the opening of the great exhibition of Italian Art at Burlington House. Our host took Elizabeth aside and said to her that I ought not to return to America and that my services were needed at home, in particular in the field of provincial art gallery direction. This field did not in the least attract me, but I was responsive to the suggestion that I could be of service in my own country. After I had taken my doctorate I agreed, at Constable's persuasion, to accept the invitation of a group of Liverpool citizens to allow my name to be put forward as a candidate for the vacant directorship of the Walker Art Gallery, which offered a challenge inasmuch as in those days this institution was the most militant and opulent provincial stronghold of the most debased kind of popular-academic art. In the fullness of time I was invited to attend an interview, at which my shyness had a farcical consequence: I was unable to utter a single syllable and in ignominious silence I retired from the ordeal and from the city.

In spite of preoccupations with writing, with degree-taking and with professional prospects, we had time left over for friends and even for expeditions abroad. One of the friends whom we liked most but saw only infrequently was Count Harry Kessler, a German with an English mother and whose father was widely but erroneously supposed to be the Kaiser Wilhelm II. Kessler was a tall man of distinguished appearance and manners, a presence that suggested the diplomat or the political general. He had indeed served as diplomatist and soldier, but simply as duties that chanced to come his way. His correctness of deportment—more correct and less relaxed than that of an Englishman of similar origins (he was apt to raise his head in an abrupt gesture of disapproval at the slightest breach of taste)— masked a passionate nature and deep convictions. In politics he was a liberal and an ardent advocate of international amity and co-operation, but his closest interests were literature, the drama and the visual arts. An admiring reference to a work of art of which he happened to be ignorant inflicted upon his system a faint but evident shock, and one might be sure that his ignorance would be promptly remedied. He was in fact an impassioned lover of the arts, their effective promoter and generous patron.

Happening to be in London in the summer of 1930 he expressed a particular wish to see me about a confidential matter of some consequence, and took me to lunch at the long-since demolished Hotel Cecil in the Strand, where he often stayed. 'You know', he said, 'how anxious I am that you and Elizabeth should come to stay with me in Weimar in June, but', he went on with evident concern, 'there's a difficulty. Maillol is to be there, with his model, Lucie Passavant; they're not married, and it occurred to me that Elizabeth might object.' I reassured him, and he looked relieved. 'That is good', he said, 'but please remember that Maillol's family know nothing of this visit and they must know nothing.'

Towards the end of lunch it became clear that my assurance about Elizabeth's probable attitude towards Lucie Passavant had not sufficed to quiet Kessler's misgivings. 'I wish', he said, 'that you would first come out to Weimar by yourself, and meet her.' To put his mind at rest, I agreed.

Kessler was away from Weimar when my letter telling him of my impending arrival was delivered, and as there was no room ready at his house, Cranachstrasse 15, nearby lodgings were promptly placed at my disposal. As soon as Kessler returned I met Maillol and Lucie Passavant, at the Cranach Press. Maillol was a thin, gnarled man of about seventy years of age, with deep eyesockets, a long inquisitive nose, a big untrimmed beard; he wore a loose-fitting tweed suit with lapels without indentations. The charm of his grave, patriarchal appearance was enhanced by the almost childlike spontaneity of his gestures—gestures which evidently reflected his childlike capacity for total absorption in the interest of the moment, which he displayed the instant after his arrival. In the course of their correspondence Maillol would seem to have complained to Kessler of trouble with his sight, for Kessler gave him a large magnifying glass on an adjustable wheeled stand, designed to spare him eyestrain while he was engraving. I have never seen a present received with such rapture. Everybody had to be initiated into the workings of the gadget—even Kessler who had probably had it made to his own design. After we had mastered its intricacies Maillol kept running it over flat surfaces and examining his fingers and other objects beneath the lens.

Lucie Passavant was a young girl of unusual beauty, who watched over Maillol with tender solicitude. I cabled to Elizabeth, who arrived next day. At the Cranach Press, which Kessler founded and in which he took particular pride and delight, a number of splendid books had been produced, including a *Hamlet* beautifully embellished with wood engravings by Gordon Craig. The occasion of Maillol's visit to Weimar, I seem to recollect, was to examine with Kessler the edition of Virgil's *Eclogues* which he had illustrated, and which had been published some four years earlier, and to work on some other engravings. Maillol seemed to enjoy Elizabeth's and my being beside him when he was at work, and watching his progress— aided, on the slightest pretext, by the mobile magnifying-glass—and so we accompanied him to the Press on several occasions.

There were many things about the Press to remind the visitor of the extent of the English contribution to European printing and lettering. The man in charge, Gage Cole, was an Englishman who had served as an apprentice to Morris at Kelmscott. A copy of Edward Johnson's *Writing and Illuminating and Lettering*, showing signs of constant but careful usage, lay open on a bench, and there was ample evidence that not only Morris but Ricketts, Emery Walker and Eric Gill were familiar spirits.

The general aspect of the Press, however, was very German and it put me in mind of contemporary wood engravings of early German presses. It was a place delightful to linger in, for it had the character of largeness and abundance as well as the cleanliness and good order that belongs to the finest products of Germany, and the dedication and skill of the craftsmen was quickly apparent. When I exclaimed in admiration of these qualities Kessler said, 'Almost everything here is inspired by England. People of your generation are so generously ready to praise the products of modern Continental presses and Continental design generally; but aren't you inclined to forget Morris and to think of the Arts-and-Crafts movement as an anachronism, if not a downright bore? You'd be surprised if you knew how honoured they are, everywhere but in England.'

Very shortly after our arrival Eric Gill walked into Kessler's house, wearing his customary short black cassock and cross-gartered yellow stockings, looking hot and tired by the long journey from London, but eager to greet Maillol. Kessler had spoken much about Gill to Maillol, who was familiar with his work, and who had looked forward to his coming.

There had been, many years earlier, an encounter between the two of a dramatic character. Gill, at Kessler's persuasion, had given his qualified assent to working with Maillol as a student, and he had gone to Marly where Maillol's studio was and where Kessler had found him accommodation. Gill, however, who had had misgivings from the first, returned to England after spending only a few hours at Marly, fearing that Maillol's mature personality would leave too heavy an impression on his own (these events occurred in 1911 and Gill had carved his first piece of sculpture only the year before), and doubting the value of the usefulness for a carver of the teaching of a modeller.

The rest of us awaited the meeting of these two with scarcely less interest than they themselves. They shook hands and exchanged friendly glances. Then they stood frozen by embarrassed disappointment, when each remembered that he was ignorant of the language of the other. Neither, I think, spoke any language but his own, although Gill may have been able to read French as well as some

Latin. Thereafter Maillol showed his benevolence towards Gill, and Gill his reverence for Maillol, but to my surprise neither made any serious attempt to communicate with the other. Gill was, of course, shown the magnifying-glass, and a little technical information was exchanged, but this represented, I believe, the extent of their intercourse. When, during the Second World War, stories were current of Maillol's collaborationist tendencies, brought to a head by the visit he paid to Paris under Nazi pressure, on the occasion of the exhibition at the Orangerie of the work of a protégé of Hitler's, the sculptor Arno Breker, I was reminded of two expressions of political opinion, vehement but contradictory, which he made during his visit to Weimar.

Maillol responded with a lively interest when I mentioned that I had visited Banyuls, the place where he was born, and had spent some time in its neighbourhood, and my observations about its architecture, local customs and the like seemed to please him, but when I spoke of the splendidly austere character of the landscape, heightened by the almost total absence of trees, his brows contracted in an angry frown. 'It wasn't always like that', he exclaimed irritably, 'it's the French who've cut down the trees.' Whether by 'the French' he meant the government, or merely intrusive speculators in timber who happened to be French, I was unable to make out, but I was left with the impression that he felt more strongly for his province than for his country. But a few days later he gave evidence of a wider patriotism. One morning I received a note from Kessler (he used to write to us, as we continued to sleep in the lodgings he placed at our disposal but spent the days with him) dated 16.vi.30, which read in part, 'If you care to come and call at my press at 4.30 *sharp* we can go together to fetch Maillol with whom I have an appointment at 4.30, and go with him to see Nietzsche's sister, Frau Fürster-Nietzsche, an old lady of 83 who is still as "going" and as pugnacious as thirty years ago'. Elizabeth, Maillol and I went with Kessler that afternoon to see this old lady, who was a remarkable person in her own right. In Weimar she was an object at once of admiration and, on account of the frustration of a project on which she had long been occupied, of commiseration: the publication of a definitive edition of her brother's works. To this end she built up a fund out of the earnings of her own industrious pen, but as a consequence of the inflation that harrowed Germany virtually the whole fund evaporated. Her great age notwithstanding she had begun to build up another fund. It appeared, however, that her understanding of her brother's philosophy did not match her ardour for its perpetuation, for she had fallen into the vulgar error of regarding it as the gospel of Fascism. She occupied herself with political agitation, and not long before our visit she had organized a local meeting at which the Italian ambassador in Berlin had harangued at length rows of Thuringian burgesses and farmers on Fascist doctrine—a harangue which left his stolid audience unmoved.

On the occasion of our visit Kessler brought a set of proofs of the edition of the *Eclogues* illustrated by Maillol to show to our hostess, who scrutinized them with evident admiration. 'This is a beautiful book,' she said, '—a very beautiful book. I know how much Signor Mussolini, who has such a love of fine books, would like to possess a copy. I wonder whether, Monsieur Maillol, you would consent, as a testimony of the admiration of France, to present one to him, inscribed . . .'

'I regret, Madame,' Maillol said, in a louder tone than he ordinarily used, 'it is not possible.' Our hostess, assuming that the refusal was due to reluctance on Maillol's part to part with a costly book, added, 'Naturally, if you will be so good as to *inscribe* it, the question of making a copy available could no doubt be arranged with Count Kessler . . .'

'I am afraid, Madame,' Maillol explained in a tone of distressed asperity, 'that it is not a question of finding a copy. I simply cannot do what you ask.'

Frau Fürster-Nietzsche was a lively and indomitable character, very much, as Kessler expressed it, 'going', and full of talk of her brother, of Wagner and of other historic figures. In response to some observation of my own, she startled me by saying, 'I remember Mazzini expressing a precisely similar opinion.' She and Maillol were respectful but conspicuously reserved towards each other: a French army was still in occupation of the Rhineland.

Next morning Maillol and I went walking. When I referred to this mutual reserve he said, 'I still find it an odd sensation to meet Germans—except of course for Kessler, my oldest and best patron, to whom I owe so much, most of all my first sight of Greece. For me, as a sculptor, everything began on that visit to Greece. It wasn't so much the sculpture that was the revelation, which was what I had expected. It was the people, the boys on the beach, getting ready to swim, drying themselves afterwards: they were the classical gods and the athletes. If Kessler had done nothing else for me—and he's done almost everything—but show me that Attic beach, I'd still owe more to him than to anyone else. That and other such sights taught me more about Greek sculpture than I ever learnt in museums.' After a pause he returned to the odd feeling that meeting Germans gave him. 'Not', he said, 'that I really feel very much of a Frenchman. In the part of the country I come from we have more in common with the people just across the Spanish frontier. I remember as a boy how angry everyone was when the French came in and cut down the trees. It ruined the land—dried it all up.'

The sun blazed down fiercely out of a sky without a cloud. From time to time Maillol looked upward with a puzzled expression. 'It's a very singular thing,' he said, 'but the sun is *really* brilliant.'

'It's midsummer', I replied, 'so why not?'

'Of course it's the time of year for sunshine, but what is singular is that it should shine so brightly *here*. Why', he continued, in a dreamy, grumbling tone, 'It's shining as brightly as it does in France, and in Germany one expects it, somehow, to be a little different, a little *greyer*, you understand.'

I noticed that he was preoccupied by something which touched him more intimately than the unexpected brightness of the sun. When we emerged from a farm track on to a broad, straight highway, he stood still from time to time, and raising a lean brown hand to his wide-brimmed felt hat, scrutinized it to the point where it disappeared on the horizon. When cross-roads opened new vistas he paused and looked long and anxiously to left and right. 'It's my son', he said. 'He's on the lookout for me, and he drives fast. But what does my family expect? My wife was my model. A beautiful model. Then', he continued, extending his arms as though embracing a stoutish figure, 'she grew out to here. Still good. But now,' and he moved his arms farther apart, 'it's too much. I must have another model. I must. And my family do not understand.'

Later on I learnt a little more about the cause of his agitation. Madame Maillol did not find it easy to reconcile herself to his use of other models, to some of whom she showed marked disapproval, in which she was encouraged by her fast-driving son. Of these other, disapproved-of models, the beautiful girl whom he had brought to

Weimar was she through whom he was able best to invoke the lyrical, autumnal mood of his latest work—the mood of a man who has outlived his most urgent emotions, yet whose memory still dwells half-passionately on the springtime of life.

In Maillol's noble and searching apprehension of form naïveté had no part, and his knowledge of European sculpture was extensive and detailed, yet in everything unconnected with his vocation he was a man of exceptional simplicity.

After a few days he returned to Paris and we never met again, but when seven years later his 'Three Graces' was given to the Tate Gallery by the National Art-Collections Fund he sent me a message by the man who had cast the group to say how happy he was that what he considered the best work of his later life should belong to the British nation. The Graces themselves were modelled from Lucie Passavant.

Kessler took us on expeditions to neighbouring towns where we used to have lunch. Every evening we had dinner in a circular, illuminated pavilion in the garden at Cranachstrasse. Meals were elaborate and somewhat ceremonious occasions, and Kessler liked them to begin punctually. On the evening of his arrival Gill was late, and Kessler, slightly irritated, decided that we should begin without him. Presently Gill came in. 'Just look at these', he exclaimed, throwing a pile of naturist and nudist periodicals on to the table with an angry gesture. 'First look at the covers', he said, insisting on showing Kessler their plump, comely young women posing nude among silver birches or on river banks, 'and then look *inside* them. Not a single proper nude. The whole thing is a swindle.' By this time Kessler was frankly disapproving. After this outburst Gill was unusually silent both at this and at all meals at Kessler's house. I was puzzled by his silences, for at home Gill was a ready and pungent talker. Yet he took scarcely any part in the lively conversations at Kessler's table. On our expeditions out of Weimar he was on the contrary in high spirits and talked with his habitual freedom. It occurred to me that, free though he was from national prejudice, Gill was more insular than I had supposed, and simply felt constrained in the presence of foreigners. When we went on these expeditions, Maillol and Lucie stayed at home, and English was the only language spoken. (Kessler had an English mother and was English perfect.) They were delightful occasions, these expeditions, only momentarily marred by Kessler's polite impatience at the time which Gill used to spend at prayer whenever we visited a Catholic church.

Kessler was fond of Gill and an ardent admirer of his work, but their relations were rarely entirely easy. One evening Kessler told us that dinner was to be a celebration of some kind, and suggested that we should change. 'But I've nothing,' Gill objected, frowning, 'to change into.' Then his expression lightened, 'Oh yes I have,' he said, 'I'll put on some *blue* stockings.' Kessler clearly considered this proposal was inadequate. This was a typical example of the trifling want of accord which prevented these two from achieving continuously tranquil relations—except when some practical matter touching Gill's art was in question, when their accord was complete.

Before our departure one act of Gill's provoked Kessler to anger. Gill showed Elizabeth, Kessler and me a sketchbook in which he had made a series of nude drawings of a girl with a fine figure who had assumed poses of a startling impropriety. 'Who', someone asked him, supposing her to be a strip-tease girl or the like, 'is the model?' 'The Deputy-Librarian at High Wycombe', came Gill's reply. Kessler, who felt extremely protective towards Elizabeth, thought it outrageous that she should be shown such drawings, and that Gill's flippancy made the outrage the less pardonable, and he admonished him severely.

Gill was inordinately sensual; he was also upright and devoutly religious. In order to prevent his sensuality from leading him into sin, into furtiveness, he made it, by giving it the utmost legitimate expression possible, a part of his day-to-day, and even of his religious life. Kessler mistook for schoolboy impropriety what I believe Gill intended as an expression of a moral attitude.

The house in the Cranachstrasse radically enlarged my own aesthetic experience. I was familiar with the work of a fairly wide range of modern British and French painters and sculptors, but, like most English people, I knew very little about the modern art of northern and eastern Europe. (Even at the time when I write these words some thirty years later such art is quite negligibly represented in British collections, both public and private, although several admirable exhibitions have made it less unfamiliar than it was then.) I was accordingly startled by Kessler's splendid collection of the work of Munch and the German Expressionists. I failed to respond to their qualities, but their vehemence and directness must have made an unsuspected impression, for I found that when I again came in contact with such works the way for an understanding of them had been prepared by what I had seen of Kessler's collection. At the time I wondered that a man so civilized, endowed with such delicate sensibilities, should have taken pleasure in an art which sprang from qualities so contrary to his own. The collection also included works by Van Gogh, Seurat, Cézanne and Renoir, a splendid life-size seated stone figure, 'Mediterranean', by Maillol, which reposed serenely in the garden, as well as several small female figures carved in box or some similar wood, which I have never seen reproduced.

Kessler was more aware than most liberals of the real character of the forces that were taking control of Germany. Of the Nazis he said to me, 'I'm grateful to them for a new experience: they've taught me how to *hate*. I don't think I ever hated before.' We left him with regret.

From Weimar we went to Caux, above Montreux, where my parents proposed to spend the summer, encouraged in this course by a friend, Sydney Schiff, who wrote under the name of Stephen Hudson. I had published not long before an appreciation of his novel sequence which seemed to give him pleasure and he had read my own novel in manuscript, in which he found 'a sense of beauty and an atmosphere of subdued poignancy' and that I was 'a congenital novelist'. We had met often in London and had become friends. The lodgings he and his wife had reserved for us at Montreux were uninhabitable and others were unobtainable; so we climbed up the mountainside to Glion, where they had a chalet, to take advantage of their extensive knowledge of the neighbourhood. We arrived about eleven, the worse for our long, uncomfortable railway journey, and our walk up the mountainside in midsummer's heat. Mrs. Schiff met us as though we were importunate strangers, explaining that Sydney was translating Proust and must not be disturbed. It was five hours before he stopped translating Proust, and emerged, radiating friendliness, which from that moment was reciprocated in ever diminishing measure. It is not often that one remembers the experience from which one learns a lesson, but as we sat in dispirited expectancy I reflected that nothing renders a man so liable to offend as inconsistency of behaviour, and that if you profess friendliness you must maintain the semblance of it if you do not wish to lose your friends.

I meditated with a new-found respect upon the conduct of an acquaintance—the future director of one of the great national art collections—who behaved with habitual discourtesy to a large circle of friends, who nevertheless remained constant. With wisdom, conscious or unconscious, he conditioned his friends to bear with his brusqueness and to welcome his smiles as shafts of sunlight from a stormy day. Callous as it was, the conduct of the Schiffs would not have made so lamentable an impression had it not been prefaced by so many professions of friendship. It was some incident of the kind no doubt that brought upon this couple so terrible a retribution from the pen of Wyndham Lewis in *The Apes of God*. Presently my parents arrived and we settled with them in a villa at Caux. Before long Elizabeth and I were anxious to be home: my future seemed to depend upon my taking my doctorate, but in a moment of reckless complaisance we agreed to sit to my father for a double portrait. For him, normally so considerate, a sitter became a subject whose only function was to remain continuously still, no matter what or how pressing his other obligations. For us that portrait came to resemble one of those youthful dreams in which the dreamer is pursued by some frightening being from which he cannot escape as his feet are caught in preternaturally dense mud. The painting was finished at last, and eventually bought by the French State, from an exhibition in Paris. Eventually we were free to go home and resume our life, barely above the level of subsistence, of hard work, punctuated by expeditions into the outside world, in the guise of self-supporting, even of modestly successful citizens.

One day, unexpectedly, at the wedding of Richard, the elder son of Walter de la Mare, we came upon Chesterton, huger even than represented in his legend, the massiveness of his head accentuated by the absurd little pince-nez which drooped as though melting on either side of his nose. His appearance was more fantastic than any caricatures of him that we had seen. The very comicality of his general appearance enhanced the one feature that was not comic: his myopic eyes, which were radiant with benignity, humour, perceptiveness and nobility. As we were introduced he turned suddenly towards us, sweeping with his stomach from table to floor a quantity of wineglasses and plates. 'One sometimes', he explained with a vague gesture, 'has insufficient dominion over the outlying parts of one's empire.' Dispensing with conventional interchanges he told us a story about an impeccably respectable writer at a public dinner horrifying an audience of brother writers by confessing to a murder and heightening his effect by giving a detailed account of how he had committed this crime, but who ended his confession thus: 'gentlemen, I know that I can count upon the heartfelt sympathy of you all when I tell you that my victim was A PUBLISHER.' He wiped his perspiring brow. 'I'm reminded of that story because, only today, by his conduct towards me, a publisher has deserved a similar fate, and has exposed me to the temptation to murder.'

We met again many members of the older generation, especially at my parents' Sunday evening gatherings, which had undergone during my absence in America a change of character in two respects: they were less firmly guided by the hosts and they were on the whole less interesting in their composition. During the later nineteen-twenties my father and my sister Rachel, who had both been seriously ill, were apt to go to bed early, a habit that in varying degrees infected other members of the family. It was accordingly said, not quite untruly, that at the Rothensteins' Sunday Evenings one suddenly found oneself without hosts and eventually had to let oneself out. But from time to time, especially when guests were invited to dinner, these gatherings were marked by the same interest and animation as their predecessors. On one such occasion there was a verbal duel between Tagore and G. P. Gooch, the historian and a neighbour on Campden Hill. The extraordinary beauty and distinction of Tagore's person, and the evocative poetry of his diction, combined to give him the aura of a mystic and even of a saint. There was, however, a dichotomy in the personality of Tagore between the prophetic, the public personality, and the private citizen and friend, which became more conspicuous, it seemed to me, after the visits he paid to the United States, where he was received with extraordinary adulation. His pronouncements, whenever he chose to assume the mantle of prophet, often bore little relation to the facts of whatever subject happened to be under discussion; a dreamy sing-song rhetoric took the place of dispassionate assessment of situations. All this showed in its least favourable light in his political pronouncements. No one knew better than he that the British presence in India was due to causes of which deliberate aggression was but one among many and that its benefits (as well as its ill-effects) were many and substantial. Yet he was capable of speaking as though

things were otherwise. One night he was expatiating upon the victim-
ization: 'the people are so poor, so uneducated, that when they do
get a little money the men go into the bad quarters and—it is
terrible—they spend it all at once, perhaps on an *umbrella*.' To every
such assertion Gooch gave a factual reply: had not the overpopulation,
he asked, nothing to do with the immense fall in the mortality rate
due to the British medical services, and so forth. Each assertion of
Tagore's was answered conclusively and by a man hardly less conscious of the justice of India's aspirations than Tagore himself.
(What I believe to be Tagore's true attitude towards the politics of
India he thus summed up in response to a question of mine: 'Of
course we Indians wouldn't rule India as well as the British—not for
a good many years, but we've the right to choose to rule ourselves,
badly if need be.') Yet in private, the mantle of prophet discarded,
Tagore was as just and as detached, as candid, as well as kindly and
amusing, as he had ever been—one of the most lovable people I have
been privileged to know. Another sage whom we saw from time to
time was Dr. Inge, Dean of St. Paul's. He also was a man of strange
contradictions: at one moment he expressed opinions that seemed in-
consistent with even the least dogmatic Christianity; at the next he
would refer to the marriage of a female relative to a layman as something as unusual as marriage to a Chinese. Unlike Tagore he could be,
was often, extraordinarily unkind. I first met him some years earlier,
when coming in late to lunch at my parents' house I found Dean Inge
seated beside my father. 'Eton', he was saying, 'has been ruined by
the vulgarities of the sons of business men. . . .' The other guest was
Sir Ernest Debenham. I also recall a saying of yet another sage,
H. G. Wells. He was irritated by my speaking of some novelist as
having a wide experience of life. 'A novelist scarcely needs *any*
experience of life,' he snapped, 'why, there's not a commercial
traveller who's not seen more of life than the most experienced
novelist—novelists in any case are too busy writing their novels. No,
the special capacity of the novelist is that of taking a *clue* from life—
from an expression on a face, a door left open, whatever you like—
and pursuing it in his imagination, building on it, eventually, but he's
no business wasting his time experiencing when a clue is all he
needs.'

On one of these evenings Max's conversational spell had an embarrassing consequence. In the spring of 1931 he and Florence came to

England from Rapallo; she to enable her to fulfil an engagement to act in a play by Pirandello which was performed at Huddersfield. Max stayed with my parents at Airlie Gardens and was in a manifestly happy frame of mind. On a Sunday Evening, after the run of the play had ended, Max was standing at one end of the drawing-room, talking his brilliant best, and a large group had gathered round him to listen. At the opposite end Florence, elated by the respectful notices her performance had received and altogether very full of her return to the stage after an absence of many years, was talking about it to a smaller group. Suddenly aware that the attention even of this little group was to an increasing degree directed at Max, she was upset, and left the room. It so happened that, a moment afterwards, showing out some departing guests I passed Florence in the hall, making for a small closet. After saying goodnight to our guests I closed the front door and returning through the hall, now empty, went into the drawing-room to listen to Max. Some time later, accompanying another group of guests to the front door, I was surprised to see, pressed against one of its glass panels from the outside, a face—Florence's face. I immediately opened the door and she entered, one arm extended straight before like a sleepwalker, at intervals calling Max's name. In the drawing-room she declared that she had been shut out for half an hour. Her words were received with consternation and incredulity. It was obvious to everyone that, had she been accidentally shut out, a touch on the bell would have secured her immediate re-entry. Max displayed his habitual tenderness and solicitude towards her—and the party broke up.

On this same visit she provoked another embarrassing situation. At the end of a play to which she had gone with my parents, they all went round to see the leading lady. On entering her dressing-room (where some members of the cast were already assembled) she uttered words of homage and threw herself on her knees. Had the leading lady been a Bernhardt or a Duse, Florence's action might have had a shadow of justification, but although she had won a high measure of respect in her profession she was a person of far less exalted attainments, and the gesture merely provoked dismay.

An old friend whose company was an unvarying delight was Athole Hay. With an audacity that proved amply justified, my father invited him to become Registrar of the Royal College of Art. He had never worked, either at Oxford or since, nor, I fancy, had he ever envisaged work of any kind as anything except as a remote possibility. The offer of work appealed immensely to his innate delight in the unexpected, and he responded to it as another might to an unforeseen chance of going on some romantic voyage of exploration. His high spirits, ready generosity, disinterestedness and a disposition to like his fellow human beings, tempered by a capacity for assessing their motives with ruthless precision, made him a resounding success. One day he surprised me by saying that he wished to marry: someone interested in painting and ten years his senior. I introduced him to Silvia Baker, a painter and a family friend, who fulfilled these and various other requirements. They married and were radiantly happy.

CHAPTER SIX

LEEDS

EARLY in 1932 an Alderman Percival T. Leigh of Leeds
wrote to ask for an opportunity of putting before me a matter
of importance. Following up his letter with a visit, he told me
that the Directorship of the City Art Gallery at Leeds was vacant,
that Professor W. G. Constable and others who had been consulted
had recommended that I be appointed. 'Some of us', he said, in a
broadish Yorkshire accent, 'are far from satisfied with the way the
Art Gallery has been run, and we want a fresh start, and after what
we've heard about you, we think you're the man to make it.' The
previous Director, Frank Lambert, had left some time previously,
and it was he who had been appointed Director of the Walker Art
Gallery, Liverpool, at the interview at which I had so ignominiously
failed. Eventually I agreed to his urgent invitation to apply, but not
without misgivings, which had several causes, among them the approach of Alderman Leigh himself, which suggested that this apparently simple invitation had devious implications which I was unable to
divine. When I visited Leeds on 21st March for the interview, I was
depressed by the Art Gallery itself and by the collection mouldering
upon its walls. There had been twenty-two applicants for the
directorship but the 'short list' of candidates to be interviewed consisted of only three names, those of Charles Johnson, author of a
popular, workmanlike book on English painting, recently published,
the Curator of the Doncaster Museum, who told me that his principal qualification was his knowledge of meteorology, which enabled
him to understand, in a manner impossible for one not so qualified,
the weather represented in paintings, and my own. After the interview it was announced that I had been recommended for appointment. 'There must be some mistake', exclaimed Johnson, evidently
distressed. The melancholy impression made by the collection and
its setting was deepened by another circumstance.

When Alderman Leigh had, in effect, offered me the post, he

promised that I should have the same salary as my predecessor, namely £650 a year, which I thought, more especially considering the eulogies of my qualifications and the declaration that 'some of us are far from satisfied with the way the Art Gallery has been run', was meagre. After the interview, on the grounds that the City's finances were adversely affected by the prevailing Depression, the salary was reduced—I was assured for one year only—to £400; and this proved, moreover, to be subject to a 10 per cent economy deduction, making £360 in all. It appeared that there were members of the City Council who regarded even this salary as quixotically over-liberal. These city fathers advocated the abolition of the post of Director altogether and the subordination of the Art Gallery to the City Librarian, a proposal, however, that aroused strong opposition. After discussion, Elizabeth and I decided to try to survive the year ahead: we were, after all, in training for this ordeal.

Sometime in June we entrained for Leeds, and as we approached our destination we peered out of the carriage window. The clear blue of the sky and the balminess of the midsummer breezes deepened the impression of shabbiness given by the small, dusty-red towns and villages we passed. (Going north you leave gradually behind the pink, variegated bricks of the home counties: the appearance of a brick with a harsh, even surface of dusty-red presently announces your arrival in a different civilization; and the acid tinge of the grass warns of a harsher climate.) On the horizon straight ahead rested a blanket of smoke; in a few minutes the train was running through fog which, though rarefied and pale, quite shut out the light and not less the warmth of the June sun, and we were among the suburbs of Leeds. The fog—the West Riding Blight, I later learnt it was called—muffled the noise of the busy city. Leaving our baggage at a hotel in which the rooms were vast but there was no running water discoverable, I went with Elizabeth to the Art Gallery, of which I was now Director. The large size and the utter dereliction of the place, my total inexperience of administration and my ignorance of provincial musuems, heightened my misgivings; had I found myself captain of an unseaworthy ship instead, they would hardly have been more serious. We had not wandered for long through the big, neglected Victorian rooms before a short, energetic man, evidently warned of our arrival, approached and shook us heartily by the hand. 'I'm a member of the Art Gallery Committee', he explained, 'and I've come to welcome you to Leeds and to arrange for you to visit my house, for I'm sure you'd like to see the few pictures I have.' We expressed our appreciation. 'But I must ask you', he said 'to *postpone* your visit for a while—in fact until November. You see, the decorators are in, and they'll not be done till then. Well, I must be going now', he said, smiling in response to our thanks, 'and probably not knowing anybody in Leeds, I thought you'd be glad for somebody to meet you.'

The sunless air, the teeming thousands of people who seemed never to have been exposed to the full light of day, the brief vistas down streets which dissolved abruptly in miasmal mist, our equivocal welcome—all this suddenly emerged for us as retribution for lives which withered under our doleful retrospective scrutiny into unredeemed chronicles of error. How otherwise explain the predicament in which we found ourselves? And we weighed with regret, against the security of an official post in purgatory, the changes and chances of our previous existence, precarious though this had always been. We remembered how about this time of year the Bluegrass region of Kentucky is transformed almost overnight, from a place temperate in climate and in aspect nearly English, into an exotic tropical paradise, resonant with the hum of insects, stiflingly crowded (spacious though it is) with luxuriant, aggressive flora. We remembered the obelisks of Manhattan, a multitude of white and greying shafts swept by an intoxicating wind. We remembered the contrasting horizontal sweep of London as we saw it from the windows of our flat on Campden Hill, the river, its axis curving broadly, here hidden by wharves and houses, there reflecting with a steely light an overcast sky. These, and all they contained, we had exchanged, at the persuasion of an unknown alderman who had climbed our many stairs, for exile in this hideous place, starvation wages and a mission the significance of which I only vaguely apprehended.

Under further scrutiny both collection and building made an even more lamentable impression than they had at first. The collection contained a number, in fact a considerable number, of pictures of beauty and interest. There were some nine excellent water colours by Cotman and three by Turner, and others by Camille Pissarro, the Sandby brothers, Sargent and a big group of drawings by Phil May. It is a curious fact about British provincial art galleries that the water colours are almost always conspicuously superior to the oil paintings—a fact that has long puzzled me and for which I can offer no explanation. There were some good oil paintings in Leeds, a Courbet, a Pourbus, a Gainsborough and a number of others. But good pictures are adversely affected by bad company; they do not shine out; rather do they merge into the prevailing mediocrity. So it was with the good pictures at Leeds: perhaps for the sake of self-preservation—for who knows what may befall a good picture within an alderman's jurisdiction?—they had taken on protective colouring and become all but indistinguishable from their drab or meretricious companions. The building, squalid itself, had fallen into an incredible state of disrepair. This state of affairs was noted not long afterwards by *The Yorkshire Post* in an article (24th September 1932) headed 'Leeds Art Gallery. Dilapidated Condition of Interior. Signs of Drabness'. 'The condition of the Gallery within doors is deplorable,' it ran, 'it ranges from dingy to dirty, from dilapidated to dangerous. The mouldings of the cornices were apparently mouldy. And patches of blistered paint and peeling paper caught the attention . . . in one corner the cornice was not only ugly with decay but possibly dangerous . . . upstairs [the wall covering] had gone too far for patching and was dismally weather-stained . . . discoloured paper was not only peeling but actually hanging in strips . . .' (How dangerous was the dilapidated state of the building was demonstrated a few weeks later. I had borrowed a case of fine renaissance glass from the Victoria and Albert Museum. As it was being set out a large piece of plaster fell from the ceiling and destroyed an outstanding example —an auspicious beginning to a career concerned with the preservation of works of art!)

On taking up my duties next day I had a heartening encounter— with my secretary, Ernest Musgrave. He was a reassuring figure, resourceful, imperturbable, conscientious, courteous, and above all dedicated. His father, I was told, had a small business that failed, and Ernest, his expectations disappointed, became an attendant in the Art Gallery, where his capabilities were recognized by my two predecessors, and he was promoted. It was he to whom I owe my initiation into art gallery administration, for I had no notion how pictures were packed, transported or insured, or how the staff entrusted with their custody were recruited and organized. Nor had I given sustained consideration to the purposes that art galleries were intended to serve. The gallery's attendants were also a delight to work with: alert, loyal, humorous and interested in the work in hand.

During the first few months I tried to alleviate the depressing conditions which prevailed by rehanging in a more spacious and logical fashion, by introducing, by way of acquisitions and loans, new blood into the collection. A splendid painting by Stubbs, 'Jupiter and Mars', was lent by Sir Gervase Beckett, and a painting by Spencer Gore, a water colour by Girtin, a drawing by Rossetti and two by Wyndham Lewis were purchased, and I persuaded Jacques-Emile Blanche to present one of his own paintings.

Reporting the arrival of the Stubbs to Alderman Leigh, I must have spoken in a tone too low to be clearly heard, for he exclaimed, 'What! Stoobs in town? You ought to have told me; I'd like to have given him a little loonch at Queens.'

'No, I meant Stubbs' *picture*', I explained.

'But where's Stoobs himself?'

'As a matter of fact, he's dead.'

'Stoobs dead!' he exclaimed, striking his forehead in affected grief, 'when did he die?'

'Oh, time passes, Mr. Alderman.'

'I want to know joost when he did die.'

'1806, Mr. Alderman.'

'Oh', he said.

Several exhibitions were arranged, among others of the work of Charles Schwandfelder, a forgotten but admirable Leeds animal painter, an almost exact contemporary of Constable's, of that of Ernest Sichel, a Bradford painter, then living, of unusual sensibility.

Beneath the galleries were two large cellars in which paintings and sculpture not required for exhibition were stored. Here, mostly undisturbed for nearly thirty years, was a miscellaneous accumulation of paintings, packing cases and plaster casts, some of these last as much as eight feet high and thick-blanketed in black Leeds soot. By spring, 1933, both were clean and well lit, and the grubby hoard that had lain there had been sorted and arranged. This Augean stable yielded a number of works of considerable interest, notably a big Riberesque 'Martyrdom of St. Sebastian'. When the picture came to light I first took it for an empty frame, so tightly packed with soot was the space between picture surface and glass. Investigation established that it had been exhibited in 1875 at the Yorkshire

Exhibition of Arts and Manufactures and afterwards presented to the Corporation by Mr. L. Wedderburn, but it had never been exhibited and there was no mention of it in any Gallery record or publication. This discovery attracted wide attention and it has been on exhibition ever since. Although previously attributed to G. B. Caracciolo, it is now attributed to Ribera himself.

By the spring of 1933 I had become convinced that the addition of a few good pictures to the collection, the bringing to light of a number of others, improvements in hanging and other reforms, however desirable in themselves, were all peripheral. The harsh fact remained that the Art Gallery was not fit to perform its proper function. Among the ugly and disorderly cities of Britain Leeds was among the ugliest and most disorderly: surely the proper function of the Art Gallery was to be a place where the standards of beauty and order would be uncompromisingly upheld, a place from which beauty and order should radiate and permeate the minds of the citizens and thus affect, even unconsciously, the way they felt about visual things, the way they made them, caused them to be made, the things they bought, and the city they lived in. How could this high ambition be remotely realized so long as the Art Gallery remained, quite simply, a place disgusting to enter. Accordingly I asked and obtained permission to close the Art Gallery, and to redecorate it entirely. I should perhaps explain that the body immediately responsible for our affairs was the Art Gallery Sub-Committee of the Libraries, Art Gallery and Museum Committee of the City Council, which consisted of a majority of aldermen and councillors and a minority of co-opted members, supposedly, and sometimes in fact, private citizens with some knowledge of the visual arts. It is, however, significant that Sir Michael Sadler, who was beyond comparison Leeds' most important art collector and patron and the Vice-Chancellor of its University, was never invited to serve. The Committee members interested themselves mainly in finance, to a lesser extent in administration; the initiative about acquisitions, loans and exhibitions was left mainly to the Director, although decisions regarding all such matters rested in their hands. They often showed prejudice both against what was unfamiliar and a strong disposition to accept gifts proffered by influential citizens, but, as far as my own experience went, they otherwise received the Director's proposals in an open-minded and friendly fashion.

The two months when the Art Gallery was closed to the public were a period of intense activity. Numerous plaster casts, chipped and filthy, their contours blurred by innumerable coats of white-wash, that encumbered one of the largest exhibition rooms I ordered to be broken up. Several citizens called to protest against the destruction of Corporation property of great value. The staff had been given instructions, whenever such protests were made, to offer the protestants the free gift of anything they cared to take away. In fact in no single instance was such an offer accepted. The roof was repaired, the damage to plaster mouldings from weather was made good. Every single room was redecorated with the wall covering best calculated to enhance the particular group of paintings hung there— a procedure fairly widespread today but revolutionary then. All this was done at a cost of £1,000 . The collection was entirely rearranged, rigorously weeded, and many works cleaned; many popular-academic works were placed in the newly organized cellars. Among these exiles were 'A Corner in the Baron's Larder', by Henry Weeks, R.A., 'A Prize in the Lottery', by Frank Topham, 'How Funny', by Henriette Bonner, 'As Red as a Lobster', by Henrietta J. Robinson, and 'In the Time of Roses', by Blanche Jenkins and scores of others of similar mediocrity. Almost a hundred pictures long lost sight of and in many instances uncatalogued were recalled from their exile, not all notable, but far superior to their predecessors on the walls. These included a fine small Reynolds, 'Portrait of Viscount Duncannon', and a fine landscape by Constable, of course the 'St. Sebastian', and a good Barker of Bath; the Tate lent 'Richmond Hill', by Turner, 'The Death of Major Pierson,' by Copley and 'Lord Ligonier', by Reynolds, and my father lent a group of drawings by contemporary British and French painters and sculptors. A special room was set aside for the work of West Riding artists. As was only just, Professor Constable was invited to perform the reopening ceremony.

I awaited the occasion with confidence, but I also anticipated criticism. The character of the collection had been radically altered from popular-academic to one which, so far as existing resources allowed, addressed its appeal to the lover of painting and sculpture and in no way to 'the man in the streets'. Moreover, there was a small group of good friends of the Art Gallery who, I suspected, had grown fond of it as it had been and might resent change.

The acclaim with which the reopened Art Gallery was received

surpassed my utmost hopes. *The Times* (3rd July 1933) carried a
special article, under the headline 'A Transformation'. This read, in
part: 'The effect produced by the redecoration of the galleries and the
rearrangement of the collection . . . reminds one of nothing so much
as the tale of the magic flute which put "everything in its right
place" . . . Hitherto the galleries have been dark and dingy . . . and
the works confused in arrangement; large pictures in small galleries,
small ones in large, with importance given to Victorian works of no
great merit . . . The contrast between interior and exterior is now
almost comic. Once inside the gallery you forget all about Leeds . . .
the gain in expansion and cheerfulness is astonishing.' *The Yorkshire
Post* devoted long, descriptive articles to it (30th June and 3rd July
1933), all highly laudatory, one headlined 'The Leeds Art Gallery
Transformed'. 'The Leeds Gallery' according to its leading article
(1st July 1933) 'now joins the minority [of provincial galleries] which
must be taken seriously by all who care for art.'

   The Art Gallery at once attracted visitors from all over the North,
and far greater numbers from Leeds itself, including members of one
category which I particularly welcomed. The Great Depression had
not yet passed and in the city the unemployed were tragically
numerous. Groups of them used to congregate in front of the Art
Gallery. After its reopening unemployed men became regular
visitors, with whom I often talked. I was impressed by the seriousness and alertness of their minds and by the way they responded to
a number of the modern works whose qualities eluded certain of the
local connoisseurs. The way in which these men, existing for month
after month, sometimes year after year, in enforced idleness and
wretched conditions, were able to preserve their faculties and to
appreciate painting and sculpture moved me to the utmost respect.

   Introducing Professor Constable, Alderman Leigh had remarked
that it was a happy coincidence that the Gallery was being reopened
on the first anniversary of my appointment. This allusion to a happy
anniversary had a mocking sound in my ears, for it had already
become apparent to me that I could not remain in the service of the
Leeds Corporation. At the end of the financial year I had reminded
him of the undertaking he had given me, and on several occasions
spontaneously confirmed, that after a year as Director I would be
entitled to the same salary as my two predecessors. Alderman Leigh
had recently told me that he could give no undertaking that my

salary would ever be raised and he declined even to allow the matter to be considered by the Art Gallery Sub-Committee.

This allusion, however, decided me to raise the matter for the last time with Alderman Leigh, who confirmed that he could do nothing and suggested that I should speak to Alderman (shortly afterwards Sir) Charles Davies, head of the Conservative Party in the city. 'Of course I haven't forgotten the promise', said Alderman Davies, 'it was you who forgot something—you forgot to get us *to put anything in writing*.' I told him that, both on account of his attitude towards the clearest undertaking and the impossibility of existing on £360 a year, I intended to resign, but I had assumed a number of obligations, to hold exhibitions and the like, and that these I intended to discharge before I left. 'Please yourself', said the Alderman, indicating that our interview was at an end.

Among projected exhibitions was one of 142 of the remarkable copies of English Mediaeval Wall Paintings by Professor E. W. Tristram, which had never been shown outside London. This exhibition—opened by Sir Eric Maclagan, Director of the Victoria and Albert Museum—enabled the public of Leeds to form a completer idea of the paintings surviving from mediaeval times in our cathedrals and churches than in the course of many months of travel.

The time came when my plans for exhibitions had been carried out and my various obligations towards the Art Gallery and to a number of artists had been discharged, and at the end of October 1933 I wrote to Alderman Leigh resigning my directorship. Alderman Leigh immediately made a wholly misleading statement to the press, which made it impossible for me to fulfil my intention of relinquishing my post without fuss. The matter became a sensation and, to my dismay, widely reported in the national as well as the local press, for I feared that I would gain a reputation for being 'difficult' and that I would not find it easy to secure another post in a profession to which I had already become deeply attached; and that such a reputation might endanger one particularly interesting prospect.

During the autumn I had received on two or three occasions an impressive visitor from Sheffield, Alderman J. G. Graves, the founder and chairman of a very large mail-order business, who told me about the art gallery, then nearing completion, that he was shortly to present to the City, and who spoke of the changes I had brought about at the Leeds Art Gallery in the most cordial terms—so cordial that I could not but construe his meaning otherwise than as an intimation that he would welcome me as director of his new foundation. Alderman Graves had invited me to lecture to the Sheffield Arts Club early in the year and had presided, giving my words, it seemed to me, almost uncannily close attention. On this occasion we had stayed at his big gloomy house in Ranmoor Road, where he showed us his collection. It was an eerie experience. The pictures, almost all of them English and predominantly Victorian, and mostly of mediocre quality, were hung from floor to ceiling in a series of rooms, originally servants' bedrooms, at the top of the house. The windows had been boarded up and there was total darkness except for the fierce beam from the electric lamp carried by our host, which he directed upon each picture successively, at which visitors were compelled to look for as long as it suited the wielder of the lamp, which was often disproportionately long. 'Watson, Weekes, both fine artists; just look at that splendid Henrietta Robertson; my finest Stanley Wood, a *great* painter', he would say, holding the works of these nonentities long and lovingly in the beam of light. Here and there was a work of superior merit. I could make nothing of this strange collection or the motives that impelled its assembly, which were the more baffling in the light of his professions of ardent admiration for what I was doing in Leeds and his apparently receptive attitude towards my opinions.

Attracted by the possibility of being associated with an entirely new venture, I told Alderman Graves of my intention to leave Leeds, and the expected invitation to become Director of the Art Galleries and the Ruskin Museum in Sheffield promptly arrived, and I was formally appointed on 10th November. Before accepting the post, however, I wrote a long letter to Alderman Graves giving in some detail my ideas as to how the new gallery should be run and emphasizing my ambition to build up a representative collection of modern British painting, and I urged him not to consider my appointment unless our views were truly in harmony.

Not all my time in Leeds had been passed in the Art Gallery. Almost everything that I observed when I emerged into the raw foggy air of the West Riding increased our sense of exile from the South, and it was not long before I was aware that most of the other Southerners in Leeds (as later in Sheffield) shared our consciousness of remaining strangers, and this knowledge helped to justify our

inability to feel entirely at home in a region for which we felt both
admiration and affection, where we had been received with so much
kindness and with which I already had many associations, for my
father was born in Yorkshire; I had cheerful childhood recollections
of Christmases spent with my grandparents in Bradford, and my
mother's family came originally from the neighbouring county of
Westmorland. There was, in fact, a frontier no less perceptible to the
inhabitants of the one side than of the other (I use the past tense,
for since I left in 1938 I have seen very little of Yorkshire and conditions may well have altered radically); for I was soon made aware of
the Yorkshire opinion of Southerners, among whom Londoners were
regarded as particularly egregious examples. This opinion somewhat corresponds to that prevailing in eighteenth-century England
with regard to Frenchmen—to the 'Monsieurs'. Southerners, that is
to say, were conceded to have the more finished manners, for what
little these are worth to the Northerner, who is inclined to regard
them as a mask of devious intentions. They were considered extravagant and pleasure-loving and to have a quite too high opinion of
their own merits, to be, in short, 'stuck-up', *fancy* sort of chaps.
These grave shortcomings appeared to excite in the Northerner not
so much hostility or contempt as an unsleeping watchfulness.

From time to time these and other regional differences were discussed in the correspondence columns of the local press. Londoners'
want of sympathy with the North, according to one contributor, had
its origin in a football season in which Arsenal suffered a series of
ignominious defeats at the hands of Yorkshire teams, which engendered, he asserted, unforgettable resentment. Few of the views
expressed revealed such want of knowledge of the metropolis, but
London's remoteness from the experience even of many of the more
privileged citizens of the North was unexpected. A married couple
with whom we were acquainted, who were widely travelled and
well-read, knew London in just the way they knew Paris, New York
and Rome; they were familiar with its antiquities, its museums and
art galleries and its big hotels, but of the more intimate, more
characteristic, aspects of its life they seemed to have no notion. But
the Londoner, except for a vague idea of the outward aspect of its
industrial cities, which chills the hearts even of those least susceptible
to their surroundings, was hardly aware of the North, or, except for
what he might have picked up from Northern music-hall humour, of

the Northerner himself. Yet in his robust music-hall mythology, especially in the ballads of which Young Albert and Sam Small are the central characters, were discoverable several distinguishing Northern traits: most conspicuously a determination never to be impressed by superiority of any sort; a frank preoccupation with material things; an indifference to 'style'; a conviction—by no means unjustified—of belonging, by virtue of an exceptional degree of uprightness, toughness and tenacity, to a superior caste. The Young Albert and the Sam Small sagas are caricatures; but there exists, in the character of Mr. Hiram Yorke in Charlotte Brontë's *Shirley*, a to my mind uniquely penetrating portrait of the generic Yorkshireman. One characteristic which, however, if my memory serves, does not belong to Mr. Yorke, but which I often met with, is a highly-developed sense of the macabre—a connoisseurship of the gloomy no more to be confused with gloom than enjoyment of the risks of steeple-chasing is to be confused with fear. Indeed the Northern town-dweller's power of survival in surroundings so forbidding would seem to argue the possession of a secret and ample fund of cheerfulness. The life in a Northern industrial city of a man with any marked disposition to melancholy could offer none but painful prospects. To a Dostoievski, a Poe or a Van Gogh, the atmosphere of Leeds or Sheffield would prove more deadly than the most severe reverse of fortune. A homely example of Northern relish of the gloomy was provided by Mrs. Flowers who came to 'do' for us each morning. One day we were struck by her air of sombre exaltation. 'I had an accident last night', she presently explained. 'We was going upstairs to bed, and I thinks I hears tapping on front door. So I turns round at top step, and I catches foot in carpet and I falls right down. I only has time to call out "Good-bye all", but before I strikes bottom I remembers *everything*, including young man I'd just read about in evening paper that was to be hung for murder, and I says to myself, "Young man, little did I think my time'd come before thine".'

The aspect of the Yorkshire temperament with which I was more particularly concerned was its response to the visual arts. Not only the general aspect of Leeds, of its Art Gallery in particular (the place above all others where its aesthetic consciousness might be expected to be most deliberately manifest), but several personal experiences suggested the prevalence, among the middle class, of visual insensibility of the most militant kind. An alderman told me that he'd once been to the National Gallery. 'But somehow', he said, 'I just couldn't fancy that.' A lady prominent in the social life of the city who, calling on my wife and instantly noting the presence of a bronze bust on the mantelpiece, exclaimed: 'I suppose that's an Epsteen. Well, I think Epsteen's *vulgar*.' These and other such utterances might have been dismissed as fortuitous, but I shortly learned that an equally unhopeful attitude flourished in academic circles. I accepted an invitation from the Education Authority of a neighbouring town to play the part of devil's advocate in a debate on modern art, to defend this activity, that is to say, against the assault of the headmaster of the local art school. When I entered the hall in which the contest was to take place it was crowded almost to overflowing by some thirty occupants, already seated and stolidly drawing at their pipes. Presently there was a stir in the aisle as two heavily breathing men trundled forward a magic-lantern so massive and stocky in construction as to put me in mind of a trench-mortar, which they presently brought to bear, at the closest range, upon a crumpled square of linen hung upon the wall. The art master opened our proceedings with animation, neglecting none of the stock indictments of the characteristic art of today: '. . . modern artists unable to draw . . . choose to depict what's ugly when so many beautiful subjects to choose from . . . don't know whether you're looking at a blue cow or an eruption of Vesuvius . . . my little boy aged four could do better', and so forth. The big mortar was then prepared for action. The beam it projected proving unexpectedly dim, it was moved closer and closer to the square of linen, and only when it was within two feet of the target was it considered to be effective. It then appeared that the monster was designed to take slides of a larger size than those which my opponent proposed to show; this difficulty he attempted to overcome by taking each slide between forefinger and thumb, lowering it into the machine, and holding it in the beam of light. In several instances it was possible to discern, as in a glass darkly, projections of the lower halves of pictures. To illustrate the theme that John Gilbert was a superlative draughtsman, a number of Sickert's free extemporizations in oil upon the older artist's themes were thrown upon the linen square as genuine works of the nineteenth-century illustrator, but the climax of the performance came when the audience was given to understand that the *coup de grâce* was at last to be delivered to the prostrate and battered body of modern art. Excitement rose. 'There's one artist, at least, who *could have been* all right: in fact', the lecturer conceded, 'he *was* all right—*until he went mad*. I'm going to show you two phases of his work. Now look: Stanley Spencer: series one—*before he went mad*; series two—*after he went mad*.' The first series consisted entirely of landscapes by Gilbert Spencer; the second of figure paintings by Stanley Spencer.

Nothing that I said (though I refrained from reference to the arbitrary attributions of the pictures shown) served to counteract the unfavourable impression of modern art which the pedagogue had given, and when the vote was taken it transpired that twenty-nine out of thirty had been cast in support of his contention, the local director of education diplomatically abstaining. When this result was announced, my successful opponent beamed: 'You know', he disarmingly said, 'I think I could have done just as well if I'd been on the other side.'

Moving around in the social life of the city, I was chiefly struck by the exceptional rigour of its tone. I remember hearing the afternoon call described of a young woman, a member of an illustrious family who had married a Leeds curate, who later became a bishop, upon the wife of a prominent citizen. Ruffled, the recipient of the call—our hostess for the weekend—dwelt ominously upon successive incidents of the unfortunate occasion: 'Do you know', she asked, 'what she was wearing? *Country shoes!* It was all too obvious she'd been out walking in the country . . . and after she'd sat down, what do you think she did? *She leaned back in her chair—right* back. "Never again", my husband said. "It may be all right in other places, but she's done for herself in Leeds".' This was a perhaps extreme, though not an uncharacteristic, manifestation of the prevailing tone. A subdued asperity was particularly evident in the attitude of the prosperous middle-class towards members of the neighbouring land owning aristocracy. This asperity is traceable, I think, not to active hostility but to an inherited attitude towards the class with which the Northern industrial and commercial classes had earlier contended with exceptional bitterness for political power. In the struggle they made use of virtue and propriety to offset the glamour of rank and lineage, an attitude implicit in Tennyson's lines about pure hearts being more than coronets and simple faith than Norman blood. The censoriousness, prevalent among the more

ELIZABETH

G. B. SHAW WITH
ELIZABETH'S SISTER
PEGGY, AND LUCY

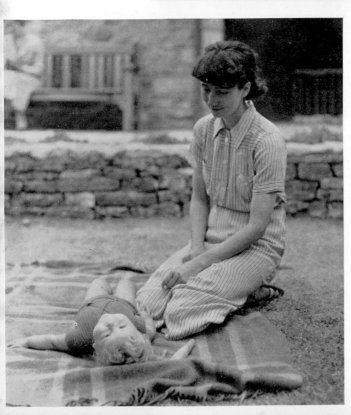

ELIZABETH AND LUCY
AT FAR OAKRIDGE

prosperous citizens of Yorkshire—which was directed to some extent to all 'outsiders'—was redeemed by an endearing characteristic: a benevolence and loyalty towards those 'outsiders' who had undergone, without marked discredit, a few years' probation, a benevolence having its springs perhaps in a feeling of grateful reconciliation towards any 'outsider', above all a Southerner, who had been able to withstand the social climate for so long. For our part we felt for the many who befriended us in Yorkshire a peculiar gratitude, for they afforded us a measure of protection against the rigours of an arctic winter. The analogy might seem strained to many men, but apt enough to most women. The Northern city gave the smallest imaginable scope for the flowering, indeed for the bare survival, of the feminine spirit. Respect for women was high; passionate emotions, however, were noticeably deficient, and of what did exist film-stars absorbed a disproportionate share, but if Greta Garbo or Marilyn Monroe had trod, incognita, the crowded pavements of a Yorkshire town, their beauty would, I suppose, scarcely have provoked a stare. 'The beautiful woman's place is the screen', would fairly have summed up the attitude of the Northern man; but feminine beauty, manifest in the flesh (more especially if heightened by make-up or hair-styling) when noticed at all was apt to be considered 'fast'. The effect of this attitude, not only on Northern social life but on Northern industry and commerce, was deleterious. An appreciable number of men in all spheres of activity were under constant pressure from their wives to find employment in the South, or, if that were impossible, to establish a residence there. Conversely, Southern wives discouraged their husbands from entering upon careers in the North. To some extent these attitudes persist, and since abler men in general enjoy the greater freedom in the choice of employment, the fact that this is continuously exercised in one direction accelerates the constant drift of talent of every kind away from the North. And not of talent only, for in spite of their constant professions of civic pride, and their quickness to react to any criticism of their native towns, the more prosperous Northern citizens are apt to migrate, so that as soon is it accumulates beyond a certain point their prosperity is frequently lost to the Northern city. For more than a century Leeds and Sheffield have produced incalculable wealth, and enjoyed revenues in comparison with which those of Venice or of Florence at the height of their prosperity were meagre.

But Venice and Florence put their limited resources to such brilliant and enduring uses as to make them places of world pilgrimage; but what have Leeds and Sheffield to show? Between them a few respectable old churches (which predate, however, the industrial age); a few mostly mediocre public buildings, a few thousand mostly dismal villas, and all these lost in a vast wilderness of slum. Again and again I urged that the sole means of arresting the wholesale and continuous flight of talent and material resources was by providing for the enrichment of life by liberal and constructive support for painting, sculpture, drama (music already enjoyed a relatively generous measure of support), and above all by the provision of a harmonious and inspiring setting for the pursuit and enjoyment of these activities. Because artists flee, at the earliest moment that enterprise or a scholarship allows, from their native county, it is not generally realized that Yorkshire, in particular the West Riding, has made a unique contribution to British art in the past century or so. Matthew Smith, Edward Wadsworth, Henry Moore, Barbara Hepworth were all born within a few miles and less than twenty-five years of one another. And these, although the most illustrious, do not stand alone. Yorkshire has given birth to a long succession of artists of unusual talent which extends right down to the younger generation active today, exemplified, for example, by Ralph Brown, Jack Smith and David Hockney. In this grimy half-lit region there is a persistent stirring of creative life (far from being confined to the visual arts), which, maybe, Yorkshire toughness enables to survive. But the grimness of life ensures that the flowering shall be elsewhere. Yorkshire has no Lowry, to remain where he is and to depict his native surroundings. All are fled, proud of Yorkshire, but living in determined exile.

The answer to any plea for the large-scale support of the amenities that raise life beyond the level of existence was always the same: such developments (though no doubt all very fine) would involve an increase in the rates. As if, in the long run, the retention within the city boundaries of a considerable part of the numerous class which pays most, per head, in taxation and makes the smallest demands upon municipal services, could raise the rates.

Full as we found our life in Leeds, we needed frequent respite from the West Riding Blight. This was found with friends in the country. Athole Hay's brother Robin (who was agent to Lord

Feversham) lived, with his three daughters, near Helmsley; his house
—a second home for us—was a place of high-spirited humour, sometimes enhanced by a visit from Athole himself. With his loud, high
voice, ascending occasionally to a scream, Athole would lure his
listeners into a world which had the appearance of fantasy yet whose
values were consistent and true. We went together into a local church
and saw what at first sight appeared to be a dull, Victorian mural
painting, representing a tree. Closer scrutiny showed it to be anything but dull: the tree had two boles, one large, flourishing and
in full foliage, a second of moderate size and fair condition. There
was also a small branch, withered and bent almost to the ground.
The first was labelled 'The Church of England', the second 'The
Eastern Church' and the third 'The Church of Rome'. In Athole's
company even such a bizarre discovery seemed very much part a of
normal life.

Other friends with whom we often stayed were Sir Gervase and
Lady Marjorie Beckett, at Newton Tower. These two were so unlike
that it was surprising that they should have become friends much less
married. He was tall, dark, a little saturnine in looks, correct, meticulous and public spirited; she was short, fair, irresponsibly and
irresistibly witty, and preoccupied with her home, family and
friends. Both of them, he from an intimate knowledge of Leeds—his
family had been Yorkshire bankers for several generations—and she
from the melancholy impression received from rare visits, sympa-
thized with our need for occasional escape.

With these friends and others we gradually came to see something
of Yorkshire, and to see it not as a county like another, but rather
(except for the absence of any sense of political identity) as a country,
like Scotland or Wales. Its great industrial cities, its seaports, its
wide tracts of splendid but desolate moor, its noble monuments of
the Middle Ages, York, Beverley, Rievaulx, Fountains, its great
houses, Wentworth Woodhouse, Castle Howard and a score of
others, the exceptional talent and self-reliance of its people and its
sheer extent, form a combination more characteristic of a country
than a county.

Leeds was distinguished from most of the other Northern cities
by the possession of a diminutive bohemia. Of this a tavern of
eminent amenity and character was the chief resort. Its name,
Whitelock's First City Luncheon Bar, misleadingly suggested an

inferior snack-counter with chromium fittings. Its location seemed
to have been chosen with a view to discouraging customers, for
although it stood in a narrow passage within a few yards of crowded
Briggate, it was virtually inaccessible to the casual seeker after
refreshment. Its seclusion gave it something of the atmosphere of
a club. The narrow long dark room, half restaurant and half bar,
with its black oak settles, embellished by brass-work of 'barley-
sugar' design, served as a meeting-place for a number of the personalities in the artistic, literary, musical and public life of Yorkshire,
as well as a large number of medical students from the Leeds
Infirmary, dog-fanciers, bookmakers and the like. The place without
doubt owed its character to the influence of the proprietor, Lupton
Whitelock, a flautist in the Leeds Symphony Orchestra, a man who,
though his smooth pink face rarely changed expression, and though
he seldom spoke, radiated a sensible cool goodwill. The prevailing
outlook at Whitelock's was one of progressive and outspoken but
rarely intemperate challenge to the more cautious opinions held
outside, more especially among the aldermen and councillors of the
city. The circumstance that Whitelock's was a resort favoured by
many members of the staff of *The Yorkshire Post* made the liberal
spirit which obtained there a more persuasive factor in the life of the
whole county than would otherwise have been the case. Under cover
of a rigid Conservative and Anglican orthodoxy this admirable newspaper consistently fostered every constructive local activity, whatever its political or sectarian implications. And at that time I do not
suppose that any English daily newspaper, with the exception of *The
Times*, allotted a larger proportion of its space to the visual arts.

Of all the frequenters of Whitelock's the most prominent and
regular was the painter Jacob Kramer, whose proud and powerful
head is familiar to many on account of Epstein's bronze of him at
the Tate. But his eyes, sad and self-mistrustful, were in curious
contradiction with his impressive head and figure. Kramer's sociable
disposition regularly impelled him to organize lunches and dinners in
honour of eminent visitors to Leeds, at which the artistic, literary
and musical society of Yorkshire used to assemble. The arrangement
of these functions, as well as the necessity of selling his pictures,
involved Kramer in a continuous series of prolonged and highly confidential negotiations with other frequenters of Whitelock's which,
although they were carried on in barely audible tones, were clearly of

the utmost complexity. The first entry of this exceptional person into England, where he was brought from Russia as a boy, passed quite unnoticed, but not many years later, at the beginning of the First World War, he returned to these shores after only a few minutes' absence, in circumstances that caused consternation. In company with some other artists he was bathing off a secluded stretch of seashore when he was caught by a current, carried swiftly along and deposited half a mile or so away upon a shallow, sandy beach, which was occupied by thousands of holiday-makers. Kramer's gradual emergence from the ocean, without clothes, spectacles or a certain command of the English language, might in any event have caused a momentary flutter of excitement. Unfortunately for him, the current which had snatched him from his decent seclusion had also caught up, and carried along in his wake, a huge horned mine. In alarmed awareness of the black, menacing form behind, he made desperate exertions to out-distance it. Whatever chances there might have been of placing limits upon the gathering excitement of his wading ashore naked and breathlessly incoherent were rendered void by his appearance of being accompanied by a vast explosive mine of probable German manufacture.

Jacob Kramer would have been a conspicuous figure in any environment; in Leeds he was a figure of fantasy. Possessed of every characteristic liable to provoke prejudice—he was a Jew, a foreigner by birth, a frequenter of shabby and even disreputable haunts, frequently drunk, even at times something of a vagrant, and eccentric—to understate matters—in some of his business transactions, he was a loyal friend, a man of delicate sensibilities, wholly without 'push' or malice and of invariable courtesy. It is to the immense credit of Leeds that it should have shown no prejudice against one who presented so easy a target for prejudice and for legitimate criticism also, and should instead have so fully recognized his almost childlike goodness and his authentic though sadly ebbing talent, and taken Kramer, not with pity but pride, to its heart.

The work of Kramer, in particular his drawings, was a good deal sought after in the city, but it was plainly apparent even to the least perceptive collector that the quality of his work declined year by year, and it was accordingly his earlier work that was most in demand. Someone would call on him and describe exactly the kind of drawing he wished to acquire—one of a kind made a decade or two earlier. Kramer, highly delighted, would tell him that by a lucky chance he knew of a drawing of the very kind his patron wanted, and he would hurry off to another patron and ask whether he might borrow, for some important purpose, an exhibition or the like, an early drawing which hung on his walls. The owner acceding, Kramer would sell it to his caller, and eventually, under persistent pressure, he would admit that the borrowed drawing was no longer available and undertake to replace it. Such negotiations, repeated again and again, involved him in a vast and unending web of negotiation, and his purpose in undertaking new work was to stop the gaps which occasionally threatened to bring the whole intricate process to a disastrous end. Eventually he came, I think, to derive as much pleasure from his elaborate diplomacy as from making the drawings which it required. Most of those made while I was in Leeds were of a very summary character. In order to simplify the making of a portrait he would place the sitter in profile close to the window in his little studio, so that half his or her face was in shadow so deep that it required no modelling—an ingenious labour-saving device. Every now and then he drew something that showed a glimmer of his earlier powers, which were considerable.

At one time he had lived in London and had contacts with the Vorticists (he contributed an illustration to *Blast*) and with Epstein and other leading painters and sculptors, and his work was beginning to win respect when he returned to Leeds, where he remained for the rest of his life. He was reticent about his reason for his premature retirement from an arena in which he might well have continued to receive the stimulus he required from his fellow artists and won a serious reputation. I had the impression that it was due to some sort of failure of confidence. About his London life he was very reserved. Occasionally he alluded to a small collection of drawings he had, presents from London friends and acquaintances such as Nevinson and Stanley Spencer, but I never saw any of them. In Leeds he gradually lost his creative urge, and I found it difficult to identify him with the powerful and dramatic 'Day of Atonement' which hung in the Art Gallery.

Kramer had a highly developed propensity to complicate an apparently simple life. He lived in two tiny rooms in an off-license house in Woodhouse Lane, yet whenever one met him he was in the throes of some complex situation which he would explain at length in a low conspiratorial mutter. One day he asked me to see him about a matter of extreme urgency. 'My God, John', he murmured, 'my God, I'm in trouble. I'm *in love*.' 'But who with, Jacob?' I asked. 'With *two* women,' he explained.

Among other visitors to Whitelock's were Monsignor John O'Connor, Rector of St. Cuthbert's, Bradford, the original of Chesterton's 'Father Brown' and the first translator into English of Maritain's *Art et Scolastique*. His great store of learning he carried in the same casual rough-and-ready way as a plumber carries his bag of tools; when a problem needed to be solved the bag was opened, the appropriate fact brought promptly out and immediately used. The operation completed, the scholarly equipment was as promptly put away, and none remained to 'embellish' Father O'Connor's cheerful, down-to-earth conversation. This excellent parish priest honoured Whitelock's only on the less informal occasions. A regular frequenter was Francis Watson, the novelist and art critic, who went to India as adviser to a Rajah who was understood to be desirous of devoting a quarter of his revenues to assembling a collection of sculptures by Henry Moore. Charles Murray, the painter, used often to come in from his caravan at Boroughbridge. His skill as an engraver gained him a prize to enable him to study in Rome, but he felt uneasy beneath blue skies, was insensitive to the splendour of classical and renaissance architecture. Declaring that Rome looked like an ice-cream cart, he left Italy and went into the North, visited Russia and Iceland, where he felt more at home, and eventually settled in a Yorkshire meadow. From these journeys he brought back a multitude of notes on minute scraps of paper; some of these he was now using as themes for compositions. A little quayside in Arctic waters, whereon two fisher-girls, wrapped in shawls, wait in driving rain for an unseen ship; a street of wooden shacks, and along it, heads down into the wind, two figures tramping through the melting snow; a churchyard in Russia, full of empty graves dug in summer for the dead of a winter which turns earth into iron—such were Murray's themes. One of his paintings, and several of his engravings, I induced the Art Gallery to buy. The Chairman called it 'a bit depressing', but it won a readier acceptance than Stanley Spencer's 'Fighting Swans', which we bought about this time—I believe the first example of this painter's work to enter a provincial collection— which one member declared he would not allow inside his house, and another that *somebody* must be pulling the Committee's leg. Upon my naming the scarcely more than nominal sum at which the picture was priced, a third Committee-man remarked that *somebody* seemed to be under the erroneous impression that the Committee was *made of brass*.

Although comments of this nature were not infrequent at the Art Gallery Committee's meetings, it would not be true to suggest that the members were in principle hostile to the newer movements in the arts; lack of comprehension was the only possible attitude that the environment in which they lived could have fostered. They were ambitious for Leeds, and imbued with a sense that they ought to keep abreast of the times in art as in other spheres. But there existed another and more cogent reason for what was at least an openness to persuasion to buy works by serious contemporary artists. For several generations the practice of collecting paintings was common among the business men of the North. An unusual number of pre-Raphaelite masterpieces had been promptly bought by Northern collectors, but such discrimination was uncommon, and by far the greater part of the numerous collections was composed of once popular 'subject' pictures by artists of the inferior sort. The endemic industrial depression which followed the First World War, and the growing difficulty of maintaining big houses, the precipitous decline in the prestige of popular-academic art, combined to dispose numbers of collectors to sell their pictures. Time after time these fetched less than a hundredth part of the sums for which they had originally been purchased. Presently every dealer was overstocked with shaggy cattle, baskets filled with puppies, carousing monks, heather-covered moors, and ladies 'dressed-up' in eighteenth-century costumes. When the dealers could absorb no more, a host of 'benefactors' made their appearance in every big Northern city, who attempted—too often with success—to present to their local art galleries pictures too large to hang, too costly to store, and too worthless to sell.

Although the average member of the local art gallery committee might well prefer, as a private citizen, pictures of this kind above all others, his opinion of their quality could not remain unaffected by their fate in the sale-room and by the evident determination of persons not always otherwise distinguished by civic spirit to present or bequeath them to civic institutions. The process of disillusionment had now gone so far as to induce in him an attitude not far short of contempt for Victorian art in its entirety; good painting, therefore, suffered in his estimation along with bad. 'Progressive' committee-men I have heard allude in slighting terms to the Pre-Raphaelites, to Watts, Stevens and Keene. I had to visit the basement of a local town hall to see an admirable Albert Moore which had been removed from the walls of the art gallery, and during the Second World War, when I remarked on the presence of an exquisite J. F. Lewis in the art gallery of a much-bombed town, I was told that every picture of any value had been sent away for safety, but a few of no consequence at all were retained so that there might be something to enliven the walls. But in spite of follies of this kind, the disillusionment of the local art-committee men with Victorian art induced in them a relative freedom from prejudice which conferred upon art gallery directors a power of initiative which they had never enjoyed before, and offered inspiring opportunities to judgment and conviction.

The Committee under which I served in Leeds included several members who cared for the arts, and its tolerance of the policy which I urged and the extraordinary responsiveness of the public to all its manifestations, gave me an exhilarating sense of usefulness.

But early one November morning we placed our few possessions in a taxicab, and as we were driven through the cold damp mist on our way to the railway station we looked for the last time at shabby Woodhouse Square—we had lived in a small flat at the top of No. 7 since our arrival—an oasis of frozen quiet among the pulsing, clattering factories that flanked it, and in a transient moment of elation we agreed that we would not have foregone a moment of the past eighteen months.

CHAPTER SEVEN

VISITS TO FAR OAKRIDGE

MY brother and sisters figure infrequently in these pages neither because I am not fond of them nor because we did not from time to time foregather. But two circumstances diminished the intimacy we enjoyed as children: I went away to school and University and emigrated to the United States while they remained at home. Between the three of them, more especially between my sisters, the early intimacy was preserved, and I became something of an outsider. My brother and I were kept in touch with each other by many shared interests which drew us closer, after a period of detachment, even than we had been as children. Rachel, our elder sister, staying with Elizabeth and me in Sheffield, became engaged to, and eventually married, our friend, Alan Ward, and remained in the North. Betty, the younger, after a promising beginning as a sculptor—I remember both Henry Moore and Barbara Hepworth speaking respectfully of her work when all three were fellow-students at the Royal College of Art—married Ensor Holiday, a doctor, and after a time abandoned her vocation.

Sometimes, occasionally at Christmas but more often in the summer, we would renew our intimacy by meeting, for longer or shorter periods, at our parents' house at Far Oakridge.

The days would be spent at work, but in the evenings Rachel, the possessor of a good small voice, would sing folk songs and persuade the rest of us to join her, and we organized charades and the like. The relative remoteness of the place favoured such diversions. But it also made us the more appreciative of the visits of friends, both our own and our parents'.

One day Bernard Shaw and his wife came to lunch. The Abyssinian War was at its height, and Shaw, an impassioned advocate of the 'civilizing mission' of Italy, argued at length that she deserved praise—in place of the blame that her aggression so widely provoked —for her self-sacrifice in attempting to put an end to the intolerable barbarism which prevailed in Abyssinia. I cannot recall a fine, in many respects a great, intellect arguing so crude a case and showing so little awareness—in fact none at all—of the moral or the political complexities of the issue. Elizabeth carried our baby daughter into the room, and Shaw interrupted his discourse to enquire whose baby she was. On being told she was Elizabeth's, he said, 'It *can't* be Elizabeth's; she's too *fond* of it for that'.

An occasional but always welcome guest was Christopher Hassall. One extremely hot afternoon in 1937 he arrived, dressed in a pin-striped dark city suit, and with no other in his bag. He had brought with him, however, a beautifully bound and admiringly inscribed copy of his recently published play, *Christ's Comet*, for presentation to John Masefield, then living at Pinbury Park—the beautiful house from which, I believe, his enraged landlord evicted him on the publication of *Reynard the Fox*. So eager was Christopher to lay his tribute at the Poet Laureate's feet that he persuaded us to set out forthwith. Pinbury is not many miles distant from Far Oakridge by road, but the sun shone fiercely down, the road was steep, the pilgrim's dark city suit fitted tightly and his arches were weak. Aware that in London he took taxis even for the briefest journeys, we marvelled at his hardihood. 'I urgently need', said Christopher through his teeth as he struggled over the last hundred yards, 'a double whisky.' At the Masefields' house visitors were usually received by Mrs. Masefield with a reminder that 'Jan' was about the Laureate's business. We waited, for a long time, that sultry afternoon, before he appeared. In the meanwhile Mrs. Masefield, sensing Christopher's exhausted state, said, 'Perhaps you would like, while you are waiting, a small glass of passion-flower juice.' Masefield welcomed us with his usual friendliness. Christopher, handing him the inscribed volume, related in a voice that trembled with emotion the touching theme of *Christ's Comet*, namely, that one of the Magi was lost on his journey to Bethlehem and spent years journeying in search of his Redeemer, finding him only at Golgotha. 'How very, very jolly—very jolly', Masefield said abstractedly, placing the book on a small table and proposing that we throw boomerangs—a pastime at which he excelled. Then after a long series of matches there was the long walk home.

A near neighbour and a frequent and most welcome visitor was James Stephens. While he would enchant the company by his copious flow of fantasy and wit, Cynthia his wife would describe, minutely, such activities as the cleaning of her sink and the disposal of rubbish. 'I brushed it', I remember her saying, 'to the end of the path and right up into the woods.' About everything except James' talk she appeared good-natured, but the rapt attention it invariably received continually provoked her. 'Don't listen to *him*', she would exclaim. 'Though it's all very well for you, I suppose, for this is the first time you've heard it, but I have to hear it *hundreds of times*.'

There were two members of our family who formed part of our life at Far Oakridge, one by very occasional visits, the other by residence in a neighbouring village. These were my father's elder and younger brothers, Charles and Albert, who fascinated me by their dissimilarity to one another and by the way in which certain of their dominant characteristics were combined in my father. Charles was severe, extremely methodical and public-spirited (he even bequeathed a substantial sum, I seem to recall, towards the redemption of the National Debt), while Albert was high-spirited, libertarian and gay even at times to the point of frivolity. The gaiety (though not the frivolity) was conspicuous in my father until his late twenties, but at the turn of the century a strong stream of puritanism asserted itself in a taste for a Tolstoyan simplicity of life, which, however, he was able only intermittently to impose upon my mother, who shared with Max Beerbohm a wish for 'richer food and poorer ratiocination'. Neither of my paternal grandparents, although extraordinarily upright, seemed to me in the least puritanical—still less frivolous. From what ancestors, I wondered, were this puritanism and this gaiety inherited? The frivolity, though not the gaiety, is dormant in our generation—except, from time to time, in me. Like my father, Charles and Albert possessed extraordinary taste. Anywhere they lived was a delight to the eye, whether Charles's forbidding stone mansion in Bradford or any of Albert's successive flats and cottages. To my father they both owed their first visual awareness, their first introductions to artists and the initial stimulus to their collecting instincts, but their visual perception was in no way, I think, inferior to his. Charles has never received his due for his prescience as a collector. It was at one time his intention to present or bequeath his collection to the Tate, but Charles Aitken, who from 1912 until 1930 had charge of its affairs, received his approaches in a manner which Charles considered slighting—a manner due more, perhaps, to a kind of frosty shyness rather than to unqualified indifference to the proffered benefaction about which, however, he can hardly have been enthusiastic. Whatever Aitken may have said, it effected a decisive change in Charles's intentions. Butler Wood, Curator of the Art Gallery in Charles's native Bradford, made no secret of the contempt in which he held the collection, which was accepted, in 1925, by the City of Manchester. Were it shown in London it would be recognized as one of the great British collections of its time, containing, as it does, outstanding examples of the work of his contemporaries whose reputations have proved most durable, among others Sickert, Steer, Augustus and Gwen John, Wyndham Lewis, Nevinson, Gaudier, Modigliani, Derain, Paul Nash, Bomberg and Max Beerbohm.

Albert was not only a dandy but he embellished everything he touched, and his manners were marked by an extraordinary but unconscious grace. I admired the way in which he used his rare social gifts to enhance his relations with his friends and, when he was Ruskin Master of Drawing at Oxford, with his students, but never in the interest of social aspiration. The memory of one example of his courtesy will remain with me always. On a cold winter's day a group of his relatives and friends stood beside him at the open grave of his gifted son, Michael. An icy blast swept across the cemetery, and Albert turned and looked to left and right with intense solicitude. We were his guests, and even at such a moment he had thought for our discomfort. As an artist he was apt to be discounted as a lightweight version of my father. In fact, except for some early landscapes, his art had an individual character, and when appropriate, a stylishness, which entitle it to far more consideration than it has received outside a circle of friends, which included, however, John, Orpen, Gilman, and Gore.

But compared, of course, with my father, everyone else who figured in our life at Far Oakridge was peripheral—even, in this environment, my mother, one of the most positive personalities I have ever known. For my father's passion for the Cotswolds and for the village and its neighbourhood was extraordinary. There was nobody thereabouts, man, woman or child, whom he did not know; there were many with whom he was on terms of friendship and many whom, in one way or another, he had helped. At the end of a hard day's painting outdoors—and, except when various illnesses forbade, almost every day, whatever the weather, was a hard day's painting outdoors—nothing gave him more pleasure than gazing intently out over the landscape. His love and his wide-ranging and intimate knowledge of the place made him the animator of all our life there.

In a quite different way my mother enjoyed it too, but not so much for itself as the object of my father's love and the focus of our family life. The beauty of the landscape she appreciated, but without any of my father's passion. Her interest in the surrounding population was scarcely less than his, but where his was almost entirely benevolent, hers was sceptical and amused. It was in the evenings, especially when friends such as the Beerbohms, the Stevenses, the Abbot of Prinknash, or our uncle Albert were present, that she became, with her reckless wit and her high spirits, most vividly herself.

My mother brought into the life of the village an element of the unforeseen. For instance, noticing among those bidding for a cottage not far from where we lived a man whose sly, rat-like face would have made him, in her opinion, an undesirable inhabitant of the village, she began, on an impulse, to bid against him. Cottages in those days, in our neighbourhood at least, were to be had for trifling sums. The rat-faced man had, however, evidently set his heart upon this particular cottage, but my mother outbid him after a duel that was the talk of the village for weeks. My father, seeing my mother landed with a cottage for which she had no use and at an exorbitant price, was not placated by her horrific description of the physiognomy of the underbidder.

These visits by my brother and sisters and myself had for all four of us, I think, the character of expeditions into the past. Our parents lived in a smaller house than the one they sold on my father's appointment as Principal of the Royal College of Art in 1920, but otherwise things were to an extraordinary degree unchanged: for many years the new house, like the old, was lit by oil lamps; the splendid countryside remained undefaced by bungalows (indeed new buildings of any kind were few and inconspicuous); traditional ways of farming continued to be followed with little modification; our few neighbours stayed where they were and newcomers were not many. There were, of course, days when the sun shone and days when snow fell, but the days I remember best were like the days that I remembered from boyhood: dry days when dark clouds flew high and continuously across the sky, and days when the clouds descending covered the hilltops and precipitated in blinding rain.

CHAPTER EIGHT

SHEFFIELD

THE big Yorkshire cities of Leeds and Sheffield are separated only by some thirty miles, but in character they are remote. The people of red-brick Leeds are inclined to be voluble and humorous, northern cockneys so to say, while the people of sombre stone-built Sheffield are dour; those of Leeds are enterprising and immensely diverse in their activities and they have made their city the shopping and amusement centre for all Yorkshire; Sheffielders are apt to continue doing what they have always done, making steel and steel products, and doing it exceedingly well. The enterprise and liveliness of Leeds were accompanied by a certain shoddiness, but the solid integrity of Sheffield seemed to involve a certain disdain for recreation and even for what elsewhere were considered necessities. The effects of this disdain we experienced not long after our arrival. Elizabeth had been ill for many weeks, and we decided to celebrate her leaving the nursing-home by having dinner out. We wandered about the centre of the city in search of some small restaurant, but we were eventually informed that there were no restaurants in Sheffield, except those at the (somewhat remote) railway stations, and were directed to the provision department of a multiple store where meals were served. We sat down and studied the menu.

'You'd best hurry,' said the waitress, 'it's near half past six and we're just closing.' We ate at home that night. The little bohemia that frequented Whitelock's and a few pubs in Leeds would be inconceivable in Sheffield: a figure such as Jacob Kramer could not have survived.

We were fortunate in discovering, within sight of the small hotel in Broomhill where we lived for a time, a house, number 6, in a regency terrace with a fine columned portico, and a biggish communal garden, known as 'The Mount'. Its architectural distinction —it resembled a big country classical house—made it a landmark in a city where, though the standard of building is high, fine domestic architecture is rare. We became extremely attached to 'The Mount' and remained there for as long as we lived in Sheffield.

Plans were made to open the new gallery in July 1934. It was one thing to take over a long established organization, as I had in Leeds, especially with the assistance of a secretary so efficient and experienced as Ernest Musgrave; it was quite another, as I quickly discovered, to create an entirely new one out of nothing. The new gallery occupied the upper part (and the Central Library the lower) of a big new civic building in Surrey Street. W. G. Davies, the City Architect who designed it, invited suggestions from me, as far as the advanced state of its construction allowed, about its interior planning, and I was entirely responsible for its decoration.

In the meanwhile I paid regular visits to Leeds, where I remained Director until some time early in the New Year. On one such visit, on 24th January, I was given the honour of a farewell dinner at Whitelock's by the Yorkshire Luncheon Group, Monsignor John O'Connor presiding, who read a message of goodwill from the Prime Minister, attended not only by artists, members of the staff of the University and of *The Yorkshire Post*, but even by the new Chairman of the Art Gallery Committee, so quickly were ruffled feelings forgotten. This occasion gave me particular pleasure because the Yorkshire Luncheon Group constituted a kind of unofficial opposition to official illiberality of word and act.

In spite of the uproar provoked by my resignation my last contacts with Leeds were singularly serene: indeed it would have taken an egregiously unresponsive nature not to have been deeply touched by the many expressions of appreciation of my work and of regret at our departure. The Art Gallery Committee had a somewhat altered complexion, owing to the Conservative Party's defeat in the Municipal elections, to which, I was told, my treatment had contributed; this was the first occasion, it was said, when an issue relating to the arts had affected the result of an election. My last task in Leeds was to organize the annual Yorkshire Artists' Exhibition (to which Henry Moore sent a stone carving, 'Mother and Child', his first contribution) which the Art Gallery Committee invited my father to open. Just before the opening I received a visit from Kenneth Clark, whom I had not seen since we were undergraduates. For an instant I scarcely recognized my old acquaintance, whom I remembered as diffident and retiring, in the person with a manner decisive, even imperious, he had become—a change due, perhaps, to the two years he had spent with Berenson in Florence, which had widened his already considerable knowledge and enhanced his self-confidence. Only a little while before I recalled that Ramsay MacDonald, then Prime Minister, dining with my parents, had asked my father whom he should appoint to the vacant directorship of the National Gallery, to which question he replied with a monosyllable: 'Clark'. Others doubt-less gave similar advice and very shortly the appointment was made.

Sheffield, where the visual arts were concerned, was considerably less sophisticated than Leeds. Leeds might have been compared with a battlefield in which serious art had been hard pressed and on balance defeated, but Leeds had however, been a battlefield, and at least as early as 1912, when Frank Rutter, a consistent advocate of modern French painting and of the New English Art Club, had been made Curator, and even earlier, good pictures were occasionally acquired and progressive ideas current. Sheffield had never been a battlefield: the Mappin Art Gallery was filled almost exclusively with popular-academic paintings mostly of inferior quality, and the interest of the Curators had been mainly in the adjoining Weston Park Museum which they also administered. Anthony Betts, head of the School of Painting at the College of Art, and my father, for whom a special visiting professorship at the University had been established, had certainly provoked some self-critical and construc-tive thinking, but only in very limited circles: the public at large the visual arts had scarcely touched. Their opportunities of seeing pain-ting or sculpture earlier than, say, 1870 and later than 1900—a few trivial examples apart—were negligible, and except for some pic-tures of rollicking monks and the like of Italian manufacture foreign art was unrepresented. The prospect of an entirely new beginning, of a new art gallery and for all practical purposes a virgin public, was exhilarating.

Alderman Graves offered as a gift to the city any works in his own possession which I should consider suitable for the new permanent collection and he agreed that I might borrow such pictures as I con-sidered appropriate from other collections. No offer could have been more generous. I could scarcely believe the good fortune that had given me, who two years before had not even thought seriously of working in an art gallery, the opportunity first of redecorating and entirely rearranging one important gallery and then of helping to decorate and even, to a very modest degree, to plan, another, and to form its collection. I have written much that is critical of the two great Yorkshire cities and expect to write more, but even though my hopes in Sheffield were destined to suffer much disappointment, nothing can ever diminish the deep gratitude I feel to both of them for having given a young tyro opportunities which, taken together, are probably without precedent in the annals of British art gallery directors. By this time I had come to know a number of my professional colleagues and was only too well aware of the bitterness and frustration felt by many of them through the want of scope for the exercise of their talents and the corroding apathy to which numbers of them fell victims. Little was expected of them except that they should avoid giving offence to influential citizens, above all by recommending the refusal of their gifts, however worthless. After a few years these unfortunate colleagues were without hope. There were centres, notably Birmingham, Glasgow and Manchester, where different conditions prevailed, but these were very few.

In Leeds I had had the advantage of the invaluable assistance of Ernest Musgrave; indeed we discussed the possibility of his applying for a post at the new gallery and I put him in touch with Alderman Graves, but without result. In Sheffield the two key members of my staff, my Assistant and my Secretary, were appointed without my being consulted, and I was inclined at first to mistrust them in consequence. Mistrust was never less justified, for I could have wished for no better colleagues than G. H. Constantine and Betty Dunster. Constantine was a respectable landscape water-colourist with some experience of the conservation of paintings. He had something of the resourcefulness and imperturbability of Ernest Musgrave, and like him he proved an excellent organizer and firm and friendly with the staff. And he was a delight to be with, but it would take a subtler pen than mine to evoke the perennial charm of this elderly quiet family man without much education, who had rarely left Sheffield or its neighbourhood. He combined an exacting standard of personal conduct with a charitable and amused understanding of human weakness, a directness of thought and speech rarely met with, and a highly developed sense of humour. In response, for instance, to an enquiry of mine about a colleague not noted for his energy Constantine replied, 'You want to know what he does? He sits, smoking his pipe, just waiting year after year for his retirement.'

Betty Dunster was intelligent, wholly trustworthy and she shared with Constantine a devotion to the new Gallery; she was pretty, looked frail, but at the end of a rigorous day's work she was as fresh as she was at the beginning. The assistance and the friendship of two such colleagues gave me confidence. The attendant staff we recruited and trained were as congenial as they were reliable and resourceful.

Our time was divided between recruiting and training attendant staff, the multifarious problems connected with the equipment and decoration of the gallery, the establishment of an office, and the assembly of loans and the formation of a collection.

Although the first impression made by Alderman Graves' collection was far from exhilarating, a closer look showed that despite its prevailing mediocrity it in fact contained a considerable number of pictures worthy of a place in the new Gallery. It was only natural that he should wish me to select the largest number that I conscientiously could, and in view of the munificence of his gifts I felt myself under an obligation to comply with his wishes even though this involved the inclusion of a substantial number of merely respectable works. He further expressed the wish that the existing attributions should not be altered, although for the time being this condition—for it virtually amounted to that—had little effect, for the immense volume of work to be done before the Gallery's opening left in any case no time for research.

I made urgent appeals in London for loans of the highest quality, emphasizing the special potentialities of a new art gallery for a public that had enjoyed fewer opportunities of seeing fine painting than any public of comparable magnitude in the country, and I was immensely gratified at the generosity of the response. The National Gallery lent paintings by Puvis de Chavannes, Claude, Cuyp and Ochtervelt; the Home House Trustees of the Courtauld Institute Cézanne's 'Card Players', Van Gogh's 'La Haie'; the Tate Degas' 'Portrait of Pellegrini', three fine Gainsboroughs and a Turner; the Victoria and Albert Museum cases of Chinese porcelain and Persian pottery, and the Royal Academy made a particularly handsome loan which included six Constables and a Reynolds. Among private collectors Hugh Walpole lent a Sickert and Edward Marsh Stanley Spencer's early 'Self-Portrait', and other collectors lent bronzes by Epstein and Dobson. There was a group of his copies of mediaeval English wall-paintings lent by E. W. Tristram, and a special display was arranged of the work of Thomas Creswick, the early Sheffield landscape painter who was singled out for praise by Ruskin. Nothing by any of these artists except Creswick, so far as I was aware, had ever been seen in Sheffield.

This collection was far from being representative of any particular school of painting: the intention behind its assembly was to widen the perspective of a public which had enjoyed negligible opportunities of becoming familiar with anything except late Victorian popular-academic painting and to give it a sight of the work of a number of the great masters. The older generation of living British painters, such men as Sickert, Steer, Augustus John, Paul and John Nash, were represented by loans of high quality but—and it may well be that I erred in being over cautious—I invited none of the more revolutionary artists such as Henry Moore, or even Matthew Smith, so anxious was I on this particular occasion that controversy be avoided, that all the exhibits should be accepted in Sheffield without question and that Alderman Graves should not come under the slightest criticism or have the least occasion to mistrust the policy upon which we had agreed. Before the opening, however, I wrote a longish illustrated article on Henry Moore in *The Sheffield Telegraph* (5th May 1934), with the double purpose of paying a tribute to a great artist—incidentally a Yorkshireman—and accustoming the Sheffield people to art of a more innovating character than could yet be seen at the Gallery.

The new Gallery, named after its donor, was opened by the Duchess of York (afterwards Queen Elizabeth) on 5th July. Until this occasion I had been unaware of her lively interest in painting: she looked at so many of the pictures with such close attention that we fell behind schedule. To my great pleasure and infinite relief both the Gallery and its contents received the highest praise, in both the national and the Yorkshire newspapers, in which there was not, so far as I can recall, a single critical word. All day long and for many weeks the people of Sheffield crowded into their new Gallery, and no one who worked there could have failed to be aware of the warmth of their appreciation, and this appreciation seemed to delight Alderman Graves. It all seemed, as the saying goes, too good to be true, but for a while this happy state of affairs prevailed. In September I outlined, on a public occasion with the Lord Mayor presiding, an art policy for the City, drawing attention to the immense over-representation of the second half of the nineteenth century and urging the acquisition of earlier paintings and of those of the best of our own contemporaries. The friendly reception of these proposals led me to believe that the time had come to show a major work by a controversial master, and Picasso's 'La Vie', an outstanding example of his so-called Blue Period, was borrowed that October through the helpfulness of T. J. Honeyman from the firm of Reid and Lefevre, who were attempting, entirely without success, to interest British public galleries in the work of this master.

On 25th July, 1935, I received, however, a letter from Alderman Graves written on the previous day proposing that 'we should now return . . . the loan pictures and rehang the vacant space from our own resources,' that is to say, that the pictures which had given Sheffield a status scarcely imaginable even a year before should be replaced by further pictures from his own collection. These were ominous words. All these pictures still in his possession had been tacitly understood to be regarded by me—who had been accorded entire freedom of choice, already exercised in the direction of his wishes to the utmost limit of conscience—as unsuitable for the Graves Gallery; to admit such works at this stage would have been to debase the currency established by the opening exhibition. From this moment there began a long conflict of wills between Alderman Graves and myself—in the course of which I was subject to heavy and continuous pressure: between his determination to impose the remainder of his collection upon the city and my determination, made painful to maintain by my deep sense of gratitude, to resist. Slowly but surely the close cooperation that had existed hitherto between us diminished. Although he could not impose his will he was able to frustrate my ideas: he declined, for instance, to allow me even to propose to our Sub-committee—among other works—Picasso's 'La Vie' as a purchase—for £4000!—a painting now worth more than twenty times that sum—a value greater in fact than that of all the hundreds of works of art then owned by Sheffield together. Some two years later we found a partial solution to the issue that divided us: Alderman Graves undertook to build an extension to the Mappin Gallery and to select himself from his own collection further pictures as a gift to be hung in this extension, and agreed that the fact that the selection was his own should be made public, and that every painting of his choice should be so labelled. This was done; the

Mappin was redecorated and rearranged and the collection aug-
mented by some 300 pictures, presented by Alderman Graves, and the
enlarged building (together with the rebuilt Museum adjoining it)
was opened by Sir Philip Sassoon, First Commissioner of Works, on
16th April 1937. (The contrast between Sir Philip, an exquisite
slender figure out of *The Arabian Nights*, thinly disguised by a suit
from Savile Row, and the raw-complexioned burly alderman was so
extreme as to make them appear quite simply to be different kinds of
human being.) The realization of this project, however, gave little
satisfaction to Alderman Graves: the extended Mappin evoked
negligible response among the public and none at all among artists
and lovers of art. He attempted, ironically enough, to turn the very
success of the Graves to his own ends by claiming that this was due
to its central location rather than to its contents, and he formed the
intention—carried into effect, I understand, after my resignation—
of making the exhibition of his gifts to the Mappin obligatory at the
Graves for fixed periods in every year.

In the meanwhile a succession of collectors, among others the
Duke of Devonshire, Earl Fitzwilliam, Lord Galway and Lady
Ottoline Morrell, lent pictures to the Graves Gallery; a particularly
illuminating collection of French Drawings from Ingres to Picasso,
assembled by Seligmann et Cie., broke its journey from Paris to New
York in Sheffield and was shown nowhere else in England; through
the cooperation of Kenneth Clark the National Gallery lent a group
of eleven examples of early Italian painting, representative of the
principal schools, including panels attributed to Botticelli and
Benozzo Gozzoli. When I thanked him Clark replied, 'It's *difficult*
for the National Gallery to lend pictures to provincial galleries:
those available either represent the Virgin or Saints, which are
disapproved of as "Roman Catholic", or else nudes, which are
considered improper, so we're delighted to be *able* to lend these to
Sheffield.' Clark paid a second visit to the Graves Gallery, arriving
on 8th November, when I took him afterwards to the Ruskin
Museum to see the Verrocchio 'Madonna', which he examined with
scrupulous care. I not only enjoyed his visit for the encouragement
I derived from it but also for his capacity for enjoying works of art
remote from his particular fields of interest, even the mediocre, and
of discerning in them at least some redeeming quality of intention or
some reflection, however faint, of the glory of some master—a

capacity, it may be observed, a great deal rarer among members of our profession than those outside it might suppose.

The opportunities offered by these and a number of other loans to the Sheffield public to widen its aesthetic experience were always warmly and sometimes enthusiastically received, but I became convinced that there was something precarious about the interest of this particular public in the visual arts, due probably to its previous privation. After much thought I decided that there was one possibility, and only one, of making the visual arts a fully accepted part of the daily life of the citizens: this was to capture the imagination of the children. In order to realize this aim I put before a meeting of head teachers a far-reaching scheme of visits by parties of children from the city's schools. The proposal was received with the utmost goodwill, and from the end of January 1935 until I left Sheffield I received two parties every week, subject only to the conditions that none of them should exceed 200, and that no child should come otherwise than of his or her own free will. In the carrying out of this scheme I had invaluable help from Constantine and invariable co-operation from the accompanying teachers. The effect upon public interest was almost immediate: there never seemed to be a time when there were not children in the Gallery on their own, and instead of their being brought, as heretofore, by their parents, it was evidently the children who took the initiative. In order to make sure that the Gallery would become known at once to every child in the city and to emphasize that it was to be visited for pleasure, I was able to arrange, through the helpfulness of the Leicester Galleries, London, for an exhibition of Walt Disney's working drawings, which showed how continuity is achieved, backgrounds designed and the like, besides the celluloid translations. Particulars were thrown upon the screen of every cinema in the region and the Gallery was in consequence invaded by hordes of children. At the Museums Conference held in Newcastle in July 1937 I was invited to give an address on the Relation between Schools and Art Galleries with special reference to the Sheffield scheme, which was, I gathered, something of an innovation.

On 16th October there occurred an event which immeasurably enriched our lives: Elizabeth gave birth to a daughter. But the baby did not flourish; she fell ill, and months after her birth her weight showed no increase. She remained a tiny skeleton, and caused us continuous anxiety. Elizabeth and I visited Canon Dolan, Rector of St. Mary's Church, to arrange for Lucy's baptism. Elizabeth, although an agnostic, was not only willing but anxious to fulfil the undertaking we gave when we were granted a dispensation to marry that any children should be brought up as Catholics. Some theological discussion arose between Elizabeth and the Canon in the course of which she made some comment on the 'Pauline theology of the Roman Catholic Church', whereupon he refused to baptise the child unless she signed a further undertaking that she be brought up as a Catholic. Considering that this demand called in question the sincerity of her original undertaking, Elizabeth refused. Shortly afterwards, in view of Lucy's precarious state of health and reluctant to cause a fuss, Elizabeth agreed to sign the second document, and I called once again on the Canon, who said that Elizabeth 'thought too much' and he doubted whether she was the right person to bring up a Catholic child and that he had some doubts as to whether he ought to perform the ceremony. I told him that I fully shared his doubts upon the latter point and that in no circumstances would I permit the ceremony to take place within his parish. A few days later with a group of our friends we drove out to an ancient centre of Catholicism, Southgate House, Clowne, Derbyshire, where the baby was baptised Lucy King in the private chapel of the Butler-Bowden family, by Father Kendal, of the Society of Jesus, who had bicycled for many miles through the driving rain. Athole Hay came from London to be a godparent; E. W. Tristram was unable to be present and Colonel Butler-Bowden stood proxy, as did Mrs. Butler-Bowden for Princess Margaret, wife of the former 'White Rajah' of Sarawak; others were Lady Matthews and Mrs. Arthur Davy. Canon Dolan won our respect by showing no trace of irritation.

It so happened that my advice was sought from time to time by the parish priest when the Church of the Sacred Heart, Hillsborough, Sheffield, was being built, and we were accordingly invited to its consecration and to the official luncheon that was to follow. (It was as a result of my advice that Eric Newton was invited to make a mosaic there.) When I asked Elizabeth whether she would accompany me, she replied that during the years of our marriage I had never asked her to do anything at all connected with my religion, and that she would certainly attend these two functions. In consequence of her own ponderings of that time she added that if among the assembled clergy she could only discern the presence of holiness as well as goodness, she might well reconsider her attitude towards the Catholic Church. I was surprised by her words, because she was deeply suspicious of Catholicism, although she had long since abandoned the Anglicanism, or, more precisely, the Episcopalianism, of her family. In the new church we scrutinized the faces of the many priests before us, faces of decent good men for the most part, decent practical men . . . then, with slight simultaneous starts, we saw a face in which shone something that was more than, goodness. In feature he was more ordinary, more commonplace, than anyone present, but his nondescript pallid features were radiant. To our surprise we found that he and Elizabeth were to be neighbours at the luncheon. She was too much overcome at the prospect and insisted on our changing places and my sitting beside him myself. They had, all the same, some conversation and this encounter affected the beginning of a change in her attitude towards the Catholic Church. The priest's name was Malachy Brazil and he was Prior of the Trappists of Mount St. Bernard, near Leicester.

Some time afterwards at my parents' home in Gloucestershire she mentioned her opinion of Father Malachy to Dom Wilfred Upson, Abbot of Prinknash, who replied, 'Yes; but,' he added ruminatively, 'I wish I had half his *business sense*.'

There was another and larger question connected with church decoration with which I was to become concerned for many years. On a visit to London I was invited by Edward Hutton, the writer and brother of our Sheffield friend Mrs. Arthur Davy, to accompany him to Westminster Cathedral, to discuss the mosaic work that was being carried out, especially that on the tympanum of the great arch. This was meretricious and inept and a gross disfigurement of the majestic interior, and he expressed dismay at the designs for further mosaics in the apse, which were of no less deplorable character. Edward Hutton told me of a project that was forming in his mind, namely an appeal to Dr. Hinsley, who had recently succeeded Cardinal Bourne as Archbishop of Westminster, to discontinue this work and to reconsider the whole question of the interior decoration of the Cathedral. I myself had been shocked by these designs when I first saw them, and had written in urgent protest a letter to *The Daily Telegraph*.[1] I eagerly associated myself with the projected

[1] 24 August 1934.

appeal, which in view of the Cathedral's being a great national monument was to be signed by leading art authorities irrespective of their faith. The effect of the appeal—which was signed by heads of the national galleries and museums, by artists and writers, and presented to the Archbishop towards the end of 1935—was the cessation of work on the mosaics.

There were during my years in Yorkshire two institutions for which I was responsible, and I have scarcely mentioned either of them, because my own contribution to their well-being was little more than nominal. I do so now, however, in the one case to pay tribute to an outstanding achievement and in the other to recall an interesting institution that exists no longer. The first was Temple Newsam House, a splendid and historic Tudor-Jacobean Mansion that had belonged to Leeds for a decade, over which the Director of the Art Gallery was supposed to exercise some ill-defined jurisdiction, and I did little beyond rearranging the pictures in a number of the rooms. In 1938, however, it was placed unequivocally under the same administration as the Art Gallery, and my immediate successors, Philip Hendy and Ernest Musgrave, made it into a model of what such a house should be. It is now a museum of the decorative arts, of conspicuous interest and beauty. The second of these institutions was the Ruskin Museum in Meersbrook on the outskirts of Sheffield. This museum was the principal achievement of the Guild of St. George, established by Ruskin in 1878 as a band of good men who would endow it with a tenth part of their incomes, and acquire land and develop it in accordance with his ideals.

This quixotic venture in the practical application of the purest and loftiest idealism never really flourished, but it did—and does—survive and it was in this body that the contents of the Ruskin Museum were vested. Ruskin himself dreamed of an ideal museum, to which the modest institution which came into being in his old age, first at Walkley and later at the house at Meersbrook placed at his disposal by the Corporation of Sheffield, could have borne only the faintest resemblance. The collection was arranged, however, in conformity with his ideas, but Ruskin himself was too old and infirm to be able to visit it. The red-brick Victorian house was a little forbidding, the collection consisting largely of Ruskin's much-loved minerals and the copies made under his instructions of paintings by Carpaccio, Botticelli and others, and drawings of buildings in which he particularly delighted and deemed to be in danger from restoration or neglect. It also contained the fascinating and mysterious 'Madonna' by Verrocchio—mysterious because there had long been doubts about its precise attribution, more especially about the background which seemed to be by a different hand from the figures. For me there was something touching and romantic about this little museum, in spite of the drabness of the commonplace little rooms, from the knowledge that everything it contained had been destined for it, and discovered or commissioned or bought and loved, by the greatest critic of the arts—for all his absurdities and contradictions—born of the English-speaking peoples, a man whose criticism was itself often great art. When I went up and wandered about there I made occasional alterations, bringing for instance an interesting object out of shadow, though sparingly, unforgetful that the arrangement, although unseen by him, had been made by those better acquainted than I with Ruskin's intentions. The Museum, in any case, had a devoted Superintendent in Miss Genevieve Pilley, a lady immersed in his teachings and who had met him as a girl. When she had taken up her post some years before, her predecessor had occupied a considerable part of the building as a residence, when it was shuttered and almost derelict, and entrance was on occasion denied to those few members of the public who found their way through a gloomy quarter of the city to visit this singular shrine. Miss Pilley soon set all to rights and looked after her charge with affectionate and scrupulous care. The master and several of the Members of the Guild of St. George (in which I was myself enrolled as an Associate) kept in periodic touch with me about the Museum's affairs and showed themselves invariably helpful and kindly.

There was another organization in which I took a more active part. The funds available for the purchase of works of art for Sheffield's municipal collection had been negligible and Alderman Graves on many occasions expressed the view that while available pictures remained in his own collection (which together with that part already presented, according to a memorandum which he circulated officially, constituted a well-balanced and representative collection of English, Dutch and French Art) expenditure upon further acquisitions was a waste of public funds. In view of the urgency of the collection's needs—it included, for example, nothing by Hilliard, Dobson, Lely, Kneller, Hogarth, Reynolds, Gainsborough, Blake,

Palmer, Turner, Stubbs, Girtin, Cotman, Stevens (in spite of his close association with the city), Madox Brown, Watts, Sickert, Steer, John, Matthew Smith, to name only a few of the more conspicuous British lacunae—a group of leading citizens came together towards the close of 1936 to form the Sheffield Art Collections Fund. Through this body a number of fine pictures have entered the municipal collection. During the first year of its existence alone were added paintings by Antonio Moro, Ribera, James Barry and William Beechey. From other sources came 'The Misses Vickers', one of Sargent's most brilliant portrait groups—which was, moreover, painted in Sheffield—and works by Walter Greaves, Spencer Gore, Stanley Spencer, Eric Gill, Wyndham Lewis, Rodin and Paul Nash. Opportunities for visits to London were less frequent than I could have wished. Alderman Graves, well aware that such visits usually led to pictures being proposed for purchase or offered as gifts or loans, was apt to oppose them, and he even on occasion had watch kept to see whether I prolonged my absences unduly. I was able nevertheless to preserve and even to extend my relations with artists.

Meeting Stanley Spencer one day in London in the summer of 1935 I was reminded that I had never been to see him in Cookham and he invited me to propose a time convenient. Not long afterwards I named a certain Sunday and received the following note in reply:

> Friday evening 'Lindworth'
> Cookham on Thames
>
> Dear Mr Rothenstein,
> I will be in on Sunday afternoon if you call. The house is in the village, at the far of a little alley that runs up alongside 'Budgens Stores'. The gate with name on it is in the left corner at top end of this little drive.
> Yours sincerely,
> Stanley Spencer
> Please excuse pencil; I have no pen that will write.

I had known him for some twelve years and ardently admired his painting, but we had not met often since my return from America and were still on somewhat formal terms. The almost total identification of Stanley Spencer with his birthplace was already well known to me; 'Cookham' indeed was the name by which he was called by

his contemporaries at the Slade, but what I had heard had not prepared me for the idyllic yet down to earth relation between Cookham
the man and Cookham the place. When I asked him whether I
might see his work, he replied, 'Of course you may, but you must see
Cookham first', and as we walked the streets he pointed out various
places of interest—places, mostly, with some particular significance
in his own life: the Methodist chapel attended by his mother's
family, the little house where he had his first lessons—they might
have been places he had longed all his life to see and was at last
granted the sight of, so ecstatic was his response. The culmination
of our tour were the church and churchyard. As he passed the lych-
gate he might have entered heaven, and his voice rose to a vehement
shrillness as he spoke of the places represented in his 'Resurrection:
Cookham' at the Tate. The contemplation of them evoked so great a
flood of early memories that, rapid as was his talk, it could scarcely
keep pace with them. It was apparent that he was one of those, like
Constable or Wordsworth, whose imaginations are at once charged
and fired by the impressions received in childhood. Although recollections about places associated with his childhood stirred him most,
the little town was far from being a museum of memories; he
delighted in the present, and recounted the histories and idiosyncrasies of the people we met; a number of them, including the most
persistent local drunk, were relations of his own. No artist, especially
no religious artist, was less of an idealist: what he loved, he loved
totally, not only selected aspects of it, the 'ugly' as ardently as the
'beautiful', the one aspect being for him the natural complement of
the other. It was this totality, this utter absence of selectivity in his
love, that chiefly prevented him from being, for all his love of God,
his fear of Judgment, his absorption in the Bible, in any dogmatic
sense a Christian. 'I'll have to turn up at the Gates of Heaven bringing all my faults,' he said to me—I won't pretend to remember
whether it was on this occasion or another—'all my faults, all my
sins, sexual and all—I couldn't bear to leave anything behind. I shall
just have to say "here I am, God, complete, with all my heavy
baggage".' Just as he rejected nothing of himself, so did he reject
nothing of his birthplace: the outcropping of 'stockbroker Tudor', of
red brick with woodwork painted white, which would have revolted
an antiquarian, the unseemliest day-tripper who would have revolted
almost anybody, all were embraced in his capacious love, seeming to

add richness and variety to the place that he regarded as holy. His conviction that Cookham was, as he put it, 'a holy suburb of Heaven' was the conviction that coloured all his paintings and drawings of it and all he said about it. A vague sense of the events, related in the Bible having taken place in the region where he was born early took a hold upon Stanley Spencer's imagination and attaches him to the tradition in which Milton, and more militantly Blake, were sharers, according to which the British Isles were the centre of all primitive and patriarchal goodness. 'Jerusalem the Emanation of the Giant Albion! Can it be? Is it a truth that the Learned have explored? Was Britain the Primitive Seat of the Patriarchal Religion?' asked Blake in his *Jerusalem*. There are no grounds for supposing that in Stanley Spencer's mind there was anything approaching an explicit historical identification of these Islands with 'the Primitive Seat of the Patriarchal Religion', and he was altogether free from the widely current heresy that the Christian religion is something which belongs essentially to the past. Indeed for Stanley Spencer past and present, the living and the dead, good and evil, all existed together in a vast undifferentiated flux.

The language in which he voiced this total love was Biblical but freely laced with racy vernacular expressions; the words poured out of him in an almost unceasing stream. Exalted by my visit I suggested to him that I should write something in the nature of a study of himself and Cookham. He seemed favourably disposed and promised to consider the project and write to me about it. His attitude, the recollection of his praise for the essay I had written about him in the 'twenties, published eventually in *Apollo*, and his willingness to help me with reproductions for my *British Artists and the War*, gave me no reason to doubt that I might count upon his goodwill. The contents and still more the tone of his promised letter (undated but postmarked 20th July) surprised me. It ran as follows:

'lindworth' Cookham on Thames

Dear Mr Rothenstein,
    I am sorry to disappoint you but I cannot permit you to write about me.
    When afterwards I thought over what you suggested doing, it seemed most distasteful to me and I do not wish you to do it.

I particularly do not wish to have anything written about me at all either my work or myself.

Yours sincerely,
Stanley Spencer

P.S.   I wish you had written to me first explaining what you had in mind, as there is nothing I am less likely to be interested in than what you proposed. But if the matter had gone on you would have found that the cost of such a venture would have made such a project impossible.

To my further surprise when we met again he greeted me with the same cordiality as he had before, and showed not a shadow of the irritability so evident in this letter. As I came to know him I understood what had impelled him to write this, in the circumstances, singular communication. Stanley Spencer on several occasions reverted to his conviction that nobody understood either him or his work except himself, and that he hoped to write a series of commentaries on his own pictures—and he showed me a number of rough pencilled drafts—as well as something in the nature of recollections of his life. I came also to understand the tone as well as the content of this letter. It was as though he were ruled by two contrary dispositions. One—and the prevailing one—was kind and generous, and at times even saintly. But without warning another was liable to assert itself, that of an irascible, suspicious little peasant, when his expression would sharpen and his voice rise to an angry scream. As the years passed the first gained an ever surer ascendancy; the other never entirely ceased to erupt, but it remained for longer and longer periods quiescent.

A painter whom I met from time to time was Paul Nash, who was as businesslike and consistent in his dealings as Stanley Spencer was the reverse. I was most anxious that 'Winter Sea', one of the finest of his water colours, in which he made use of a post-cubist style to enhance the impressiveness and the actuality of the subject, should be acquired by the Sheffield Art Collections Fund. As soon as it arrived he wrote (18th October 1937) enquiring about the decision in order that a reproduction of it in a forthcoming publication should be correctly captioned, and (21st October) voluntarily reducing the price from 25 guineas to £20, but adding, 'I regard it as one of my best drawings; and you will understand one parts with these always reluctantly.' The purchase was duly made, but I heard nothing from the artist. Late the following month I received a letter that I transcribe in full as it is one which recalls so clearly the inflexion of his voice:

3 Eldon Road, Hampstead N.W.3.
November 28, 1937

Dear John Rothenstein

You must think me very odd. I have got into a thoroughly bad complex about writing letters—simply *not* writing them—irrationally obstinately not. Please try to excuse me, and believe how delighted I was to hear you had succeeded in persuading Seffield (sic) to purchase my 'Winter Sea'. Also, I must express my appreciation of that gesture by the Sheffield Art Collections Fund in paying the commission due to the Society.

I hope to hear from you eventually that the Graves Art Gallery has admitted the drawing to its collection.

You once promised to get into touch with me when you came to London. We should be so pleased if you would come and lunch here when you have time to spare. If she is with you of course come with your wife. Will you let us know? Again, my thanks and congratulations.

Yours sincerely
Paul Nash

About this time the possibility of my writing something on him was evidently the subject of discussion between us, for I recently came upon a letter which accompanied various documents likely to serve this purpose. This came to nothing and only one of these documents survives, but as it is a clear and concise statement (in his own handwriting) regarding his aims and the development of his art it seems well worth reproduction here. (So completely had I lost sight of it that I made no allusion to it in my chapter on Paul Nash in the second volume of my *Modern English Painters*.)

This statement runs as follows:

Dear John

Here are the promised references. Keep the catalogue if you like as I have others but send me back the pages from AXIS.

I have 'made a statement' also which I hope is the kind of thing you want. I will now map out my pictures on the pages and let you have the plan as soon as it is ready—In haste.

P.N.

Since I began, in 1928, to exercise invention instead of depending solely on an interpretation of the natural scene, I have made pictures of two kinds side by side.

On the one hand, direct studies of landscape and sea scape, on the other, imaginative compositions treated in a variety of ways but whose content still is, for the most part, a presentation of recognisable, natural forms.

The character of these presentations led me to be invited to take part in the International Surrealist Exhibition of 1936. That association with the Movement greatly stimulated my interest in Surrealism. Through the medium of its ideas I have found, since then, an increasing inspiration, and I have sought by a variety of means—painting, 'collage', object-making, photography, and even writing to evolve my own concept of its application to pictorial art.

My attempts to write about both Nash brothers in the 'thirties were frustrated. I was commissioned to prepare a monograph about John Nash which was to follow one already published about Paul. This indeed I had completed when it became apparent that something had gone amiss with the arrangements for its publication. In fact it never appeared. My MS was shown to Paul, who going over it with John made a number of criticisms. In an undated letter from his house at Meadle, near Aylesbury, John wrote that Paul 'seemed to think that you had not "got me right",' and that he 'would like to talk to you himself' and 'I was "dumb" about myself'. It was no doubt Paul's wish to set me right that impelled him to send me a long letter mainly about John. Unfortunately the end is missing. As an authoritative account—however fragmentary—of an artist of unusual gifts by a highly articulate and even more gifted brother, it merits publication:

3 Eldon Road, Hampstead, N.W.3

May 25, 1938

Dear John

I can't sleep so I may as well try to get this long-postponed letter written to you. I was at Oxford last night speaking to the

Arts Club; it seems to have irritated my chords in some way with the result that I can't stop coughing for more than a few minutes, and that is the knell of sleep.

. . . . . .

Now, as to the subject of your essay. When J left Wellington he was supposed to go to Oxford. The project fell through and no one seemed quite certain in what direction he would steer. By way of filling in time he took a job as reporter on the local newspaper and it was while he was at this peculiar game that he began to make quite frequent drawings. Most of these were humorous and fantastic but now and then he would make a note of some landscape seen while he was bicycling about the country. One of these, a view over flooded meadows at night, I remember impressed me very much and I began to encourage him to do more of this sort of thing. All the same he went his own way mostly and I was careful not to try any special pressure. I think my own practice of continual drawing influenced him. We had drawn, as it were, side by side, since we could hold pencils. It was natural for him to fall into line again now that the interruptions of 'school' were over and we could spend more time together.

He then came across a Slade friend of mine Pellew Harvey. They in turn became great friends and Pellew who had done much to help me in my first stages seemed able to get Jack going in earnest. They spent a holiday together—I think in Norfolk—and from this appeared the first authentic, convincing signs that Jack had something to say and was going to say it in the medium of some kind of art, as opposed to literature, or diplomacy or divinity or whatever other fields of operation had been considered for him. I remember I told my father when I had seen these first watercolours that he might as well make up his mind to it. Jack, I felt certain, was going to be an artist.

Pellew's example and encouragement continued and rapidly bore fruit. I adapted and enlarged for his purpose the technique of watercolours washed over waxy chalk areas which he, Pellew, used so skillfully in his own work. But what he picked up from seeing me draw and paint and what he got similarly from Pellew was the only schooling in art he ever had. From the beginning he was practically self-made.

What I miss in your account of J's development is any reference to the extraordinary vision of his first pictures. They were, if any pictures ever were, the products of a fine naivety; as authentic as that of the Douanier Rousseau's. If a number of these were collected they would represent a unique passage in the history of English art. By the same token one of the most interesting aspects of J's development is his deliberate *re*construction. It was like a choir boy with a lovely natural treble who must begin again when his voice breaks. You have . . .

How ambivalent relations between brothers, and between artists, can be, was exemplified by a further response of Paul to my essay on John. Having made these and other suggestions regarding my first draft and expressing a wish to discuss the amended version, he invited Elizabeth and me to lunch with him at his house in Eldon Road. Welcoming the prospect of further suggestions for its improvement I read my essay aloud. The final paragraph stirred him to sudden and extreme agitation, and, instead of making the expected suggestions, Paul said, with the utmost deliberation, 'It was I who encouraged Jack to be a painter; and I'm still not sure that I did rightly: I don't know whether he has a painter's imagination.' What caused this agitation I have no certain means of knowing, but I had a strong sense that he felt my conclusions about the art of his brother to be more applicable to his own. Paul's words astonished me, and I might have doubted having heard them, although they were repeated in slightly differing terms, had not Elizabeth heard them also.

The house at Eldon Road, like so many artists' houses, had a style as distinctive as its owner's paintings. But in contrast to many places where artists live and work the house in Eldon Road and every object in it—including the objets trouvés, the pieces of strangely gnarled roots, stones sculptured by the sea, the leaves and even the stuffed owl occupying one of the armchairs—were immaculate. The studio no less than the drawing-room: Paul Nash would not have tolerated the room where he pursued the central activity of his life to be less elegant and less tidy than any other. Of the artist himself his friend Herbert Read well wrote: 'If an earlier intention had been carried out he would have been a naval officer, and he carried over, into his actual career, some of the swagger of the rejected career—art, for him, was to be a Senior Service. His clothes were not

conventional but they were always well-cut; his manners were perfect . . .' He wore that day a painting coat of brown cloth but which
had the look of suede, with cuffs, and his carefully cut hair was
brushed straight back. He was always frank about the difficulty of the
artist's lot, and not less frank about the necessity of taking every
possible measure to make a success of his career as an artist, though
never at the expense of his art. In fact he thoroughly enjoyed the
element of 'promotion' that this involved. Like other artists, but to
an even greater degree than most, he was preoccupied, I think, by
his posthumous fame, and his meticulous tidiness in everything that
pertained to his art was prompted in part by the desire, not to impose
his own assessment of his achievement, but to leave it beautifully
framed, comprehensively catalogued and 'placed' so as to give poste-
rity the best possible opportunity of passing favourable judgment.

Another painter with whom I had occasional encounters was
Ethel Walker, who wrote me long letters about her doings which
expressed her uninhibited delight in her own works. '. . . It would
give me the greatest satisfaction,' ran one, written from her house at
Robin Hood's Bay on the Yorkshire coast, dated 9th April 1934, 'if
"Woman of Samaria" was chosen, because I love it. I have priced it at
£150. Is that possible, do you think. If not shall I say £125? I am at
least £30 overdrawn at the bank, besides which I owe my builder
here £81 for saving my house here from being precipitated into the
sea through the past 2 years storms by its dangerous clay foundation.
He has now pierced down to the solid rock, building a high cement
wall extending 40 feet in length and made it safe for 100 years . . .
but not having sold anything since last March this £81 has not been
forthcoming for him. . . . I have at Cheyne Walk the "Invocation"
which I wrote to you about, but that wd be about £400 in price.
Mr. Wethered says it is a masterpiece.' I went from time to time to
her studio, at 127 Cheyne Walk, and enjoyed her confidence in the
immortality of her work, as well as her courage and her candour.
And who would not have enjoyed the extremes to which she carried
bohemianism of living, extremes that it takes the prosperously
brought up to achieve. One day I went there to tea.

'Do you mind fetching the cake,' she asked me in her deep voice,
'it's under the bath.' I brought it, deep-furred with dust which she
blew away with a few vigorous puffs. A fellow guest called out in
dismay:

'I've upset the milk.'

'That's all there is,' came the gruff reply, 'but it doesn't matter, I can soak it up with my body sponge and not much will be wasted.' The effect of such happenings was heightened for me by the contrast between them and the lyricism of the young girls in arcadian landscapes and other idyllic children of the imagination of our hostess who gazed from wall and easel. But in those days I knew Ethel Walker only slightly.

One of the artists who came to stay with us in Sheffield was Edward Ardizzone. Anyone meeting him for the first time would have taken this stoutish figure for an example of that rare bird, 'a typical Englishman', of Dickensian stamp in his middle forties, an impression that further acquaintance would have tended to confirm. He was in fact born in China, of Italian descent on his father's side, and in his middle thirties. Of his drawings I particularly admired the long series of pen-and-ink and water colour he made of the life in and around the big Victorian public houses in the neighbourhood of his house in Maida Vale, in which he seized with a warmly sympathetic insight their opulent classical architecture, their fullblown, pretty barmaids and their varied customers, the dependable, the wan, the brazen, the sly. Before going to the Gallery in the morning I gave him an indication of the whereabouts of the public houses likely to disappoint him least. He appeared at lunch time enraptured.

'My dear John, how can you,' he exclaimed, 'be so modest about your Sheffield pubs? I spent the morning in magnificent places, with big classical columns—and what barmaids! splendid creatures!' I asked where he had been, and some days later followed his vague gesture: but I never discovered any place remotely answering to his description.

It was on one of my visits to London during the same year that walking, as I thought by myself, round the Courtauld Institute, which then occupied the beautiful Adam House, 20 Portman Square, presented by Samuel Courtauld, I became aware of somebody following in my footsteps, who was scrutinizing the pictures with unusual attention. Presently looking round I found myself face to face with Roger Fry. The former friendship between him and my father had become clouded and I felt some resentment at the hostile attitude that he had from time to time shown towards him. If Fry was aware of some reserve in my response to his greeting, he did not show it but he spoke to me with more than his accustomed warmth. I told him of the Graves Gallery's possession of his portrait of Edith Sitwell.

'Ah,' he said with his wild smile, so attractive because it seemed somehow beyond his control, 'I've been hearing great things about what you've been doing in Sheffield; I must give you one or two of my pictures.' A few moments after he had wandered into an adjoining room I heard his returning footsteps. When he reappeared his smile was wider still. 'I wouldn't like you to think,' he said, 'that I intended to saddle you with pictures painted by me; what I had in mind was one or two of the French things I've acquired from time to time.'

I never saw him again: shortly afterwards I heard that he was dead. The news made me sad: the art world of London would have remained a more complacent, more provincial place without his crusading zest, his extraordinary power of communication, his enthusiasms. To be sure, certain of his enthusiasms for the young contemporaries in whom he saw the heirs of Cézanne and Matisse were wildly misdirected, but that he deepened the general understanding of many of the masters, old and recent, is beyond question. What strain, I wonder, mingled with his solid English Quaker ancestry could have produced his strangely foreign look, enhanced when he smiled his wild, wide, thin-lipped, slightly assymetrical smile? The invariable kindness he showed me was not prompted, I think, by any particular liking or regard, but because I was a friend of his son Julian with whom I was at school, and, like my father, he would have deplored a quarrel between fathers impairing the friendship between sons. I remembered his first lecture at Bedales, given not long after the Second Post-Impressionist Exhibition, on the superiority of an apple by Cézanne to a godlike and heroic centurion by some Victorian, and I used to stay at the Gallic villa he built near Guildford.

Julian, fond though he was of his father, rebelled somewhat against his almost exclusively aesthetic and intellectual preoccupations. His own, so very different, were eventually to make him a cattle rancher and secretary to the British Columbia Beef Cattle Growers Association. At Cambridge he took Agriculture and rowed in his college eight. Although Julian followed his father to King's some time elapsed before their relationship became generally known to his fellow undergraduates. A group of the father's admirers then persuaded the son to give a luncheon to enable them to meet him. One day the chief aesthetes of Cambridge (according to a common schoolfriend of Julian's and mine who was present) were assembled round a table which, however seductive the talk of Roger Fry, the guests could not but notice was bare of cloth, of silver, of everything. After a time their growing uneasiness at its continued bareness became apparent. Suddenly there was a loud crash as a cascade of tins and of tin-openers struck the table. 'Set to, you bastards,' shouted Julian at the sophisticated company.

It was, I think, during 1936 that my work in Sheffield began to yield me less and less satisfaction. The Graves Gallery had been opened and the foundation—although no more—of a collection of paintings had been laid; an influential group of interested friends had rallied around it, and mainly through the activities of this group and the conducted visits of school-children there was a steadily growing public response to serious painting, though not perhaps to sculpture, for which it had been possible to do little. In the face of the persistent opposition of Alderman Graves to a purchase grant of any magnitude, the prospects of building up the collection at all substantially were slight. I was accordingly coming to feel that in the particular circumstances I had already made the contribution that such qualities as I possessed enabled me to make of an opportunity, unique in my generation of directors of art galleries, of a fresh beginning. My relations with Alderman Graves grew ever more tense and unhappy, yet they never seemed to approach more closely to breaking point. I had no shadow of doubt that I acted rightly in resisting his attempts to impose the remainder of his collection upon the Gallery that bore his name, with the inescapable consequence of destroying the only possibility that the people of Shffield had ever enjoyed of possessing an institution from which they might derive standards of order and form and colour, and which they might rightly regard as an oasis in the midst of the ugliness and disorder that stretched away, beneath its low pall of smoke, on every side. But my consciousness of acting rightly scarcely made my struggle with this old man the less hateful: his, after all, was the dream of this new gallery, his the money that brought it into being, and his the invitation that made this unique opportunity mine. Yet here was I obstructing the full realization of his hopes, and giving other benefactors part of the credit that he felt should have gone to him. I came to believe that what was now called for was a director who by a persuasiveness superior to my own would succeed where I had failed and reconcile Alderman Graves to the new beginnings and win his support for the formation of a collection that would fulfil the hopes that his generosity had aroused.

The city itself for both Elizabeth and me became more and more oppressive: the mile after mile of little blackened houses beneath the dirty sky, the pinched people lacking both the power to extract pleasure from their sombre environment or the will to change it. If the poor were joyless and apathetic the lives of the rich seemed stultified by their excessive caution. One day a friend suggested that I might give some advice to a well known citizen about the decoration of a house which he considered buying. I was driven by my friend to a semi-detached villa of modest size to call for the citizen in question, and we drove together to the house, a historic mansion outside the city. After giving the advice required and restoring the citizen to his pokey home, I said to my friend that I doubted whether people accustomed to living in so meagre a fashion could have any notion of what it cost to maintain a house of such a size. At this my friend laughed. 'You really need not worry about him,' she said, 'he's chairman of one of the largest businesses in Sheffield and quite apart from what he derives from that he has had an income of £12,000 a year from birth.' Any thought that this and some other instances of excessive caution were unusual was dispelled by a friend ideally qualified to offer an opinion, the doctor with the most fashionable practice in the city. Discussing over dinner at his house the difference in spending habits between North and South, I said that in the North people seemed unprepared to take risks in the way that a young man in the South might, for instance, borrow enough to enable him to study abroad for a year, and that the rich seemed unhappy if they were compelled to spend more than half their incomes. 'If you were to make it a *quarter* you'd be nearer the mark,' said the doctor and invited the opinions of the other guests. There was no dissenting voice.

My growing restlessness was not all of it the result of my own parochial or personal concerns. I felt the chill of the shadow cast by the coming war. First there was the Spanish Civil War. Like most of my generation I took a radically over-simplified view of this conflict, seeing it as in the main a struggle between a somewhat anarchical liberalism and 'fascism', a view that found confirmation in the evident sympathy and eventual help forthcoming for the 'fascists' from the Nazi and the Fascist powers. Then there was the crushing and humiliation of the Jews of Germany. To me this was a growing nightmare; that any human beings should be so used, and they the helpless fellow-countrymen of Isaiah, of Moses, of St. Paul, of Spinoza, and of Our Lord himself, seemed a particular enormity and a portent of impending, of immediately impending disaster. To share at such a time the blood of both criminal and victim is a searing experience. But a nightmare darker still was the crass complacency and the nerveless half-faith in 'understanding' that afflicted our own country. Our enemies, the enemies of everything that we held precious, made no secret of their intentions. One evening in Paris I met for a drink the correspondent of *The Times*. When I arrived at the café he was sitting holding his head in his hands, seeming to hear nothing, to see nothing.

'If I stay here much longer I shall lose my reason,' he presently almost shouted; 'day after day I send dispatches to my editor, with irrefutable evidence that the Germans intend to attack and soon; irrefutable evidence about their preparations. Do you suppose Geoffrey Dawson will publish them? Either they go into the waste-paper basket; that's the best that can happen; more often they're published with the key facts blue-pencilled, so that what appears actually fosters this complacency that looks like being the end of us all. And the same sort of thing happens to what's sent by my colleagues in Vienna, Rome and of course Berlin.'

I became aware of being a bore to my friends and others by advocating—as though the advocacy of an obscure provincial art gallery director could accomplish anything at all in a field so remote from his own—the concentration of all our resources upon the building up of a fleet of bombers, while our industry could work undisturbed and we were still able to import freely from abroad whatever was needful to expedite this programme. My not numerous friends in the Armed Forces seemed to be as 'unprepared' as 'public opinion'—with one notable exception, a young Engineer acting from 1935 until 1939 as Adjutant to the 58th Divisional Engineers, Sheffield Territorials, who during the course of long discussions showed that he fully shared my anxieties, if he did not, perhaps, fully endorse my over-simple programme. (His name was Richard Lloyd, and before many years had passed he had become a Major-General and Director of Military Intelligence.) So certain was I of the imminence of war and of the obligation of everyone who felt as I about the issues involved that I put down my name for the Officers' Emergency Reserve. I cannot even now but think that a thousand-bomber raid the night that the Nazis attacked would have made our prospects less sombre, or even the threat of such a raid.

There was one friend who took an even darker view of things than I: my old friend Jacques Blanche, with whom I was in intermittent correspondence during my years in Leeds and Sheffield.

'You, happy English,' he wrote from Paris on 22nd May 1936, 'do not realize the slightest bit what is going on in this country, but you will soon have to, I fear. Apart from the general terrible situation I had a very bad time. . . . I should feel glad to present your Sheffield Gallery some of my English pieces, always eager to have as many of my own works as possible safely kept in England . . .' Again, from Offranville, on 30th June:

Dear John

Just arrived, after the terrible days when one hardly was sure of being able to motor out of Paris safely. It was a very narrow escape of the fiercest revolution ordered by the IVth International from Moscow. No actual government left. The supposed ended strikes, still raging throughout the country. A sort of interval, but sounding more ominous for August.

This state of things cannot go on; alas as to what shall be the future shape of an inevitable dictature, takes, I fear the worse is likely, I mean that of the Soviets. Even here, in this usually calm, old fashion village, everybody has a strange disquieting feeling, peasantry being inspired by the new spirit of communist Syndicates. No plans allowed us; we just wait and see. . . . Supposing you stopped at Dieppe on your way, let me know.

Conder letters? Where are they, I wonder? Would you tell me who a Mr. James Laver (as far as I can read his signature), from the Victoria and Albert Museum, is? I answered a letter from him, about James Tissot, but never got a reply. He intends writing a book, or an article, and wants particulars of Tissot's private life—the most mysterious man I ever knew—absolutely forgotten over here, I am sorry to say. His best early work, vanished, the few pictures of his in the Luxembourg ought to have gone to the Louvre—but there is no trace left . . .

Yrs affecly

J.E. Bl

And yet again, from London, on 3 September,

'Fancy, John! We heard yesterday from one of the heads of the Victoria and Albert. . . . M. Leon Blum had just sent over, to be trusted to the museum his precious silver plate and other belongings of his! ! ! ! The amount of French, presently in England, come with a view you can easily guess—is reported to be enormous . . . Do you follow the frightful events—Spain? It seems as thought (sic) the whole human kind was determined to commit suicide. I wonder how we still are able to keep one's head upon onc's sholders (sic).'

His distress was far greater than mine: he had lost faith, entirely, in his country, whereas I believed that mine might still withdraw its head from the sand. With a tried recipe in mind I went to see Blanche, and proposed to him, as I had to my father in the days darkened by illness just before my departure for America, that he should write his memoirs. My father, after a briefly hesitant beginning, had derived enormous satisfaction and benefit to his health from the recovery and ordering of his memories. My proposal to Blanche was more specific. Blanche was fascinated by England, which for him was still the aristocratic Edwardian England of his memories. The highly privileged friends with whom he mostly foregathered on his visits to London and the relative stability he found there in comparison with Paris prevented his perceiving that this was an England that survived only for the very few. English was his second language, he spoke it almost perfectly and wrote it, with frequent mistakes due rather to impatience than ignorance, as fluently as a native. From the moment we met he would question me immediately and closely about England, eager to hear personal gossip and about the prevailing tendencies in politics, art, literature and the social structure. What I told him served to stimulate his own teeming memories of his English friends—and enemies. What I accordingly proposed to Blanche was that he should write his

English memories, and in English. Oddly enough the idea was one that had never occured to him; he received it with enthusiasm and in accordance with his exceptional capacity for translating ideas immediately into action, he began to write at once. Shortly afterwards he showed me the first chapters in MS, and on 7th August he wrote from Offranville:

My dear John

Already 101 pages out of the book you red (sic) the first pages of, have been sent to be typed. According to Messrs. Dent's suggestion, the ready chapters shall be sent over, as soon as ready and corrected. But what I miss badly, are several details I must make sure of, which you took note of: for instance dates of the first *International*, *Whistler* president, the second; *Rodin*. Names of artists on the Board (I was one)—and names of exhibitors—at least the most interesting ones.

The name of several societies of the independent English painters who had held shows formerly—(one, at the Egyptian Hall, Piccadilly, round about 1885—your father was the inspiring spirit, I think I remember).

Where, and *when* did Sickert start a class—(Charlotte Street?) I suppose, before 1914. Who were the marking students? And the *London Group* who first assembled in Dieppe, at Sickert's house, Neuville? Gore and several whose names I forgot.

Now—about my sendin (sic) some of pictures of my collection —and some of my works *on loan*, to Pub. Galeries, England— could you help me? How should I approach curators?

Things are turning more and more ominous. Day after day something happens just enough to make one shiver. The example of Spain is deplorable, not to say more. I do not feel like writing more about it, my dear John. War was expected to break out—as usual—in the Balkans and Central Europe. Is a new one likely to start from Spain, Mediterranean, North Africa? The unexpected seems to be our lot, all over the world!

> In great haste
>
> Ever yrs affly
>
> J.E. Bl

Portraits of a Lifetime was published the following year and *More Portraits of a Lifetime* two years later. In the Prolegomena he expresses in graceful terms his gratitude to me for suggesting a task which would take his mind off the preoccupation with the present but 'one nevertheless that fills a man in his declining years with dread, for the November, if not the December, of his life has come with the sunset of the civilization whose child he was'.

It was our daughter Lucy—she was the most zestfully adventurous and happiest child imaginable—who brought light into the gathering gloom. At a very early age she showed herself unusually responsive to beauty. She talked continually but only uttering meaningless sounds until one day out walking we passed a lilac in resplendent bloom and she cried out, 'Init marbrous'. These were her first coherent—or almost coherent—words. But responsiveness to beauty was not quite her most conspicuous trait. We came to know Mr. A. V. Alexander, afterwards Lord Alexander but then Member of Parliament for the Hillsborough Division of Sheffield, a Labour politician of ability and impressive presence. After attending the opening of one of the Gallery's exhibitions, he invited Elizabeth out to tea, taking her to the Café of the Cooperative Funeral Parlour—he was one of the most influential figures in the Cooperative movement. Shortly afterwards he came to lunch with us and the occasion was one of some importance to me. Our serious discussion of some civic issue was disturbed by a series of shattering crashes. It occurred to us that a length of heavy coping or a window casement might have fallen. We went upstairs to the nursery, to find that Lucy, still too young to stand up straight, had with infinite labour ranged all her possessions on the window ledge, and pushed them over. In short she was a boisterous baby, caring for nothing so little as want of attention. Greatly as she added to the joy—and the eventfulness—of our lives, my restlessness increased, as my sense of usefulness diminished. In the evenings I worked on a Life of Conder (about whom I had a quantity of unpublished information) but this too failed to assuage my restlessness, which was further increased by invitations to lecture in the United States and Canada, seconded, so far as the Dominion was concerned, by Mr. Vincent Massey, High Commissioner in London, a collector of painting, and shortly to become a Trustee of the National Gallery, who came to visit the Graves Gallery. I know few more ardent enjoyers of painting than he.

My book on Conder involved a considerable volume of correspondence. One letter I received, because it conveyed so forthright an opinion about a figure whose character has sometimes been called in question, should be made public.

Heytesbury House, Wiltshire.

6.10.36.

Dear Mr. Rothenstein

I am very glad to lend you R[obert] Ross's letters to Conder, as I think that they are a good testimonial to his qualities, which I remember with deep affection and gratitude.

As you already know, Robbie Ross was a man of boundless generosity and impulsive chivalry. (Forgive me for taking this opportunity of reasserting his merits.)

With all good wishes,
Yours sincerely
Siegfried Sassoon

Early one morning in March, 1938, I received a telephone call from London to tell me that J. B. Manson, the Director of the Tate Gallery, had provoked a sensational incident in Paris by getting drunk at the luncheon held to celebrate the opening of an important exhibition of British painting at the Louvre, and by shouting interruptions at the speakers and running eventually more or less amuck, and that this had started numerous rumours, among others that he had been asked to resign. These rumours must have been heard by almost every art gallery director in the country and innumerable others with the most intense excitement, for the directorship of the Tate was generally regarded as the most interesting post in the art world of Great Britain. I tried to subdue my own agitation with the reflection that, so far as I was aware, no member of the staff of a provincial gallery had ever been appointed to the headship of a national one. I had for years had a special feeling for the Tate. Ten years earlier, almost to the day, I had written to my father from Lexington, '. . . when (if ever) I return permanently, there is one place where I would love to work. That is the Tate . . . I cannot imagine anywhere I would rather be . . .'

A few weeks later Elizabeth went to London to see a doctor and had tea with Eric Newton, art critic of *The Sunday Times*, with whom we had become friendly when he was working in Manchester as art critic to *The Guardian*. Eric Newton said to her that he supposed that I had applied for the by that time definitely vacant directorship, that I was the right person for the post and that he would do anything possible to assist my candidature. '*Apply*,' Elizabeth exclaimed, and told Eric Newton that my father, who had been a Trustee of the Tate himself until five years before, had said to her that for anyone to apply would be unthinkable, and that candidates must be invited. (So as to avoid the temptation of speaking on my behalf he retired to Far Oakridge.) A few days later Eric Newton telephoned to her to say that friends had induced him to apply himself and that he hoped that she would not consider him disloyal to me for doing so, adding that all the other applicants had already been interviewed, the post being held open to enable him also to be interviewed, the trustees not having been satisfied. Elizabeth immediately taxed my father with having so gravely misinformed her. Much upset he offered to act contrary to his principles on such matters by consulting Lord Balniel, a Trustee, over the telephone. Lord Balniel told him that I was very young for the post but I must certainly apply and instantly. Elizabeth telephoned to me in Sheffield to tell me how matters stood. I went to London next morning, writing my application in the train, and had it delivered by hand. On the Sheffield-bound train next day Leigh Ashton, of the Victoria and Albert Museum, came and sat with me.

'I've put in for the Tate,' he said.

'But why, Leigh, when you've never been particularly concerned with European painting or sculpture and you'll probably be the next Director of your own Museum.'

'The Tate,' he replied, 'is six years nearer.'

When I arrived at the Graves Gallery I found a telegram from the Tate asking me to attend an interview the following afternoon. Once again I went to London, and I was interviewed, searchingly but benevolently, by the Tate Trustees, who had been especially convened, namely Sir Evan Charteris, Chairman, Lord Balniel, Lord Sandwich, Augustus John, Sir William Reid Dick, Lord Bearsted, Sir Edward Marsh, Sir Walter Russell, Lord Howard de Walden and Sir Kenneth Clark.

The interview was so momentous for me that it made nervousness seem irrelevant and petty and in any case I was aware that the extraordinary opportunities given me in Leeds and Sheffield had taught me a good deal about art gallery policy and administration, but nevertheless all recollection of those three quarters of an hour has been obliterated from my memory. Yet again I went back to Sheffield only to find a summons from Sir James Rae, the Under-Secretary of the Treasury, to call on him next day. In this fusty but impressive place where I had never been before I was invited to sit down opposite a smallish, keen-eyed man with a reassuring presence.

Without preliminaries, he said, 'I am authorized by the Prime Minister to offer you the vacant directorship of the Tate.'

After my acceptance we had some half hour's talk; in spite of its desultory character I was aware of being probed by an experienced mind, mostly about administration. I volunteered the information that among several serious intellectual deficiencies I suffered to an unusual degree from an inability to deal with figures, finding even addition and subtraction laborious and the more exacting exercises beyond me. He replied that I would not be called upon to deal with figures and that financial responsibility for the Tate rested in the hands of the Director of the National Gallery, who was Accounting Officer for both institutions. Then he said, with a sharpness of tone I had not heard in his voice before, 'the Treasury has not for some time been satisfied with the state of affairs at the Tate, and we wish to assure you of full support in any changes you may consider it proper to make.'

I telephoned to my father, and he, my mother, Elizabeth and I all met for tea at the Annexe to the Athenaeum Club.

'It is the happiest day of my life,' my father said, and remembering my many failures and that I had not always been an easy son, his happiness meant much to me.

A few days later, on 4th May, I received formal confirmation of my appointment in a letter from Sir James, in which he expressed the hope that the Corporation of Sheffield would release me as early as possible. It was announced next day and *The Evening Standard*, having no photograph of me, reproduced my likeness from 'The Princess Badroulbadour', a painting in the Tate of my two sisters and myself in fancy dress, by my father, made when I was six or seven years old.

I spent the next few weeks in Sheffield to make everything ready for my successor. I continued with my work—in particular the close supervision of the cleaning and restoration of a remarkable frieze in oil on paper (belonging to the Corporation) representing the industries of Sheffield by Godfrey Sykes, a gifted but forgotten Yorkshire friend and pupil of Alfred Stevens, of whose work we had held a small exhibition at the Gallery, in 1935, and the designer of the old cover, with 'The Sower', of *The Cornhill*, which was admired by Thackeray and inspired a poem by Hardy.

My appointment to the Tate—the only post I had ever been ambitious to occupy—affected me so intensely that for the moment its significance was more than I could contemplate. My chief thought was for the friends who have figured little or not at all in these pages, but without whose support we could scarcely have endured our years in Yorkshire: so let me name them now with gratitude: Gervase and Marjory Beckett, of Kirkdale Manor, Nawton; Ronald and Vera Matthews, of Aston Hall; Robin Hay, of Helmsley; Sydney and Nita Atkin, and Alice Davy, of Sheffield, whose homes were as our own and with whom our serene friendships had no history. For Yorkshire itself, in spite of its grim twilight air, and the narrow cautious way of living that prevails over much of it, I had formed a deep attachment: there is a toughness, a kindness, a candour and an innate liberality of mind that inspire lasting affection and respect.

On the morning of 1st June, leaving Lucy with friends, Elizabeth and I drove away from No. 6, The Mount, with gratitude and regret mingled with an exhilarating sense of high expectation.

INDEX